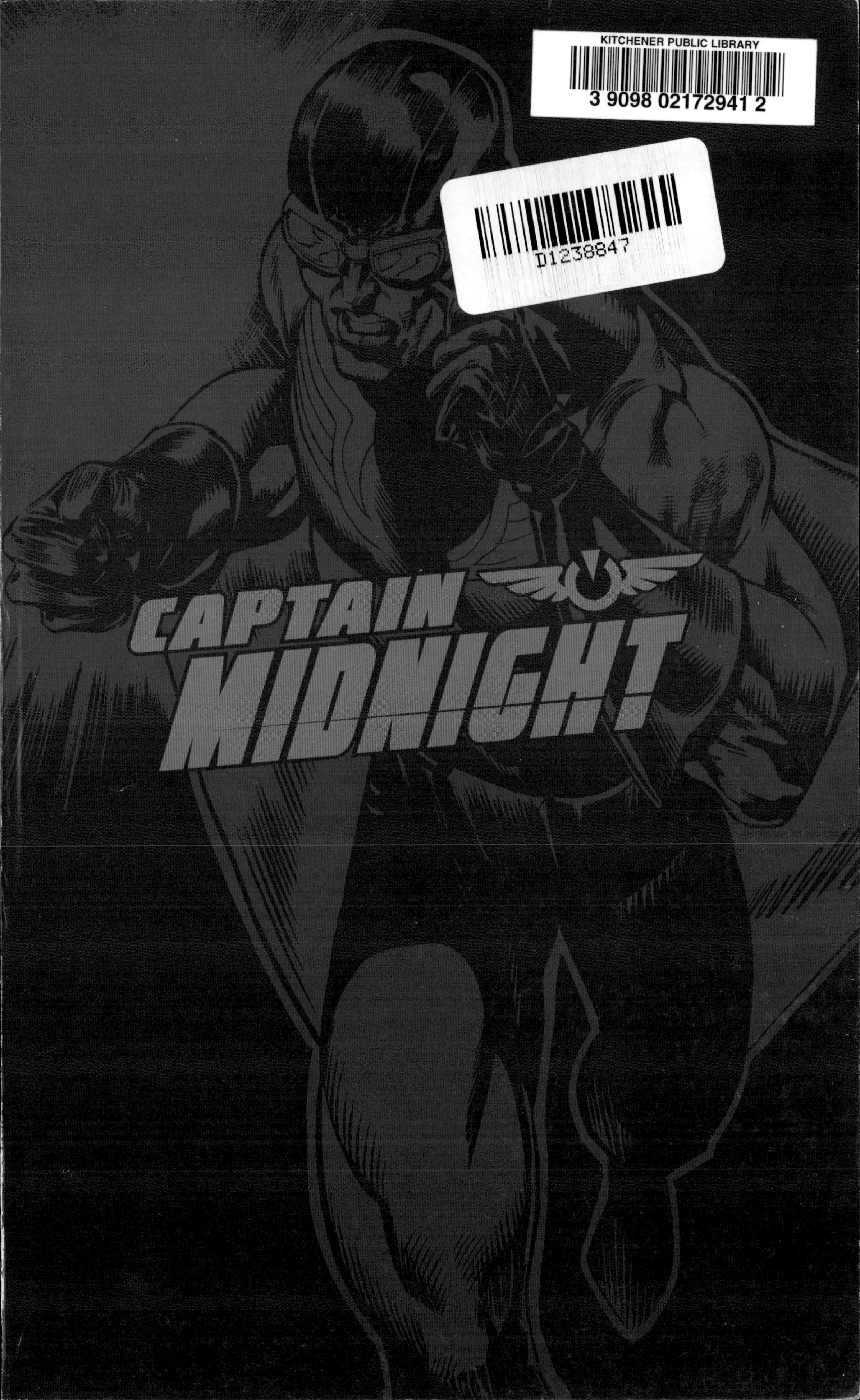
CAPTAIN
MIDNIGHT

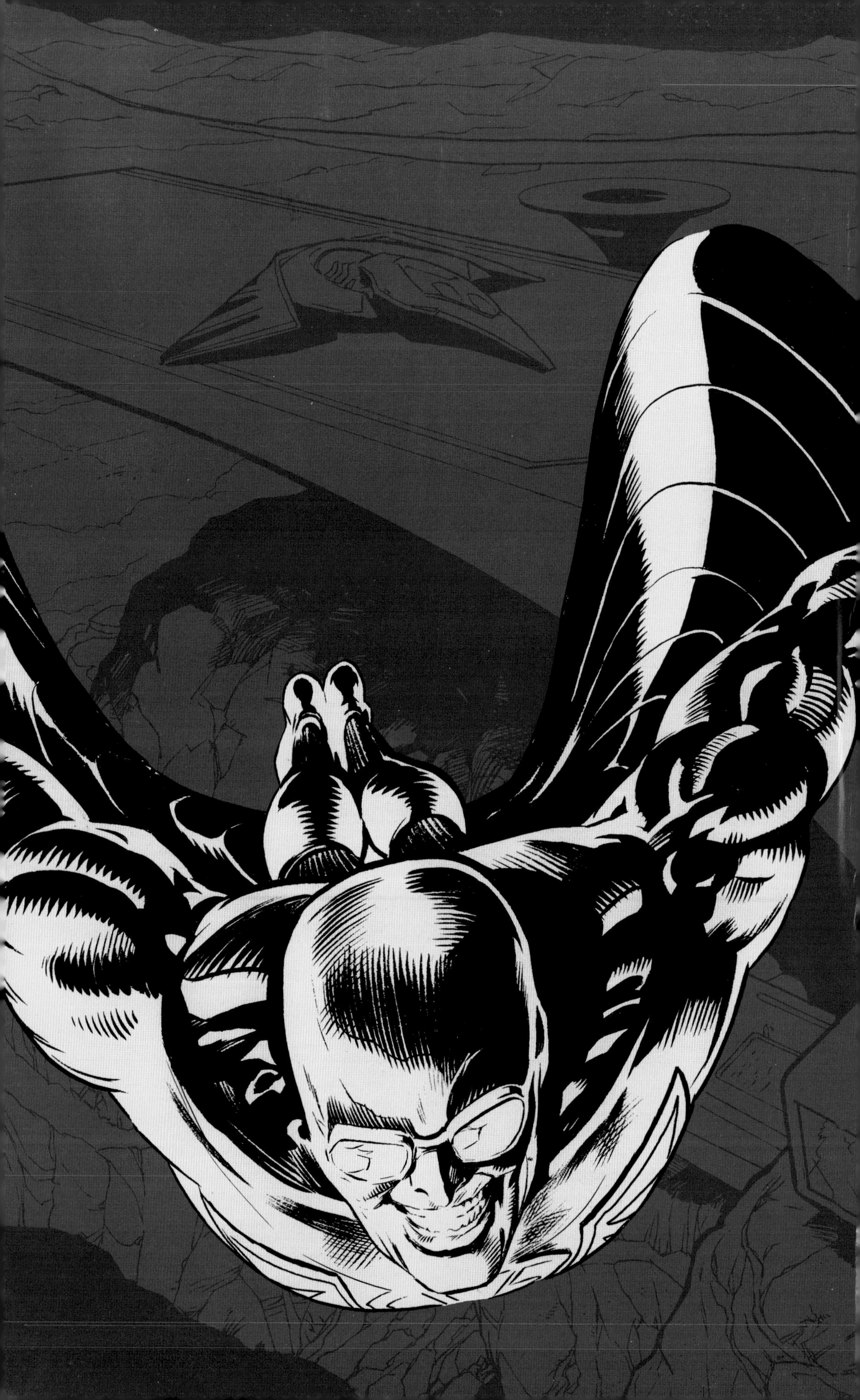

CAPTAIN MIDNIGHT

VOLUME 3 · FOR A BETTER TOMORROW

STORY BY
JOSHUA WILLIAMSON

ART BY
FERNANDO DAGNINO

COLORS BY
JAVIER MENA

LETTERS BY
NATE PIEKOS OF **BLAMBOT®**

COVER BY
FELIPE MASSAFERA

CHAPTER BREAK ART BY
FELIPE MASSAFERA
(CHAPTERS 1–3)

FREDDIE WILLIAMS II
AND **JEREMY ROBERTS**
(CHAPTER 4)

DARK HORSE BOOKS

PUBLISHER.................MIKE RICHARDSON
EDITOR.....................JIM GIBBONS
ASSISTANT EDITOR........SPENCER CUSHING
DIGITAL PRODUCTION........ALLYSON HALLER
COLLECTION DESIGNER........NICK JAMES

Special thanks to Mike Richardson, Randy Stradley, Scott Allie, and
David Macho Gómez and Spanish Inq.

Mike Richardson, President and Publisher | Neil Hankerson, Executive Vice President | Tom
Weddle, Chief Financial Officer | Randy Stradley, Vice President of Publishing | Michael
Martens, Vice President of Book Trade Sales | Anita Nelson, Vice President of Business
Affairs | Scott Allie, Editor in Chief | Matt Parkinson, Vice President of Marketing | David
Scroggy, Vice President of Product Development | Dale LaFountain, Vice President of
Information Technology | Darlene Vogel, Senior Director of Print, Design, and Production |
Ken Lizzi, General Counsel | Davey Estrada, Editorial Director | Chris Warner, Senior Books
Editor | Diana Schutz, Executive Editor | Cary Grazzini, Director of Print and Development
| Lia Ribacchi, Art Director | Cara Niece, Director of Scheduling | Tim Wiesch, Director of
International Licensing | Mark Bernardi, Director of Digital Publishing

Published by Dark Horse Books
A division of Dark Horse Comics, Inc.
10956 SE Main Street
Milwaukie, OR 97222

First edition: September 2014
ISBN 978-1-61655-231-2

1 3 5 7 9 10 8 6 4 2
Printed in China

International Licensing: (503) 905-2377
Comic Shop Locator Service: (888) 266-4226

CAPTAIN MIDNIGHT VOLUME 3: FOR A BETTER TOMORROW

This volume collects Captain Midnight #8–#11 from the ongoing series from Dark Horse
Comics.

CHAPTER 1

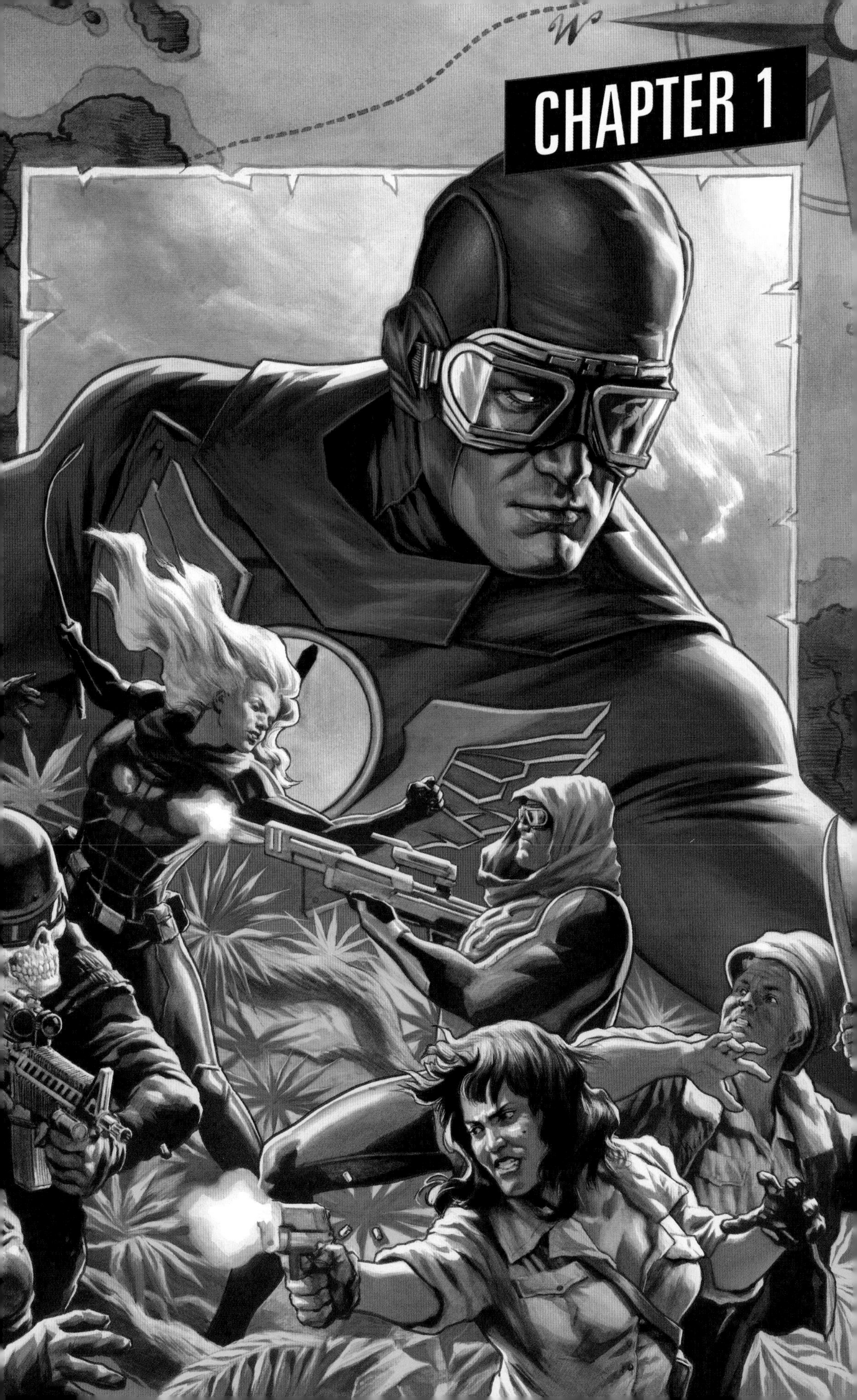

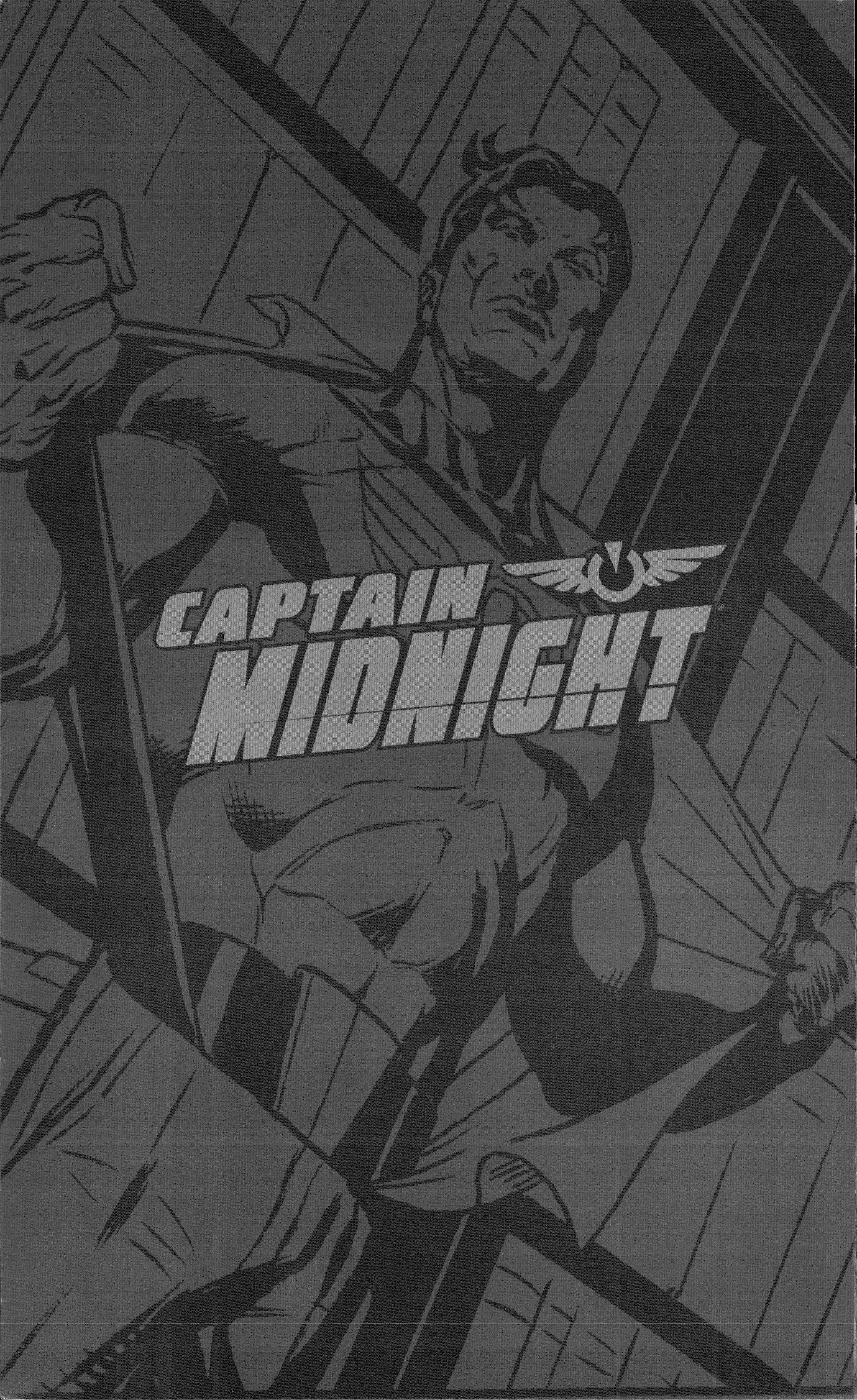
CAPTAIN
MIDNIGHT

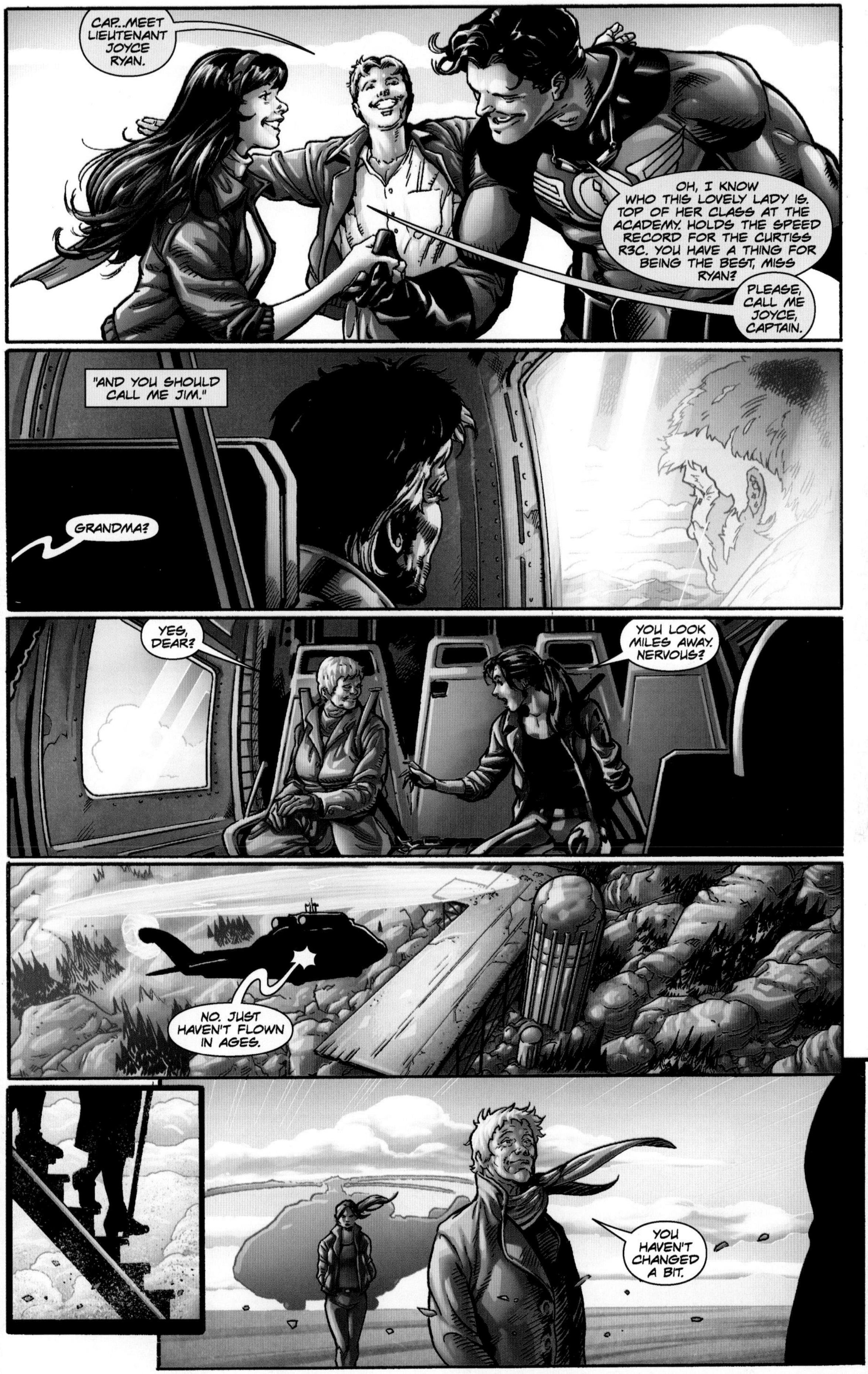
CAP...MEET LIEUTENANT JOYCE RYAN.
OH, I KNOW WHO THIS LOVELY LADY IS. TOP OF HER CLASS AT THE ACADEMY. HOLDS THE SPEED RECORD FOR THE CURTISS R3C. YOU HAVE A THING FOR BEING THE BEST, MISS RYAN?
PLEASE, CALL ME JOYCE, CAPTAIN.
"AND YOU SHOULD CALL ME JIM."
GRANDMA?
YES, DEAR?
YOU LOOK MILES AWAY. NERVOUS?
NO. JUST HAVEN'T FLOWN IN AGES.
YOU HAVEN'T CHANGED A BIT.

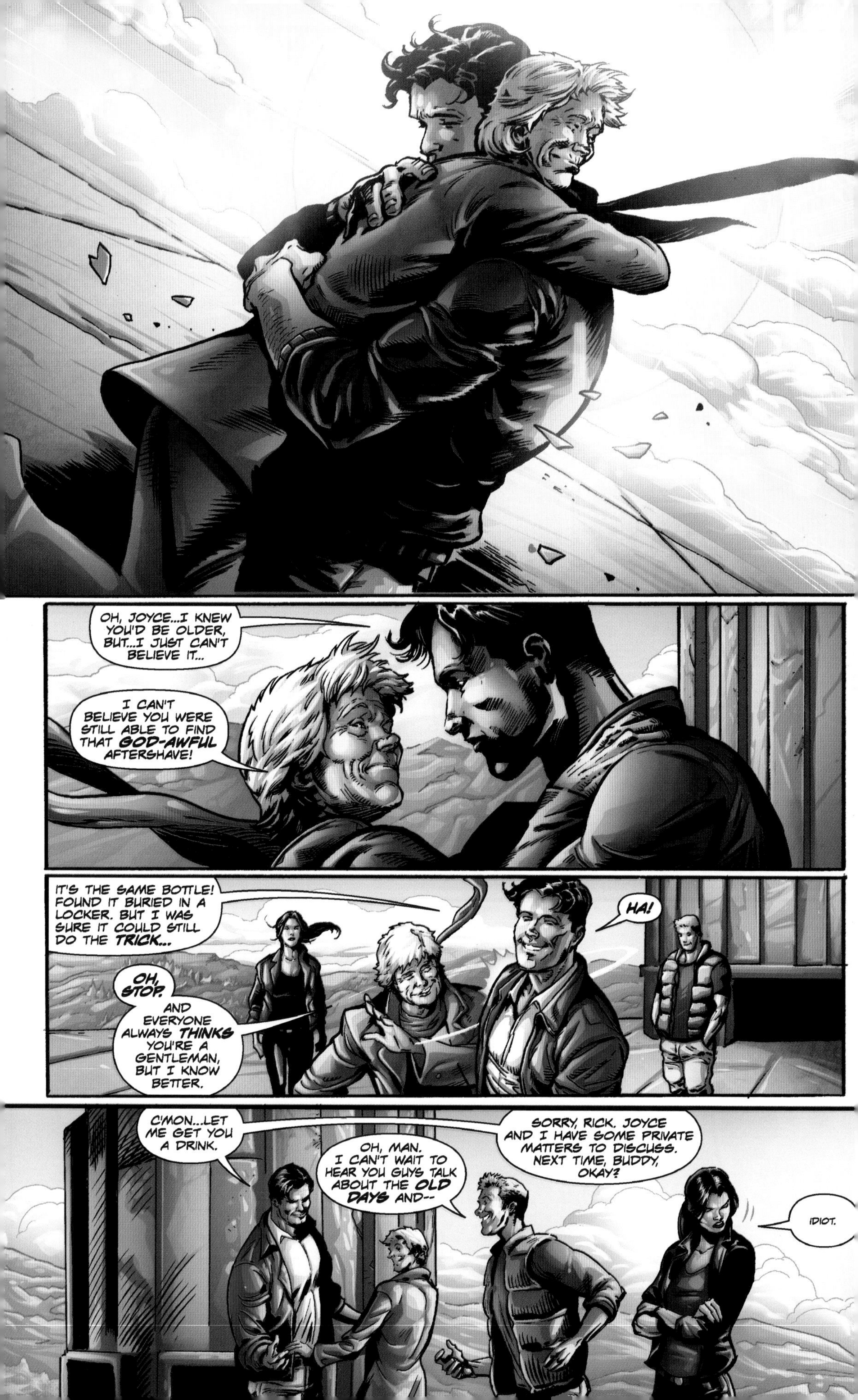
OH, JOYCE...I KNEW YOU'D BE OLDER, BUT...I JUST CAN'T BELIEVE IT...
I CAN'T BELIEVE YOU WERE STILL ABLE TO FIND THAT GOD-AWFUL AFTERSHAVE!
IT'S THE SAME BOTTLE! FOUND IT BURIED IN A LOCKER. BUT I WAS SURE IT COULD STILL DO THE TRICK...
HA!
OH, STOP. AND EVERYONE ALWAYS THINKS YOU'RE A GENTLEMAN, BUT I KNOW BETTER.
C'MON...LET ME GET YOU A DRINK.
OH, MAN. I CAN'T WAIT TO HEAR YOU GUYS TALK ABOUT THE OLD DAYS AND--
SORRY, RICK. JOYCE AND I HAVE SOME PRIVATE MATTERS TO DISCUSS. NEXT TIME, BUDDY, OKAY?
IDIOT.

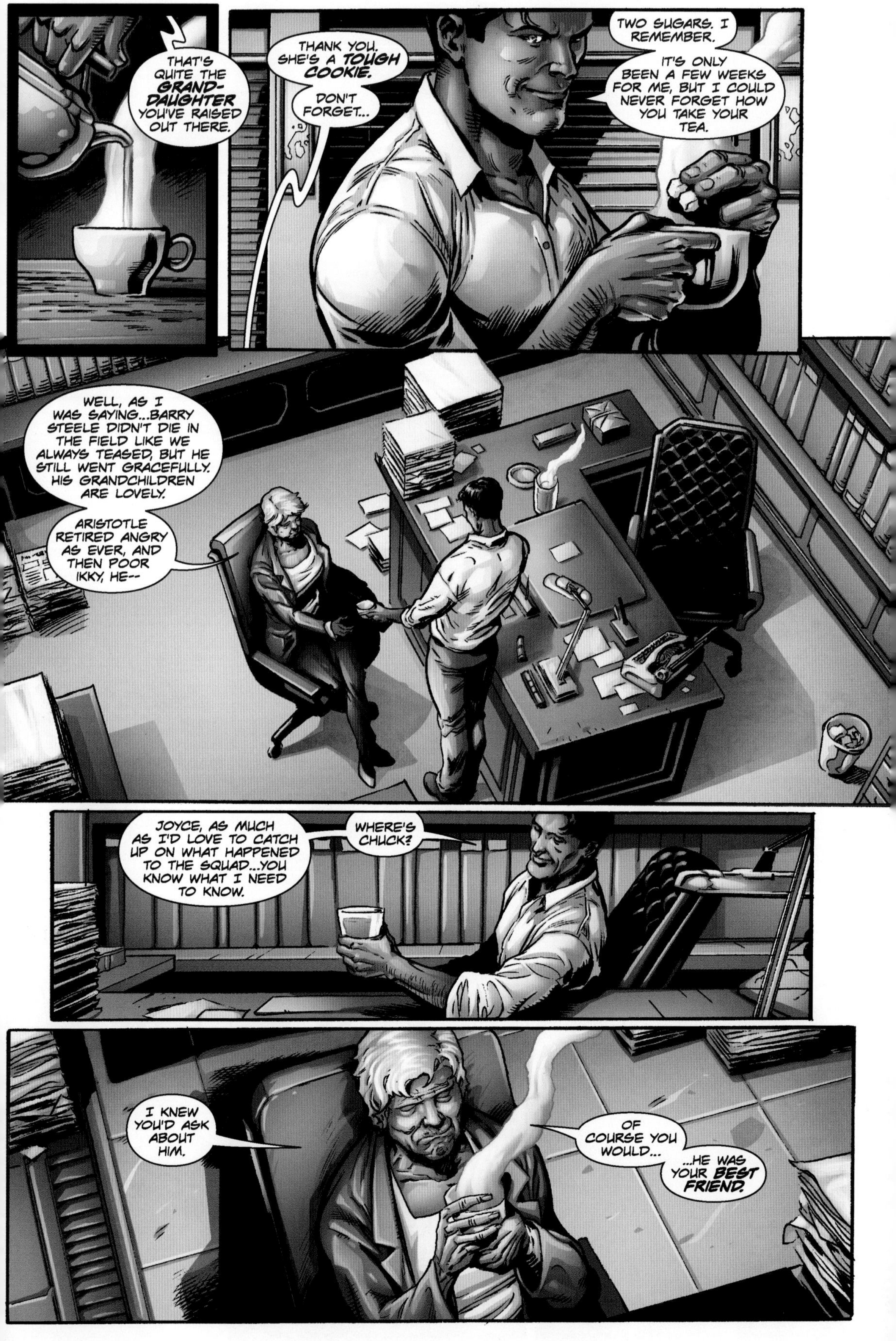
THAT'S QUITE THE **GRAND-DAUGHTER** YOU'VE RAISED OUT THERE.
THANK YOU. SHE'S A **TOUGH COOKIE.**
DON'T FORGET...
TWO SUGARS. I REMEMBER.
IT'S ONLY BEEN A FEW WEEKS FOR ME, BUT I COULD NEVER FORGET HOW YOU TAKE YOUR TEA.
WELL, AS I WAS SAYING...BARRY STEELE DIDN'T DIE IN THE FIELD LIKE WE ALWAYS TEASED, BUT HE STILL WENT GRACEFULLY. HIS GRANDCHILDREN ARE LOVELY.
ARISTOTLE RETIRED ANGRY AS EVER, AND THEN POOR IKKY, HE--
JOYCE, AS MUCH AS I'D LOVE TO CATCH UP ON WHAT HAPPENED TO THE SQUAD...YOU KNOW WHAT I NEED TO KNOW.
WHERE'S CHUCK?
I KNEW YOU'D ASK ABOUT HIM.
OF COURSE YOU WOULD...
...HE WAS YOUR **BEST FRIEND.**

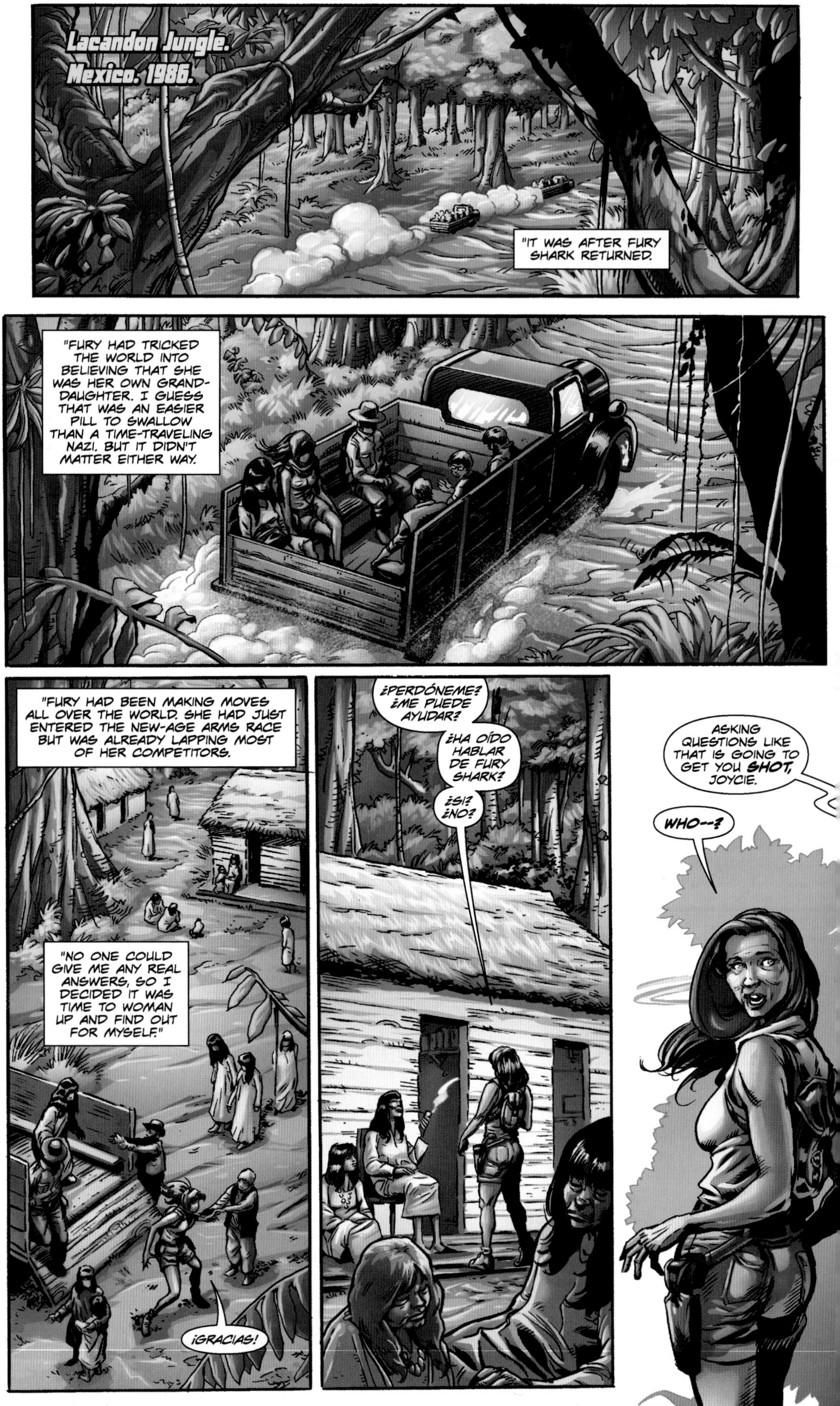
Lacandon Jungle.
Mexico. 1986.
"IT WAS AFTER FURY SHARK RETURNED.
"FURY HAD TRICKED THE WORLD INTO BELIEVING THAT SHE WAS HER OWN GRAND-DAUGHTER. I GUESS THAT WAS AN EASIER PILL TO SWALLOW THAN A TIME-TRAVELING NAZI. BUT IT DIDN'T MATTER EITHER WAY.
"FURY HAD BEEN MAKING MOVES ALL OVER THE WORLD. SHE HAD JUST ENTERED THE NEW-AGE ARMS RACE BUT WAS ALREADY LAPPING MOST OF HER COMPETITORS.
"NO ONE COULD GIVE ME ANY REAL ANSWERS, SO I DECIDED IT WAS TIME TO WOMAN UP AND FIND OUT FOR MYSELF."
¡GRACIAS!
¿PERDÓNEME? ¿ME PUEDE AYUDAR?
¿HA OÍDO HABLAR DE FURY SHARK?
¿SI? ¿NO?
ASKING QUESTIONS LIKE THAT IS GOING TO GET YOU SHOT, JOYCIE.
WHO--?

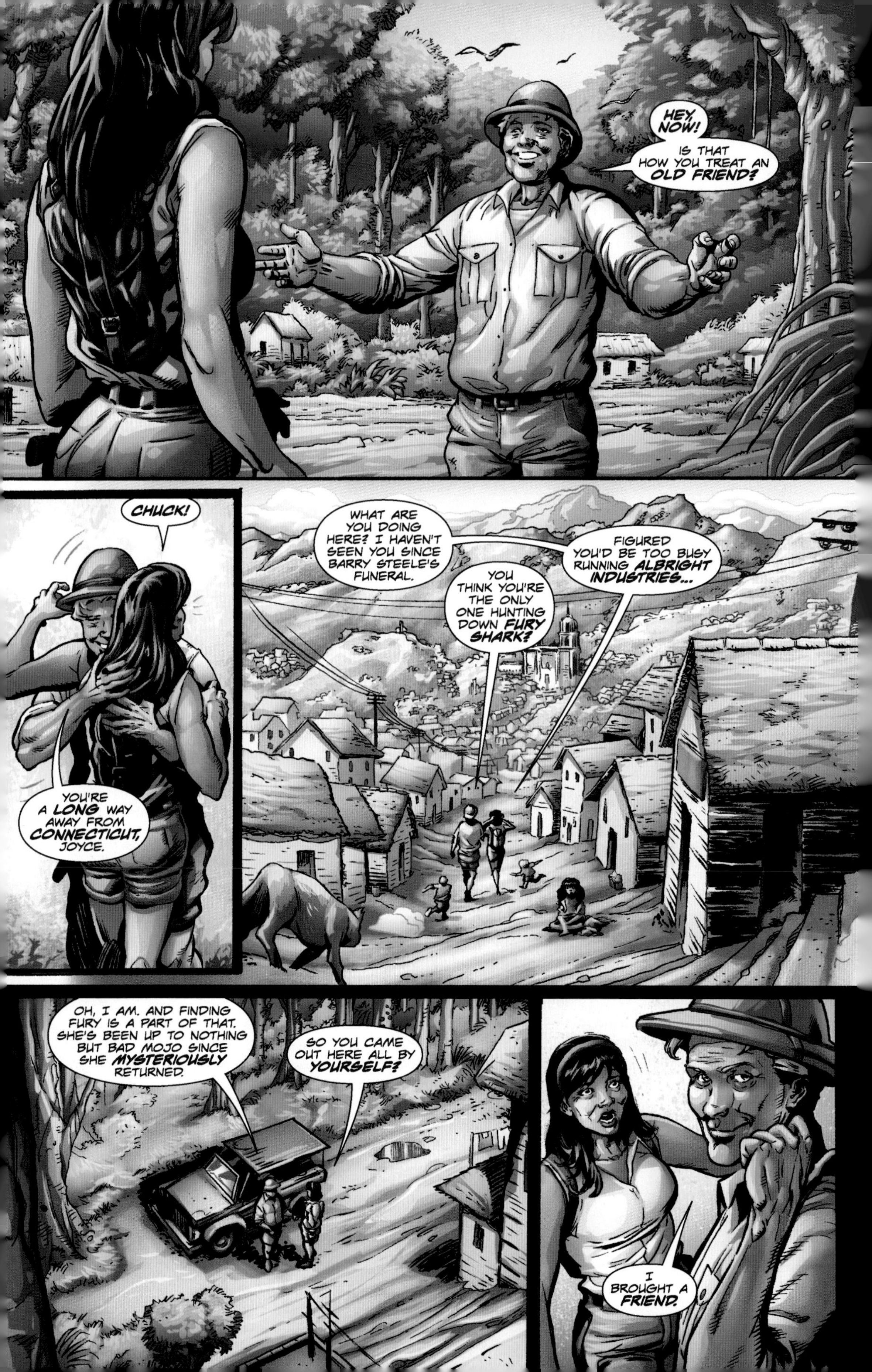
HEY, NOW!
IS THAT HOW YOU TREAT AN OLD FRIEND?
CHUCK!
YOU'RE A LONG WAY AWAY FROM CONNECTICUT, JOYCE.
WHAT ARE YOU DOING HERE? I HAVEN'T SEEN YOU SINCE BARRY STEELE'S FUNERAL.
YOU THINK YOU'RE THE ONLY ONE HUNTING DOWN FURY SHARK?
FIGURED YOU'D BE TOO BUSY RUNNING ALBRIGHT INDUSTRIES...
OH, I AM. AND FINDING FURY IS A PART OF THAT. SHE'S BEEN UP TO NOTHING BUT BAD MOJO SINCE SHE MYSTERIOUSLY RETURNED.
SO YOU CAME OUT HERE ALL BY YOURSELF?
I BROUGHT A FRIEND.

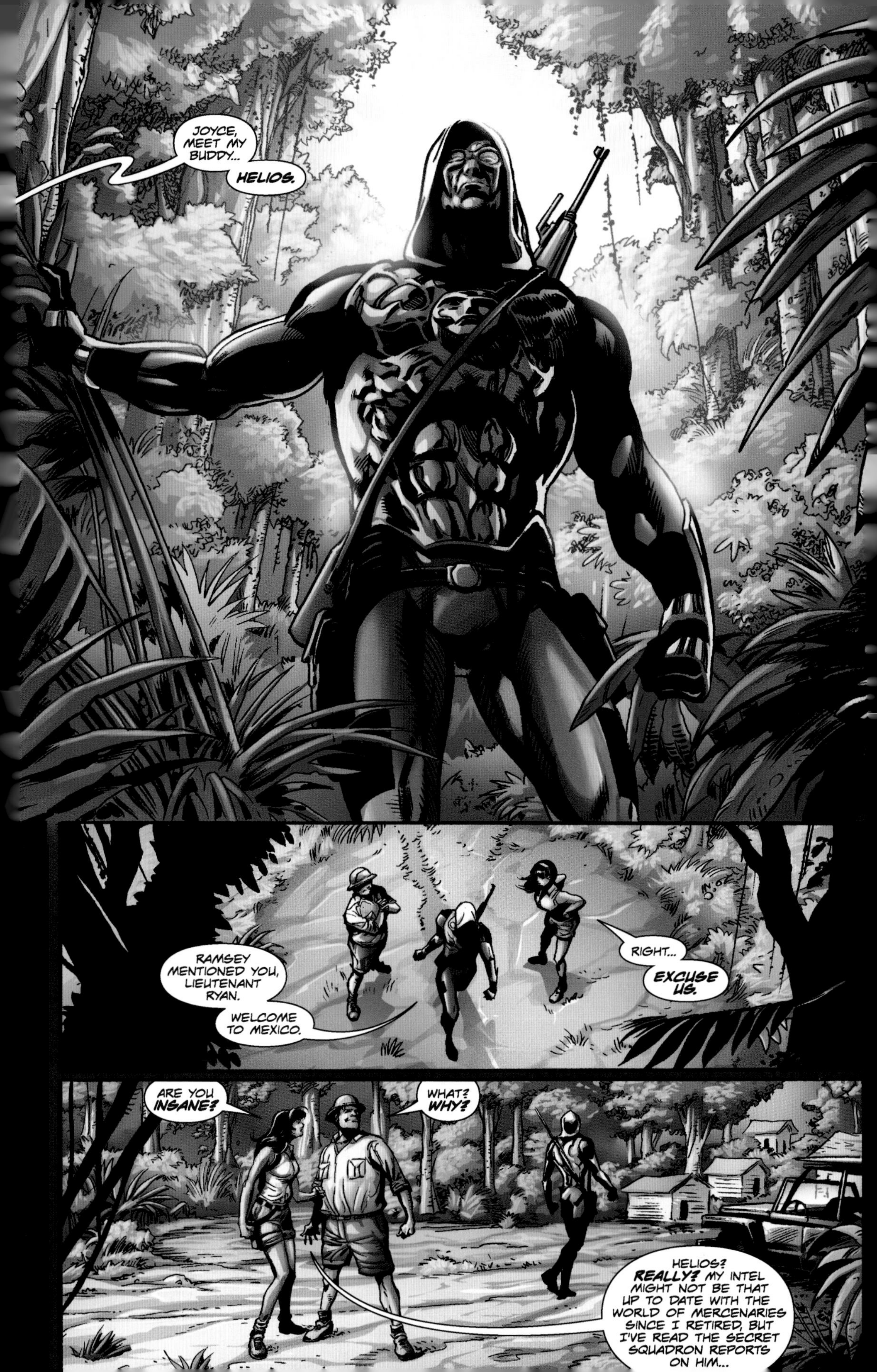
JOYCE, MEET MY BUDDY...
HELIOS.
RAMSEY MENTIONED YOU, LIEUTENANT RYAN.
WELCOME TO MEXICO.
RIGHT...
EXCUSE US.
ARE YOU INSANE?
WHAT? WHY?
HELIOS? REALLY? MY INTEL MIGHT NOT BE THAT UP TO DATE WITH THE WORLD OF MERCENARIES SINCE I RETIRED, BUT I'VE READ THE SECRET SQUADRON REPORTS ON HIM...

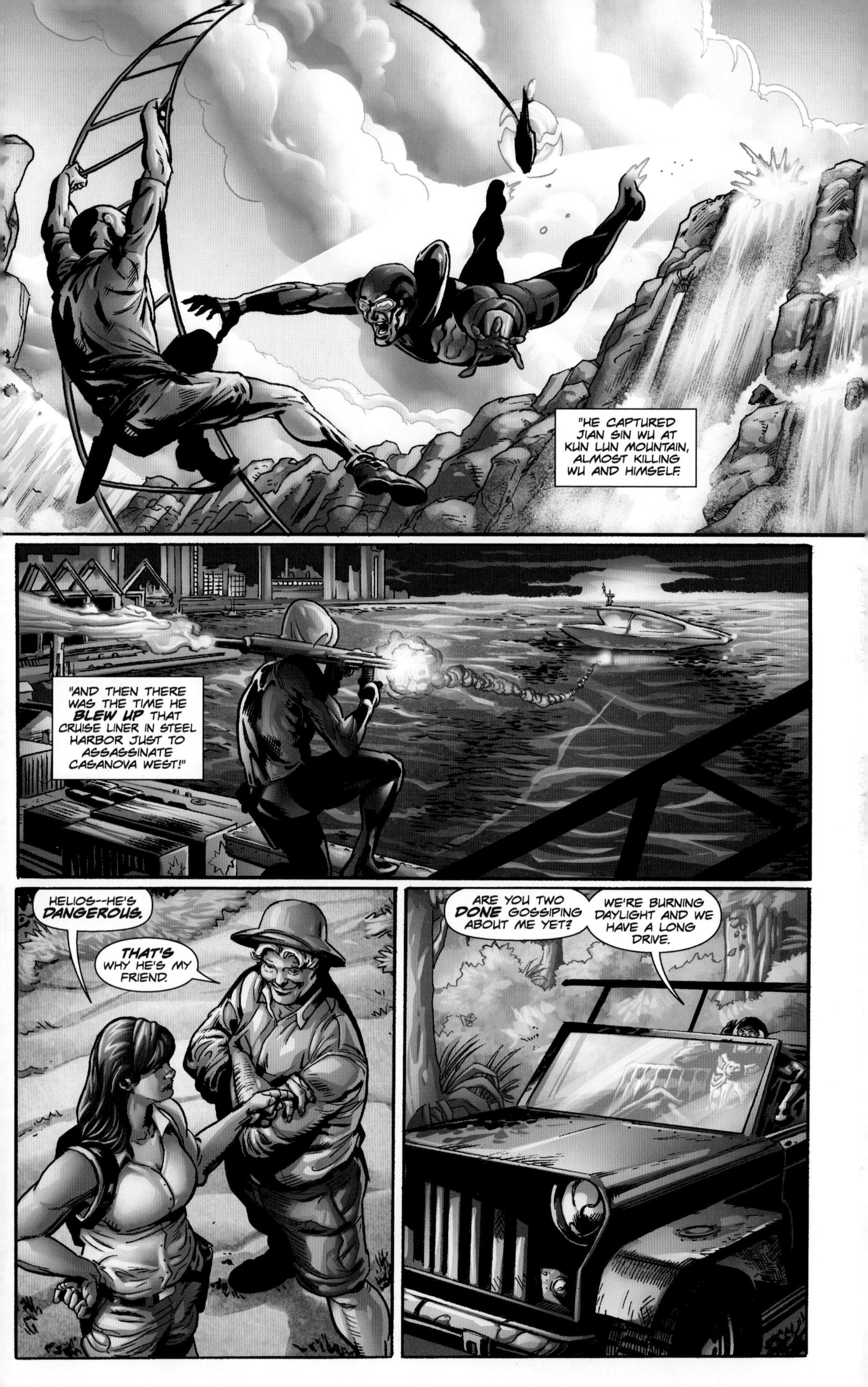
"HE CAPTURED JIAN SIN WU AT KUN LUN MOUNTAIN, ALMOST KILLING WU AND HIMSELF.
"AND THEN THERE WAS THE TIME HE BLEW UP THAT CRUISE LINER IN STEEL HARBOR JUST TO ASSASSINATE CASANOVA WEST!"
HELIOS--HE'S DANGEROUS.
THAT'S WHY HE'S MY FRIEND.
ARE YOU TWO DONE GOSSIPING ABOUT ME YET?
WE'RE BURNING DAYLIGHT AND WE HAVE A LONG DRIVE.

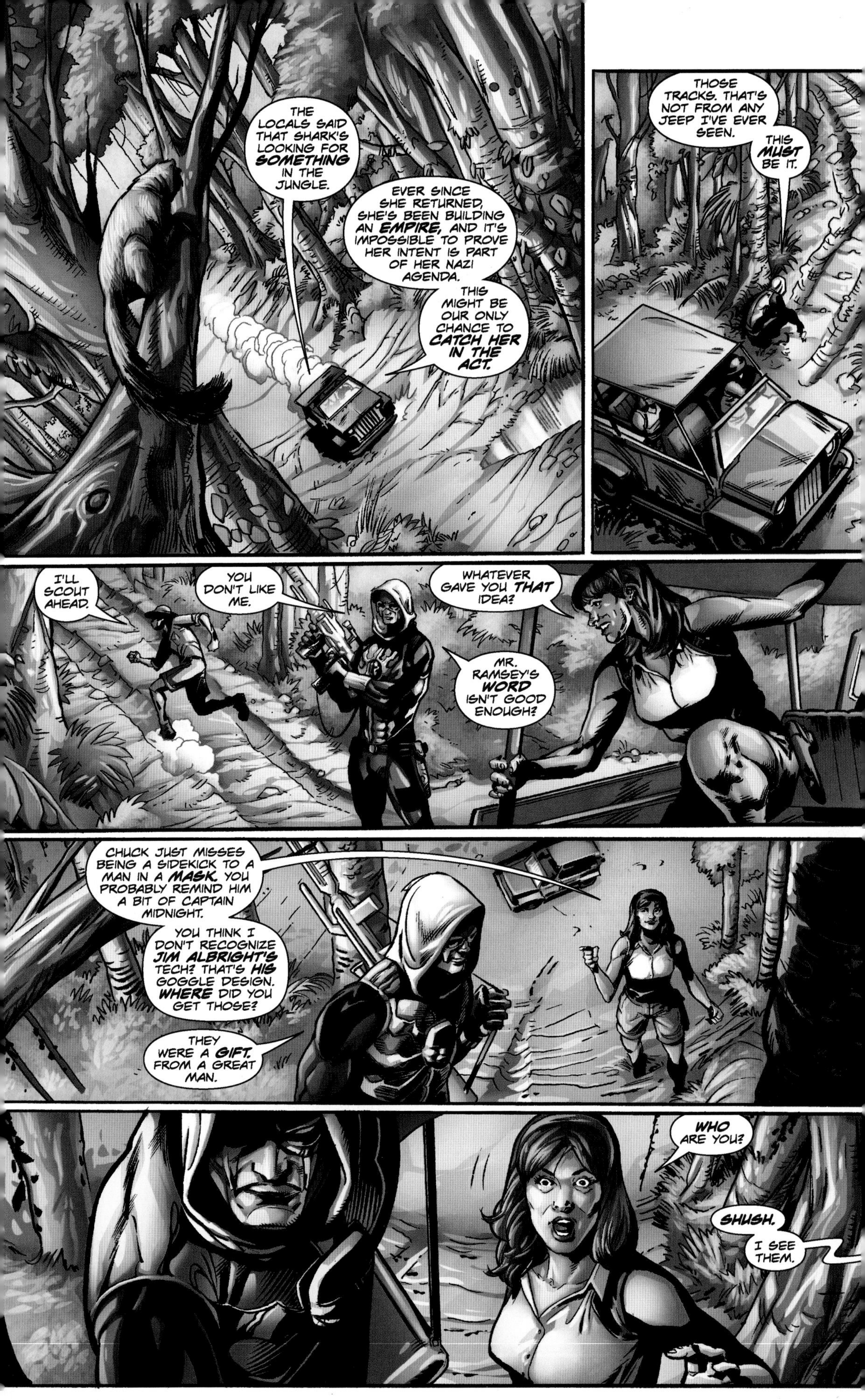
THE LOCALS SAID THAT SHARK'S LOOKING FOR SOMETHING IN THE JUNGLE.
EVER SINCE SHE RETURNED, SHE'S BEEN BUILDING AN EMPIRE, AND IT'S IMPOSSIBLE TO PROVE HER INTENT IS PART OF HER NAZI AGENDA.
THIS MIGHT BE OUR ONLY CHANCE TO CATCH HER IN THE ACT.
THOSE TRACKS. THAT'S NOT FROM ANY JEEP I'VE EVER SEEN.
THIS MUST BE IT.
I'LL SCOUT AHEAD.
YOU DON'T LIKE ME.
WHATEVER GAVE YOU THAT IDEA?
MR. RAMSEY'S WORD ISN'T GOOD ENOUGH?
CHUCK JUST MISSES BEING A SIDEKICK TO A MAN IN A MASK. YOU PROBABLY REMIND HIM A BIT OF CAPTAIN MIDNIGHT.
YOU THINK I DON'T RECOGNIZE JIM ALBRIGHT'S TECH? THAT'S HIS GOGGLE DESIGN. WHERE DID YOU GET THOSE?
THEY WERE A GIFT. FROM A GREAT MAN.
WHO ARE YOU?
SHUSH.
I SEE THEM.

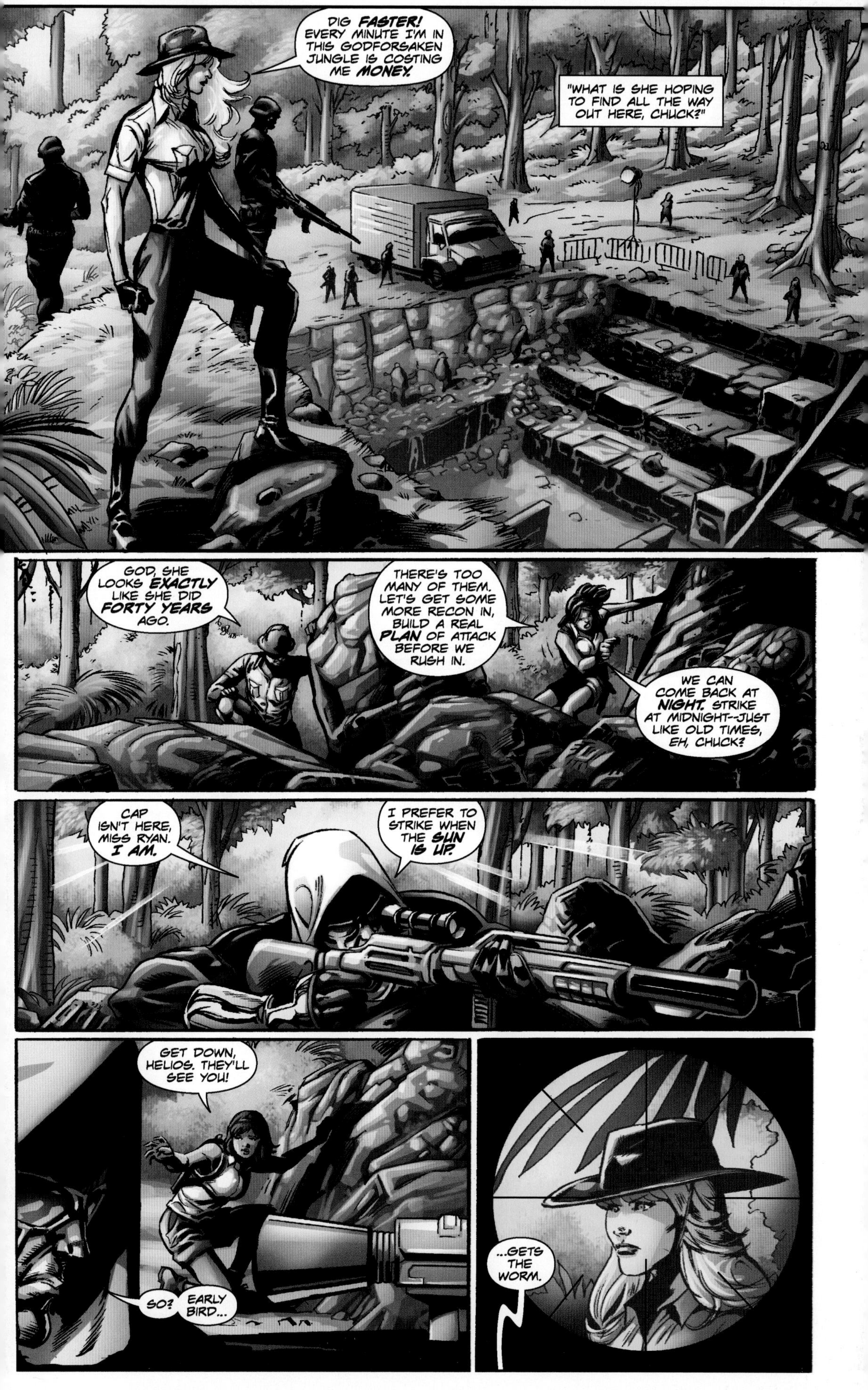
DIG FASTER! EVERY MINUTE I'M IN THIS GODFORSAKEN JUNGLE IS COSTING ME MONEY.
"WHAT IS SHE HOPING TO FIND ALL THE WAY OUT HERE, CHUCK?"
GOD, SHE LOOKS EXACTLY LIKE SHE DID FORTY YEARS AGO.
THERE'S TOO MANY OF THEM. LET'S GET SOME MORE RECON IN, BUILD A REAL PLAN OF ATTACK BEFORE WE RUSH IN.
WE CAN COME BACK AT NIGHT. STRIKE AT MIDNIGHT--JUST LIKE OLD TIMES, EH, CHUCK?
CAP ISN'T HERE, MISS RYAN. I AM.
I PREFER TO STRIKE WHEN THE SUN IS UP.
GET DOWN, HELIOS. THEY'LL SEE YOU!
SO?
EARLY BIRD...
...GETS THE WORM.

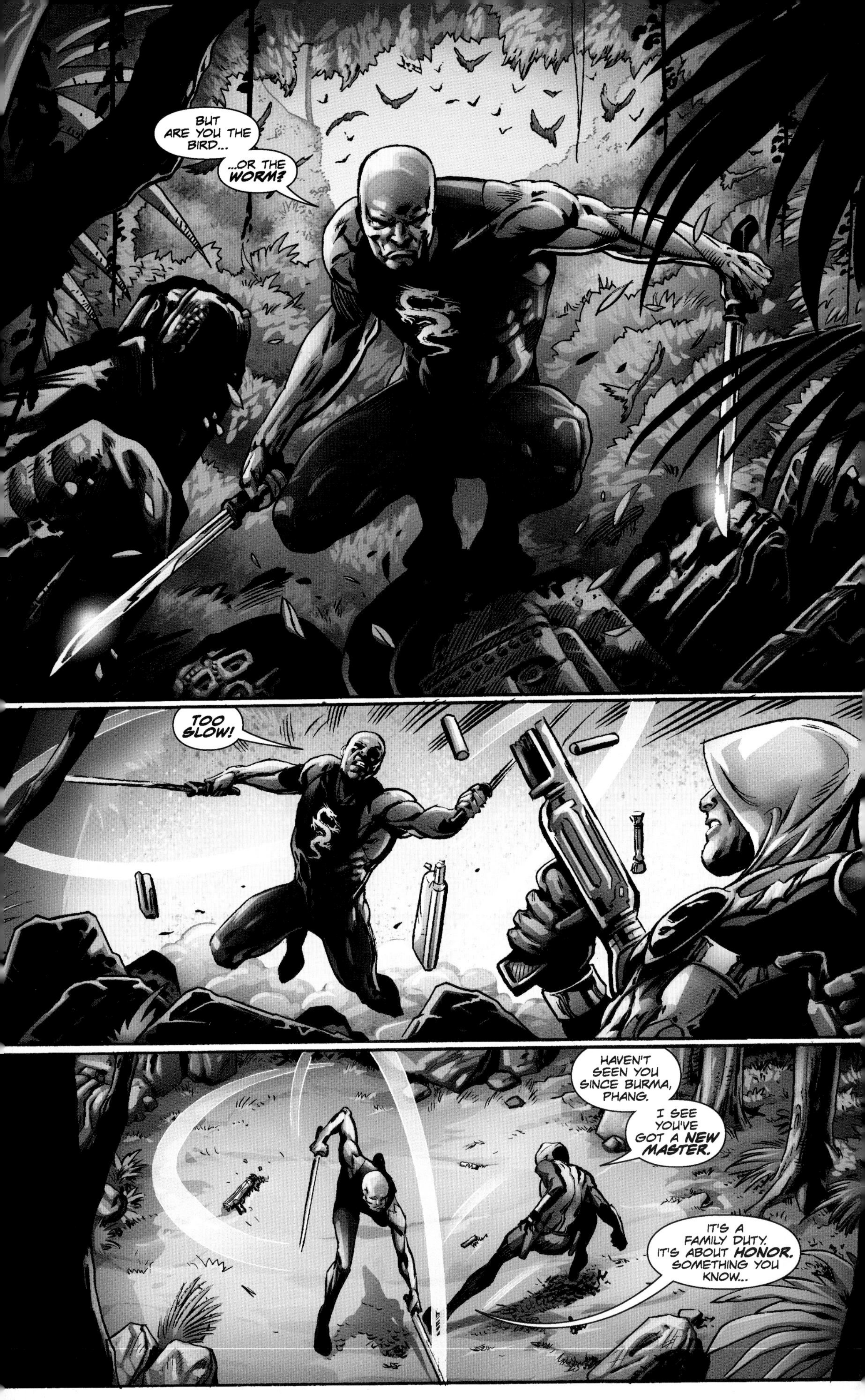
BUT ARE YOU THE BIRD...
...OR THE WORM?
TOO SLOW!
HAVEN'T SEEN YOU SINCE BURMA, PHANG.
I SEE YOU'VE GOT A NEW MASTER.
IT'S A FAMILY DUTY. IT'S ABOUT HONOR. SOMETHING YOU KNOW...

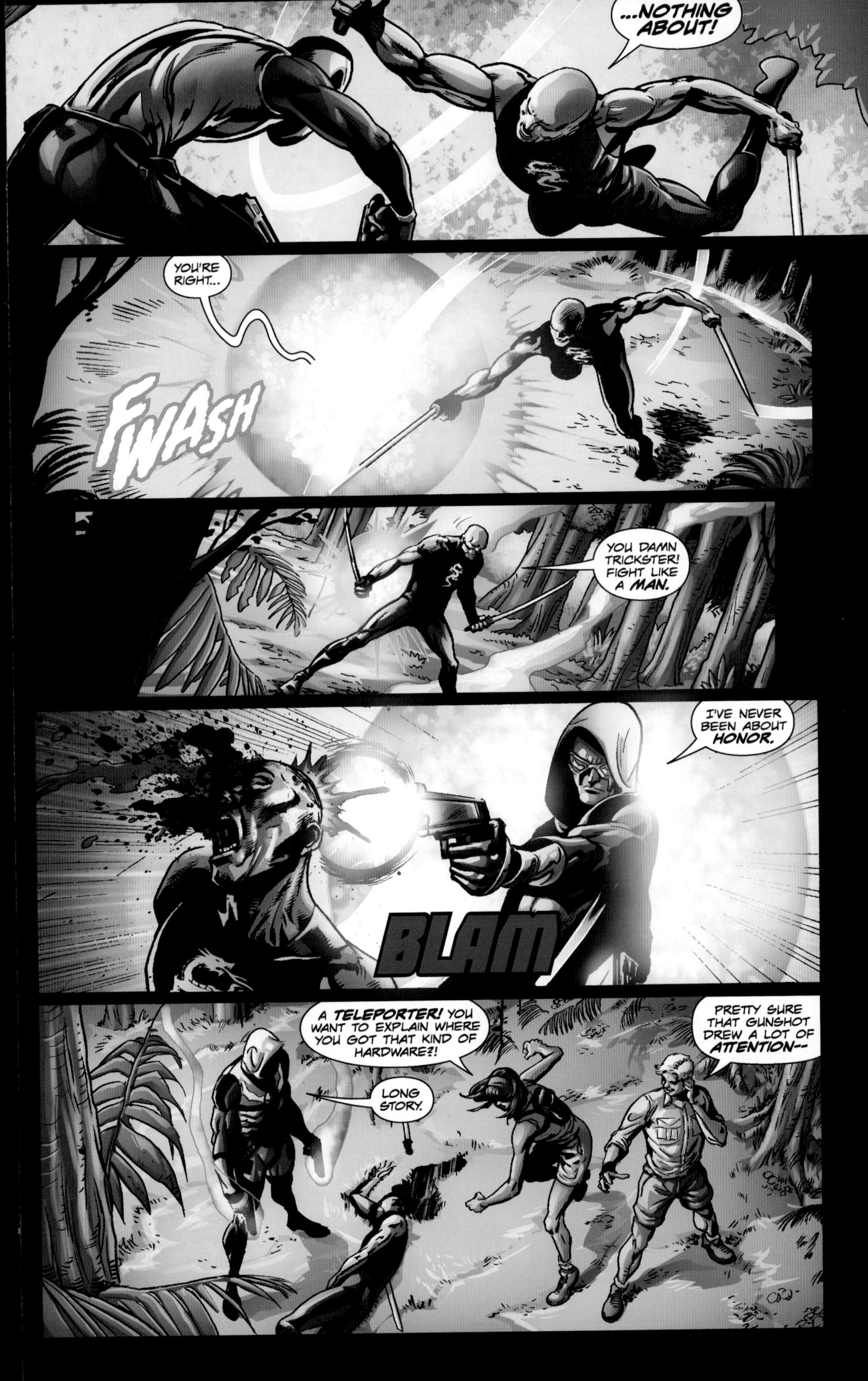
...NOTHING ABOUT!
YOU'RE RIGHT...
FWASH
YOU DAMN TRICKSTER! FIGHT LIKE A MAN.
I'VE NEVER BEEN ABOUT HONOR.
BLAM
A TELEPORTER! YOU WANT TO EXPLAIN WHERE YOU GOT THAT KIND OF HARDWARE?!
LONG STORY.
PRETTY SURE THAT GUNSHOT DREW A LOT OF ATTENTION--

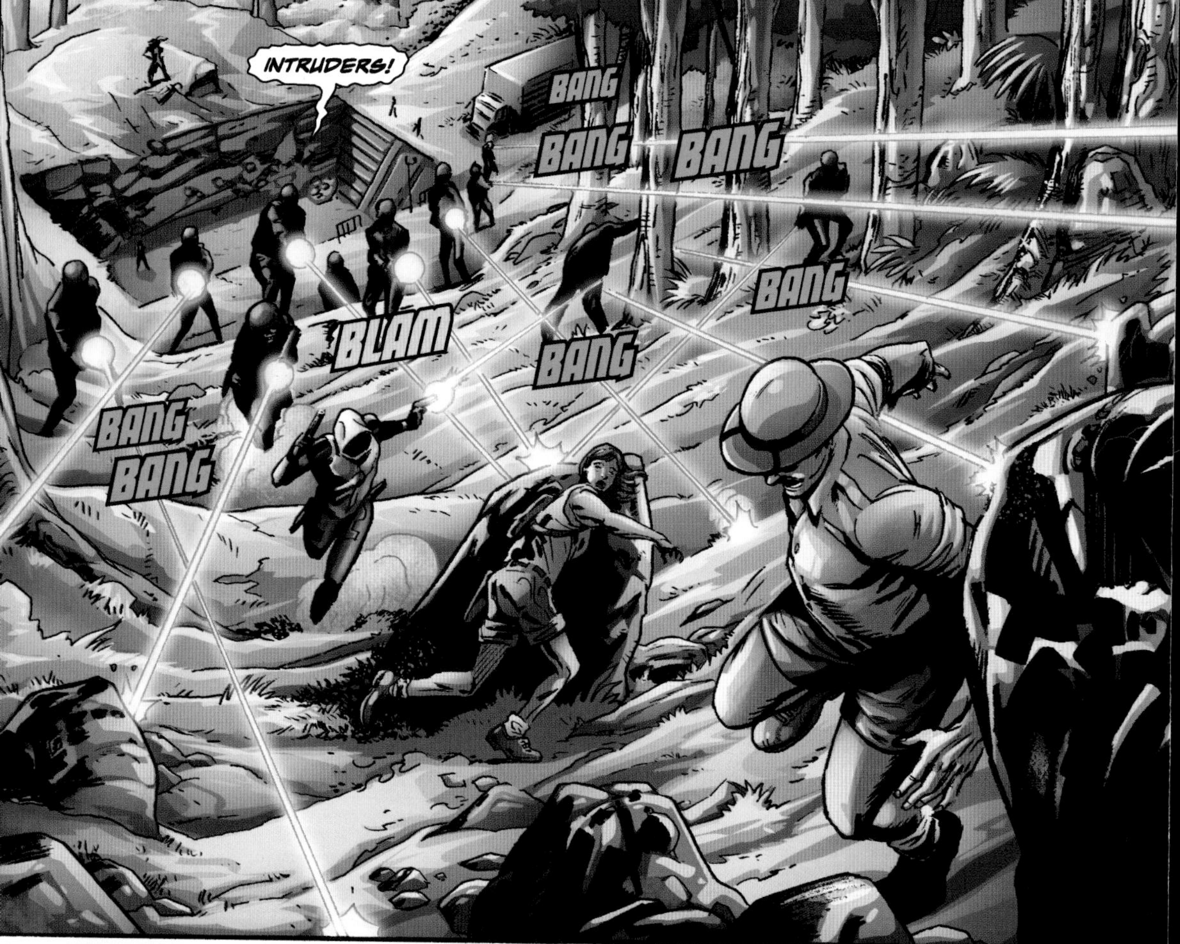
INTRUDERS!
BANG
BANG
BANG
BANG
BLAM
BANG
BANG
BANG
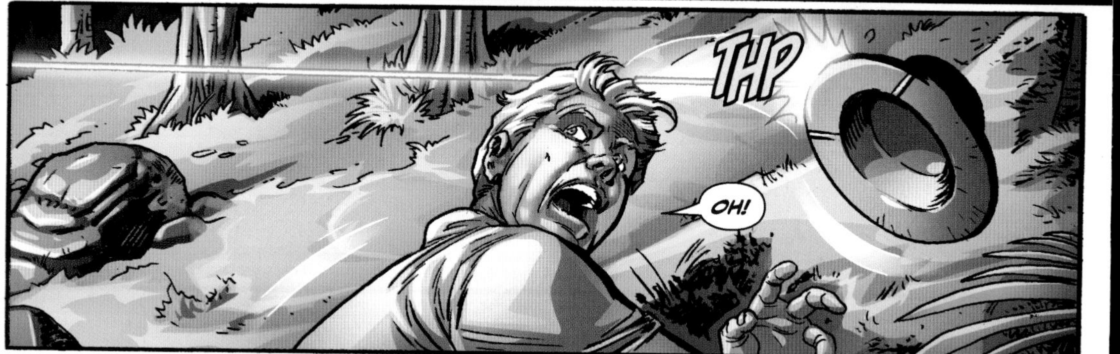
THP
OH!
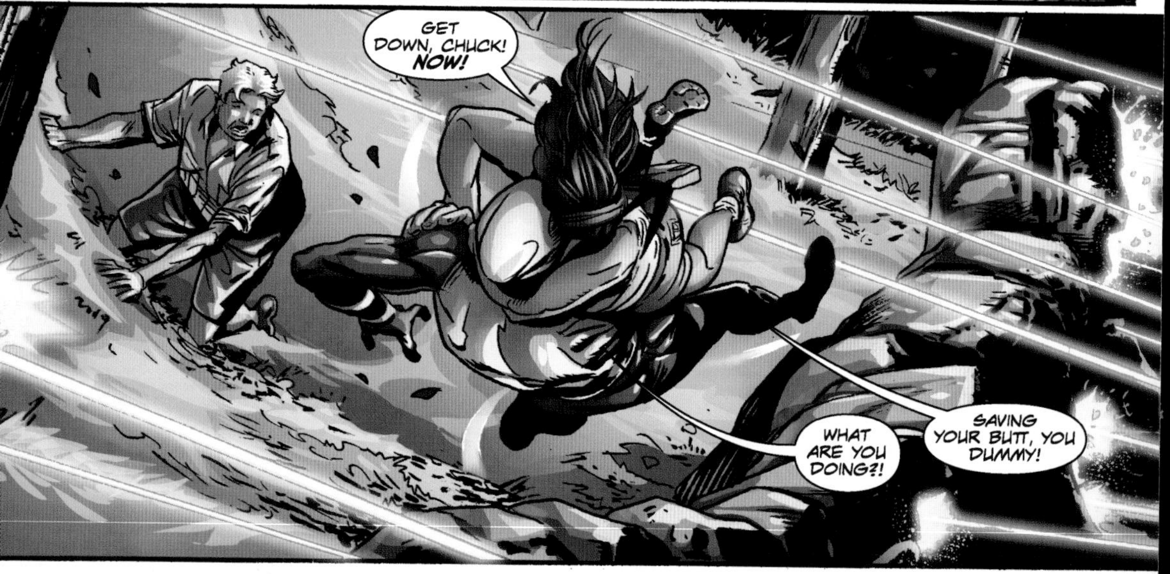
GET DOWN, CHUCK! NOW!
WHAT ARE YOU DOING?!
SAVING YOUR BUTT, YOU DUMMY!

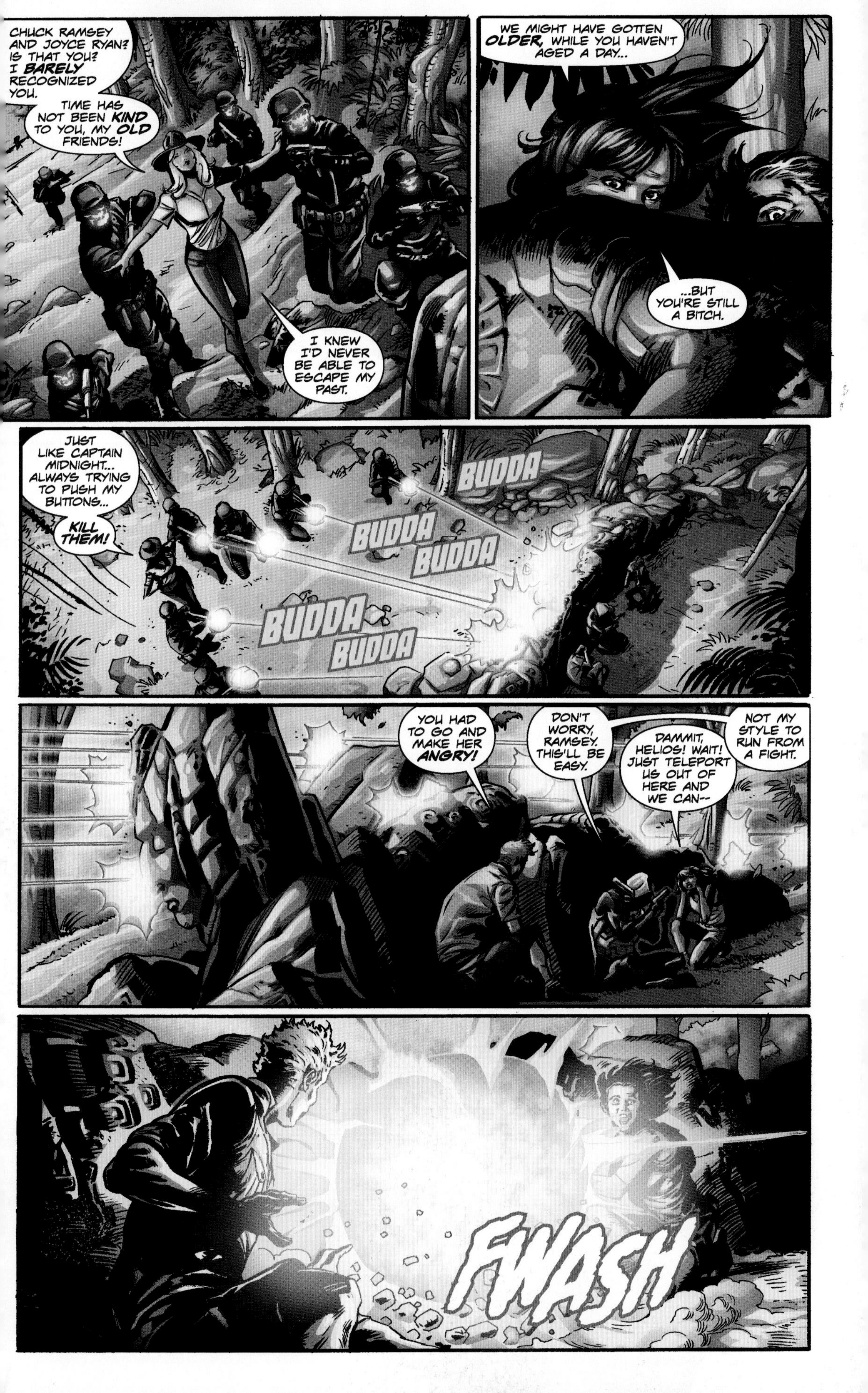
CHUCK RAMSEY AND JOYCE RYAN? IS THAT YOU? I BARELY RECOGNIZED YOU.
TIME HAS NOT BEEN KIND TO YOU, MY OLD FRIENDS!
I KNEW I'D NEVER BE ABLE TO ESCAPE MY PAST.
WE MIGHT HAVE GOTTEN OLDER, WHILE YOU HAVEN'T AGED A DAY...
...BUT YOU'RE STILL A BITCH.
JUST LIKE CAPTAIN MIDNIGHT... ALWAYS TRYING TO PUSH MY BUTTONS...
KILL THEM!
BUDDA
BUDDA
BUDDA
BUDDA
BUDDA
YOU HAD TO GO AND MAKE HER ANGRY!
DON'T WORRY, RAMSEY. THIS'LL BE EASY.
NOT MY STYLE TO RUN FROM A FIGHT.
DAMMIT, HELIOS! WAIT! JUST TELEPORT US OUT OF HERE AND WE CAN--
FWASH

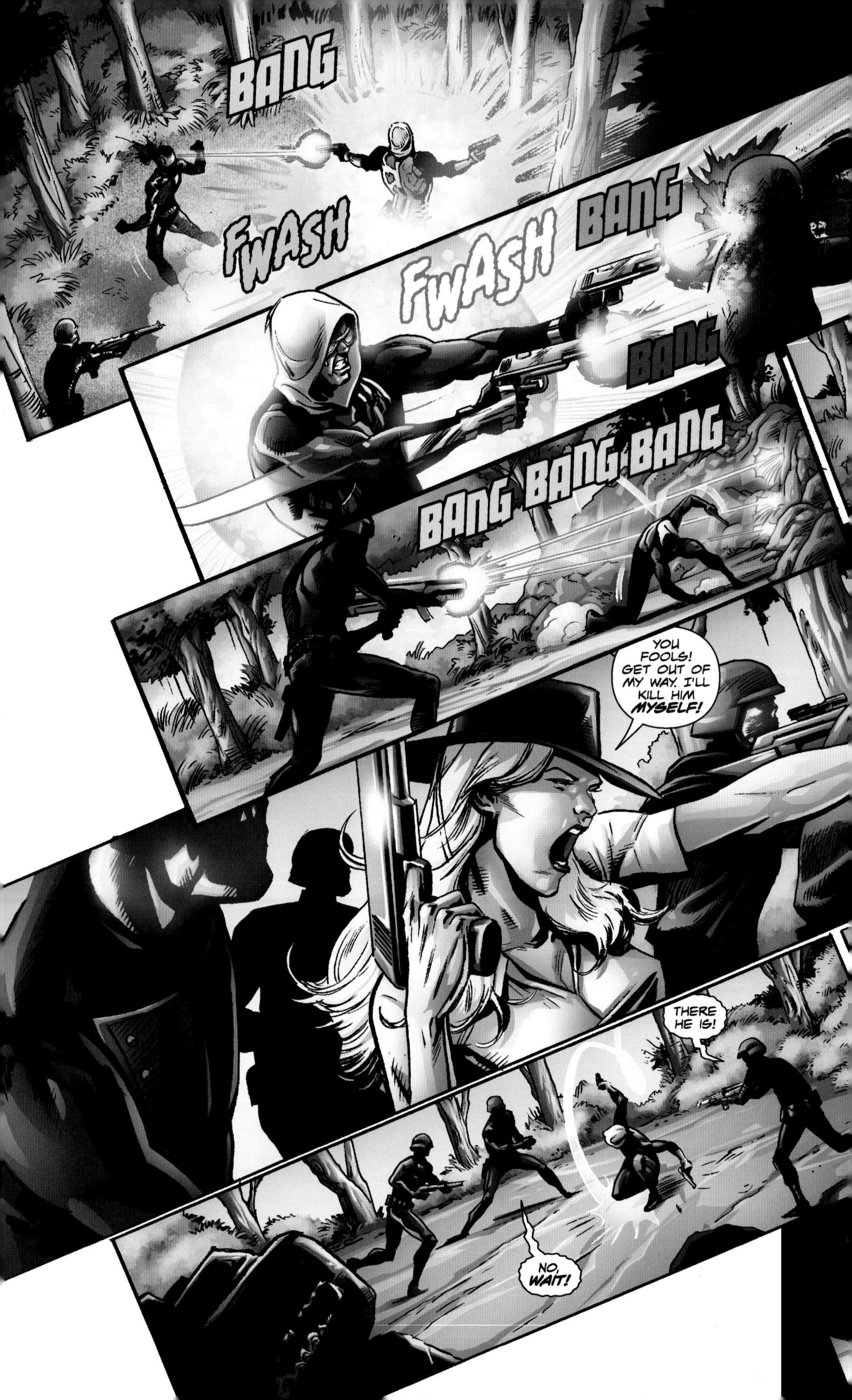
BANG
FWASH
FWASH
BANG
BANG
BANG BANG BANG
YOU FOOLS! GET OUT OF MY WAY. I'LL KILL HIM MYSELF!
THERE HE IS!
NO, WAIT!

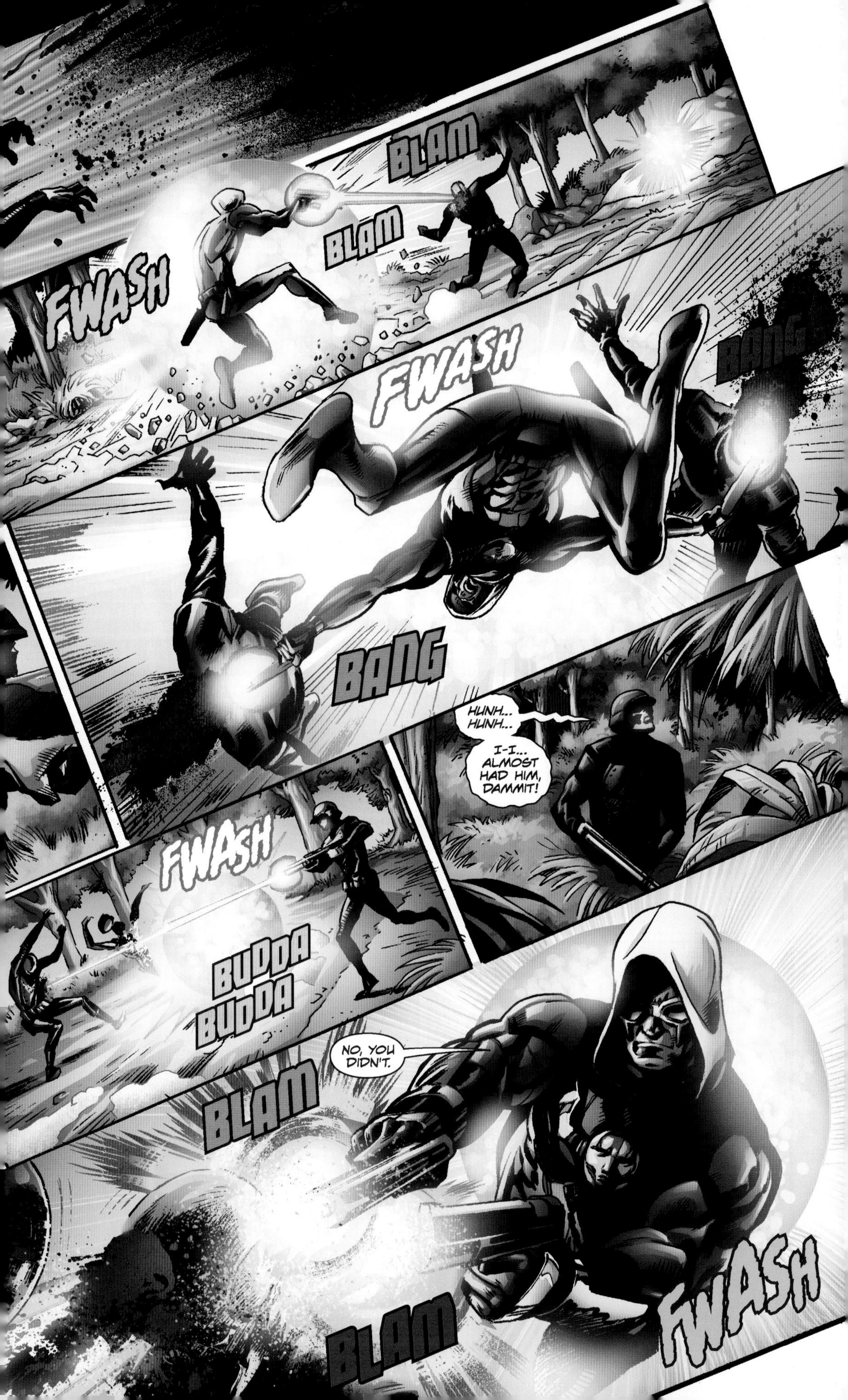
BLAM
BLAM
FWASH
FWASH
BANG
BANG
HUNH... HUNH...
I-I... ALMOST HAD HIM, DAMMIT!
FWASH
BUDDA BUDDA
NO, YOU DIDN'T.
BLAM
BLAM
FWASH

UGH.

NICE TRY, BUT I ALWAYS HAVE *MORE* WRAITHS!

THERE WILL BE *NO* ESCAPE!

THAT WAS A COMPLETE WASTE OF TIME. CAN YOU STILL TELEPORT US OUT OF HERE?

NO... THAT WAS *TOO MUCH.* IT'S GOING TO TAKE A MINUTE.

WE DON'T HAVE A MINUTE!

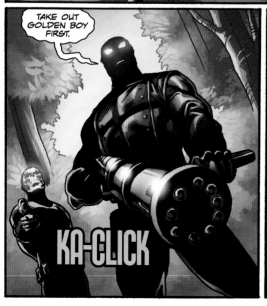

TAKE OUT GOLDEN BOY FIRST.

KA-CLICK

BLAM

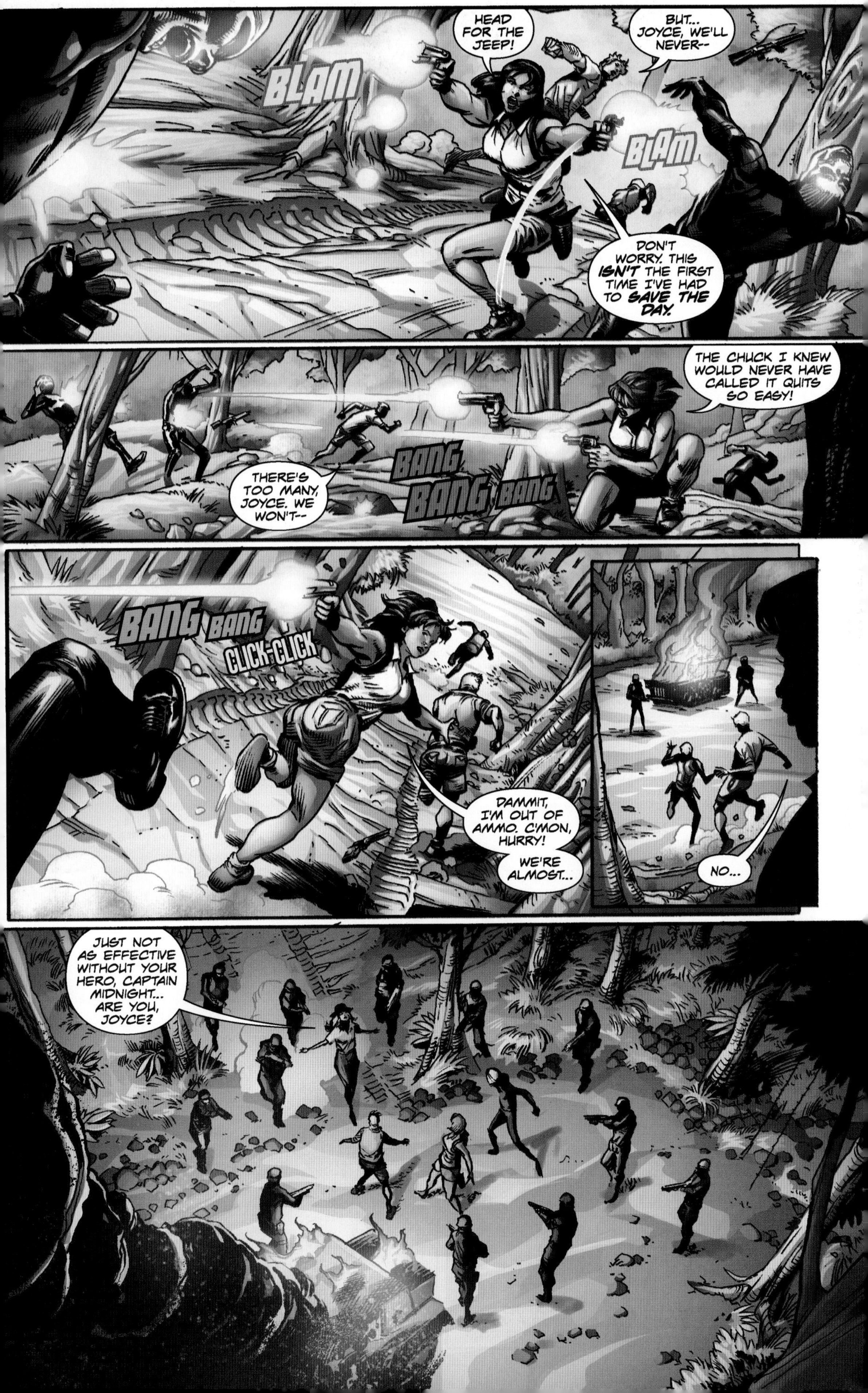
HEAD FOR THE JEEP!
BLAM
BUT... JOYCE, WE'LL NEVER--
BLAM
DON'T WORRY. THIS ISN'T THE FIRST TIME I'VE HAD TO SAVE THE DAY.
THE CHUCK I KNEW WOULD NEVER HAVE CALLED IT QUITS SO EASY!
THERE'S TOO MANY, JOYCE. WE WON'T--
BANG BANG BANG
BANG BANG CLICK-CLICK
DAMMIT, I'M OUT OF AMMO. C'MON, HURRY!
WE'RE ALMOST...
NO...
JUST NOT AS EFFECTIVE WITHOUT YOUR HERO, CAPTAIN MIDNIGHT... ARE YOU, JOYCE?

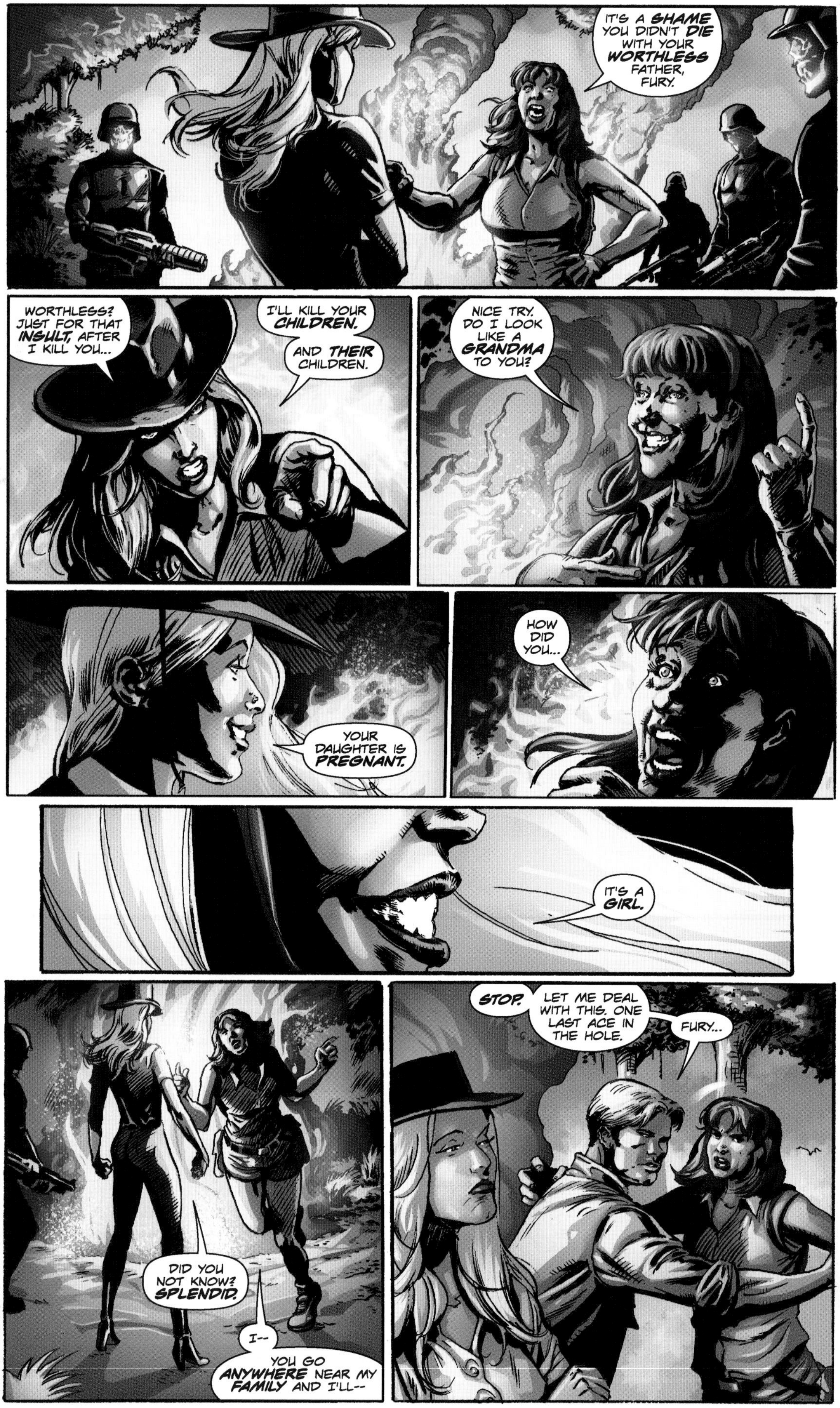
IT'S A SHAME YOU DIDN'T DIE WITH YOUR WORTHLESS FATHER, FURY.
WORTHLESS? JUST FOR THAT INSULT, AFTER I KILL YOU...
I'LL KILL YOUR CHILDREN.
AND THEIR CHILDREN.
NICE TRY. DO I LOOK LIKE A GRANDMA TO YOU?
YOUR DAUGHTER IS PREGNANT.
HOW DID YOU...
IT'S A GIRL.
DID YOU NOT KNOW? SPLENDID.
I--
YOU GO ANYWHERE NEAR MY FAMILY AND I'LL--
STOP.
LET ME DEAL WITH THIS. ONE LAST ACE IN THE HOLE.
FURY...

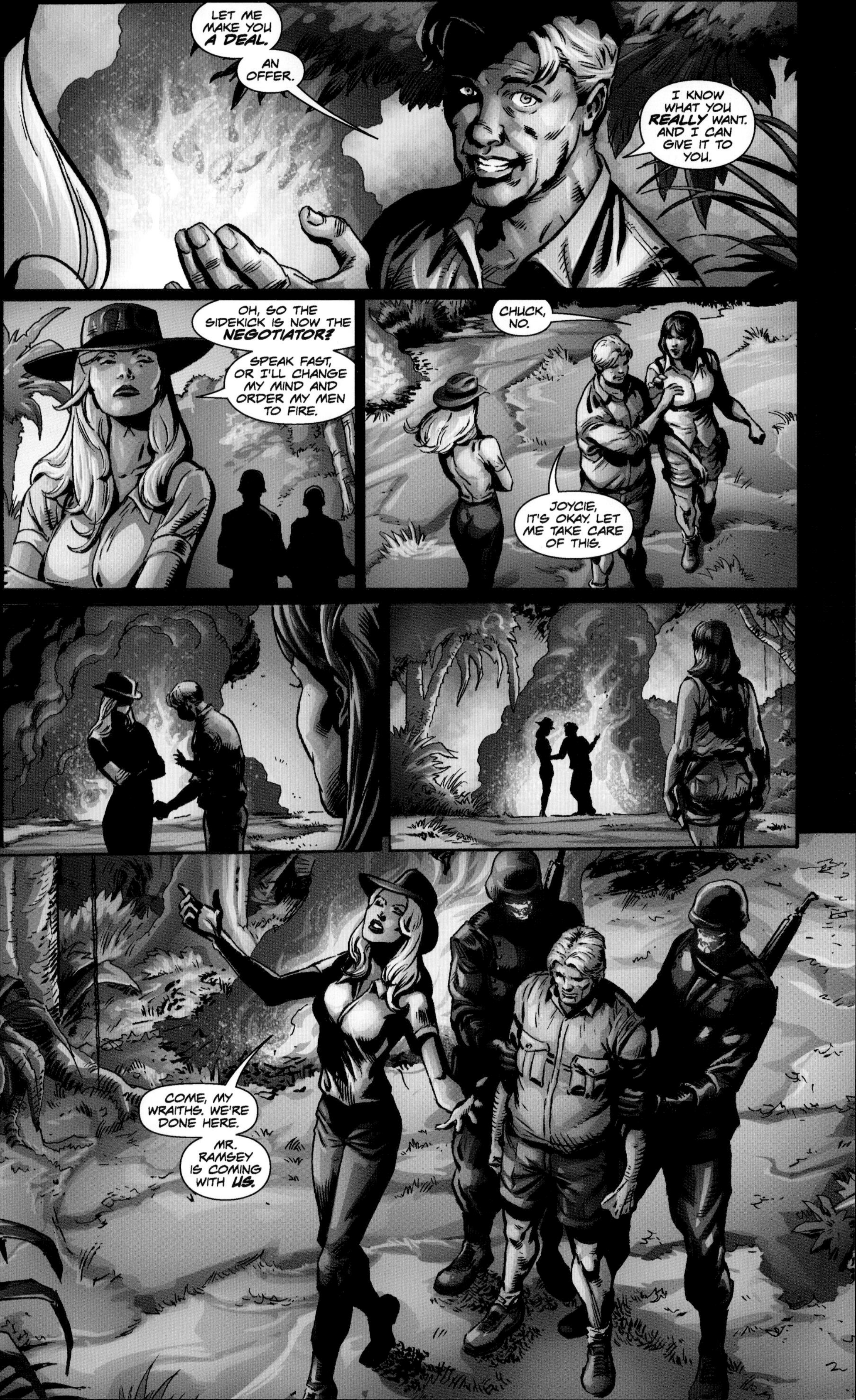
LET ME MAKE YOU A DEAL.
AN OFFER.
I KNOW WHAT YOU REALLY WANT. AND I CAN GIVE IT TO YOU.
OH, SO THE SIDEKICK IS NOW THE NEGOTIATOR?
SPEAK FAST, OR I'LL CHANGE MY MIND AND ORDER MY MEN TO FIRE.
CHUCK, NO.
JOYCIE, IT'S OKAY. LET ME TAKE CARE OF THIS.
COME, MY WRAITHS. WE'RE DONE HERE.
MR. RAMSEY IS COMING WITH US.

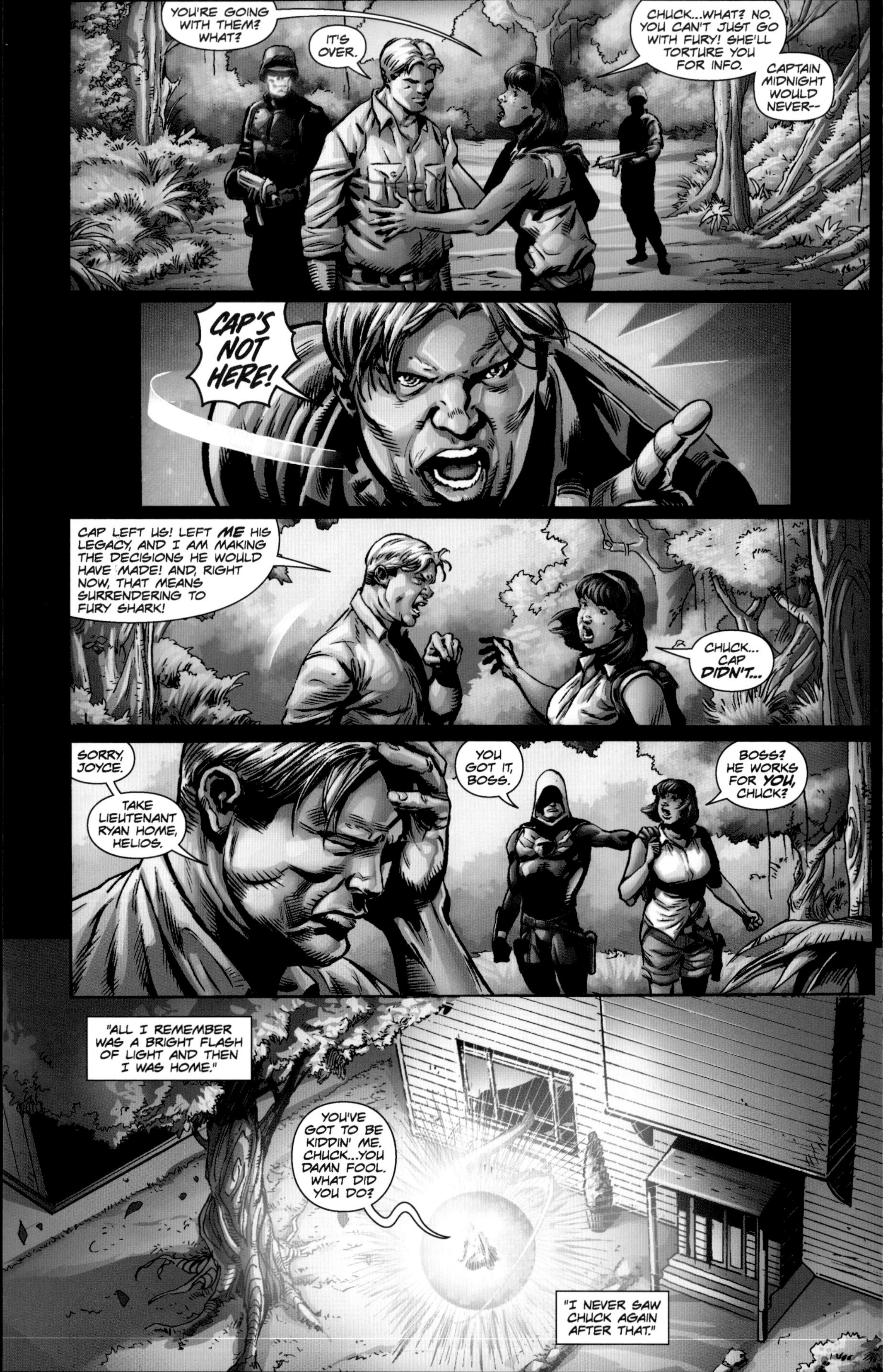
YOU'RE GOING WITH THEM? WHAT?
IT'S OVER.
CHUCK...WHAT? NO. YOU CAN'T JUST GO WITH FURY! SHE'LL TORTURE YOU FOR INFO.
CAPTAIN MIDNIGHT WOULD NEVER--
CAP'S NOT HERE!
CAP LEFT US! LEFT ME HIS LEGACY, AND I AM MAKING THE DECISIONS HE WOULD HAVE MADE! AND, RIGHT NOW, THAT MEANS SURRENDERING TO FURY SHARK!
CHUCK... CAP DIDN'T...
SORRY, JOYCE.
TAKE LIEUTENANT RYAN HOME, HELIOS.
YOU GOT IT, BOSS.
BOSS? HE WORKS FOR YOU, CHUCK?
"ALL I REMEMBER WAS A BRIGHT FLASH OF LIGHT AND THEN I WAS HOME."
YOU'VE GOT TO BE KIDDIN' ME. CHUCK...YOU DAMN FOOL. WHAT DID YOU DO?
"I NEVER SAW CHUCK AGAIN AFTER THAT."

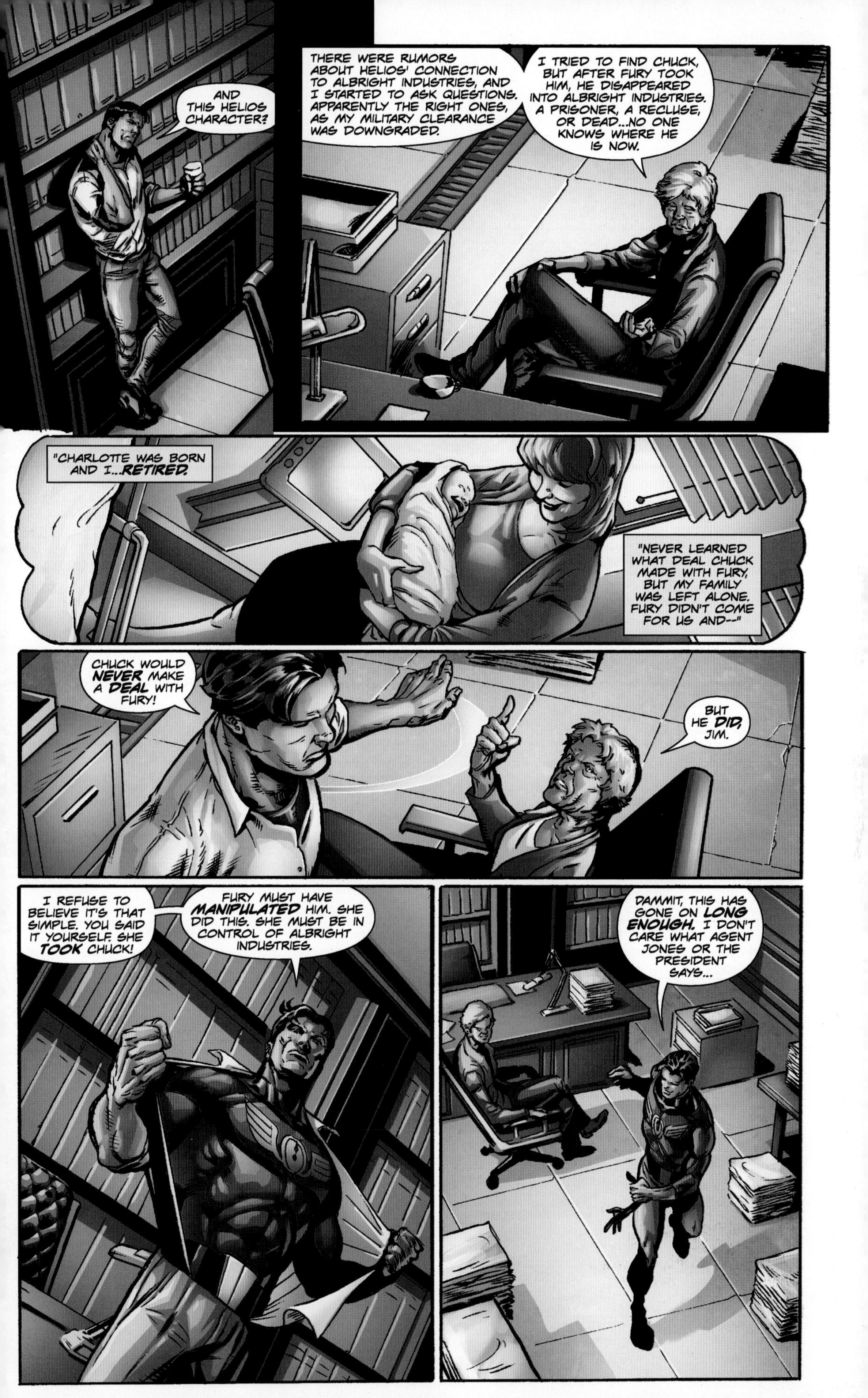

AND THIS HELIOS CHARACTER?
THERE WERE RUMORS ABOUT HELIOS' CONNECTION TO ALBRIGHT INDUSTRIES, AND I STARTED TO ASK QUESTIONS. APPARENTLY THE RIGHT ONES, AS MY MILITARY CLEARANCE WAS DOWNGRADED.
I TRIED TO FIND CHUCK, BUT AFTER FURY TOOK HIM, HE DISAPPEARED INTO ALBRIGHT INDUSTRIES. A PRISONER, A RECLUSE, OR DEAD...NO ONE KNOWS WHERE HE IS NOW.
"CHARLOTTE WAS BORN AND I...RETIRED.
"NEVER LEARNED WHAT DEAL CHUCK MADE WITH FURY, BUT MY FAMILY WAS LEFT ALONE. FURY DIDN'T COME FOR US AND--"
CHUCK WOULD NEVER MAKE A DEAL WITH FURY!
BUT HE DID, JIM.
I REFUSE TO BELIEVE IT'S THAT SIMPLE. YOU SAID IT YOURSELF. SHE TOOK CHUCK!
FURY MUST HAVE MANIPULATED HIM. SHE DID THIS. SHE MUST BE IN CONTROL OF ALBRIGHT INDUSTRIES.
DAMMIT, THIS HAS GONE ON LONG ENOUGH. I DON'T CARE WHAT AGENT JONES OR THE PRESIDENT SAYS...

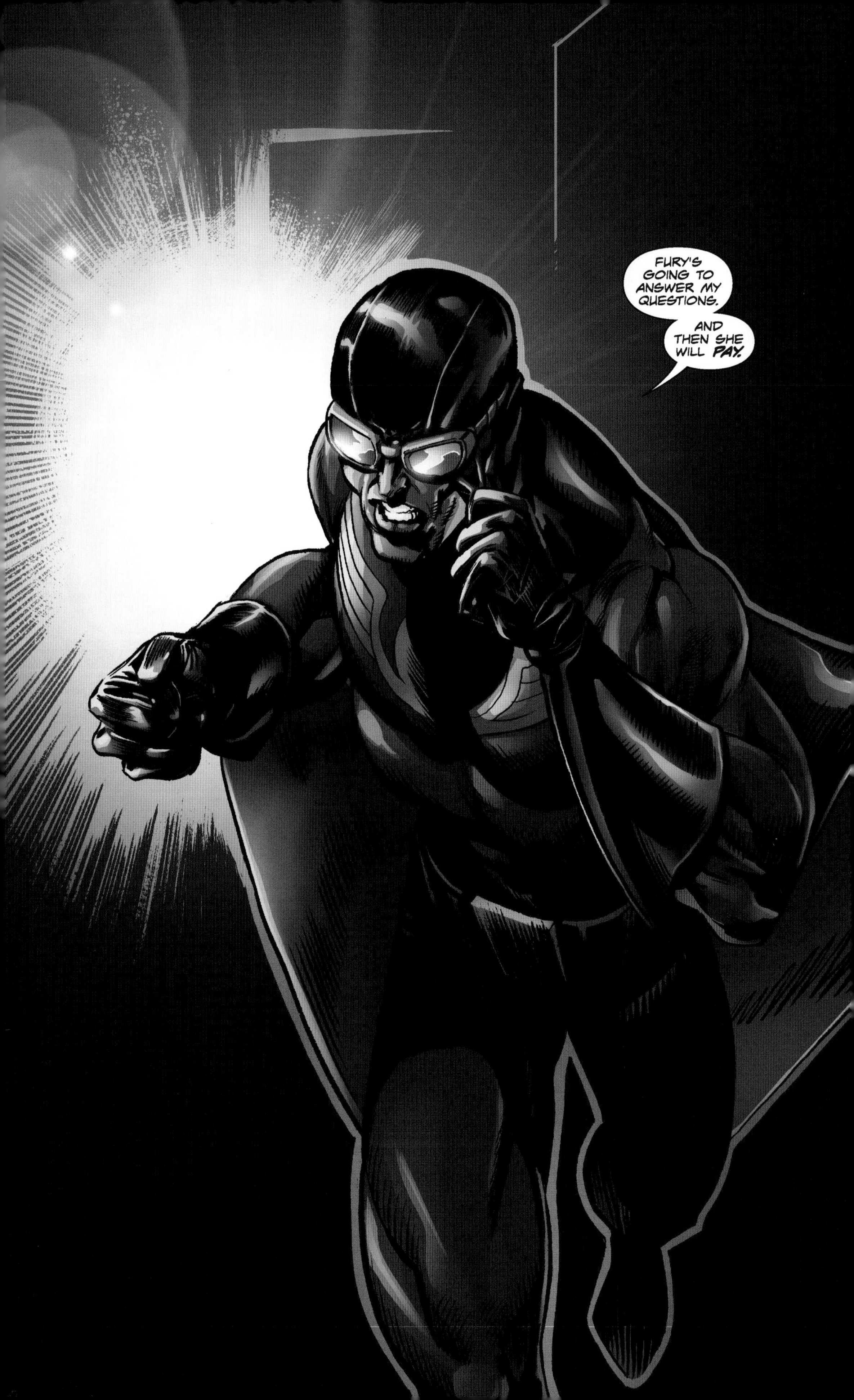
FURY'S GOING TO ANSWER MY QUESTIONS.
AND THEN SHE WILL PAY.

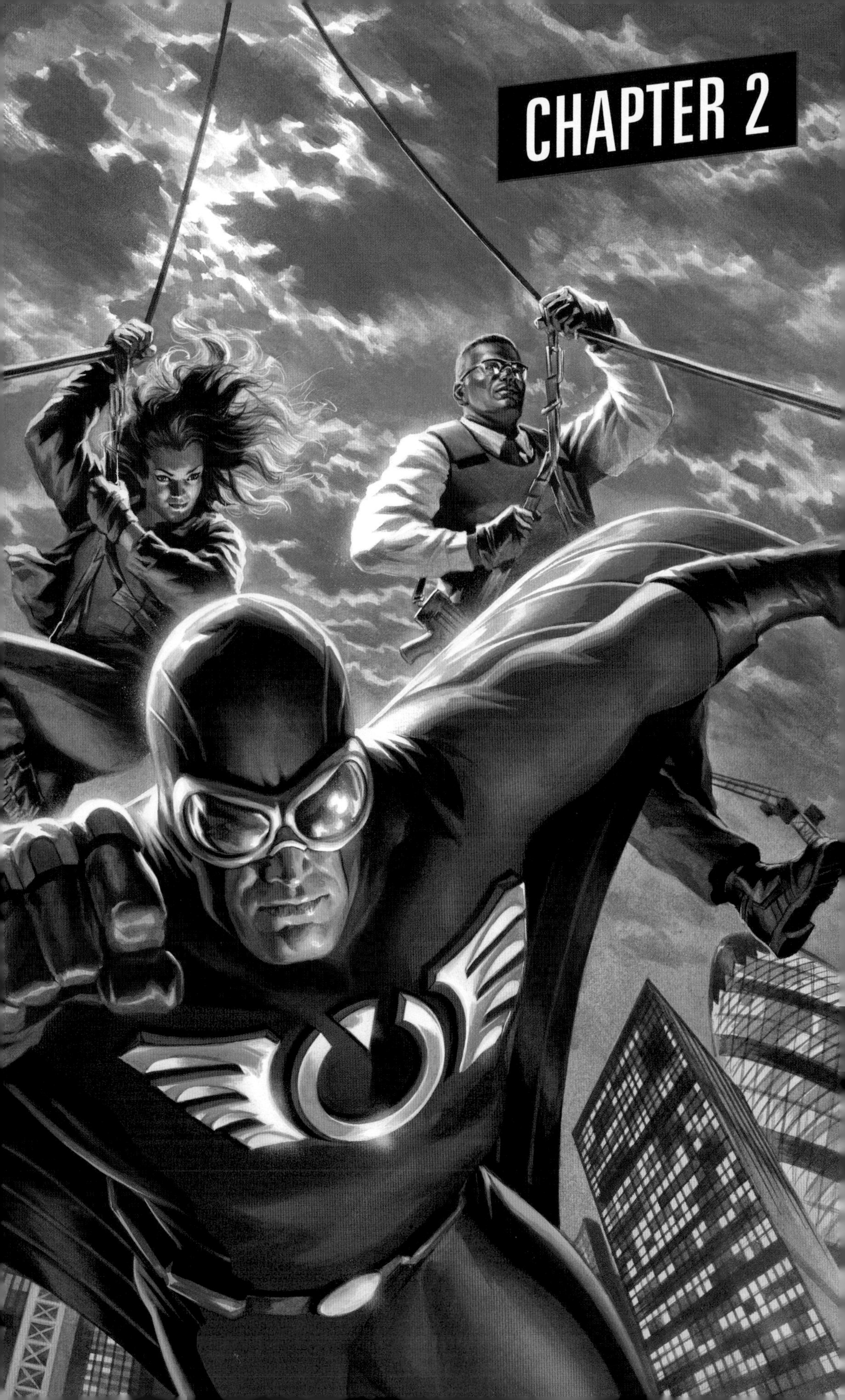
CHAPTER 2

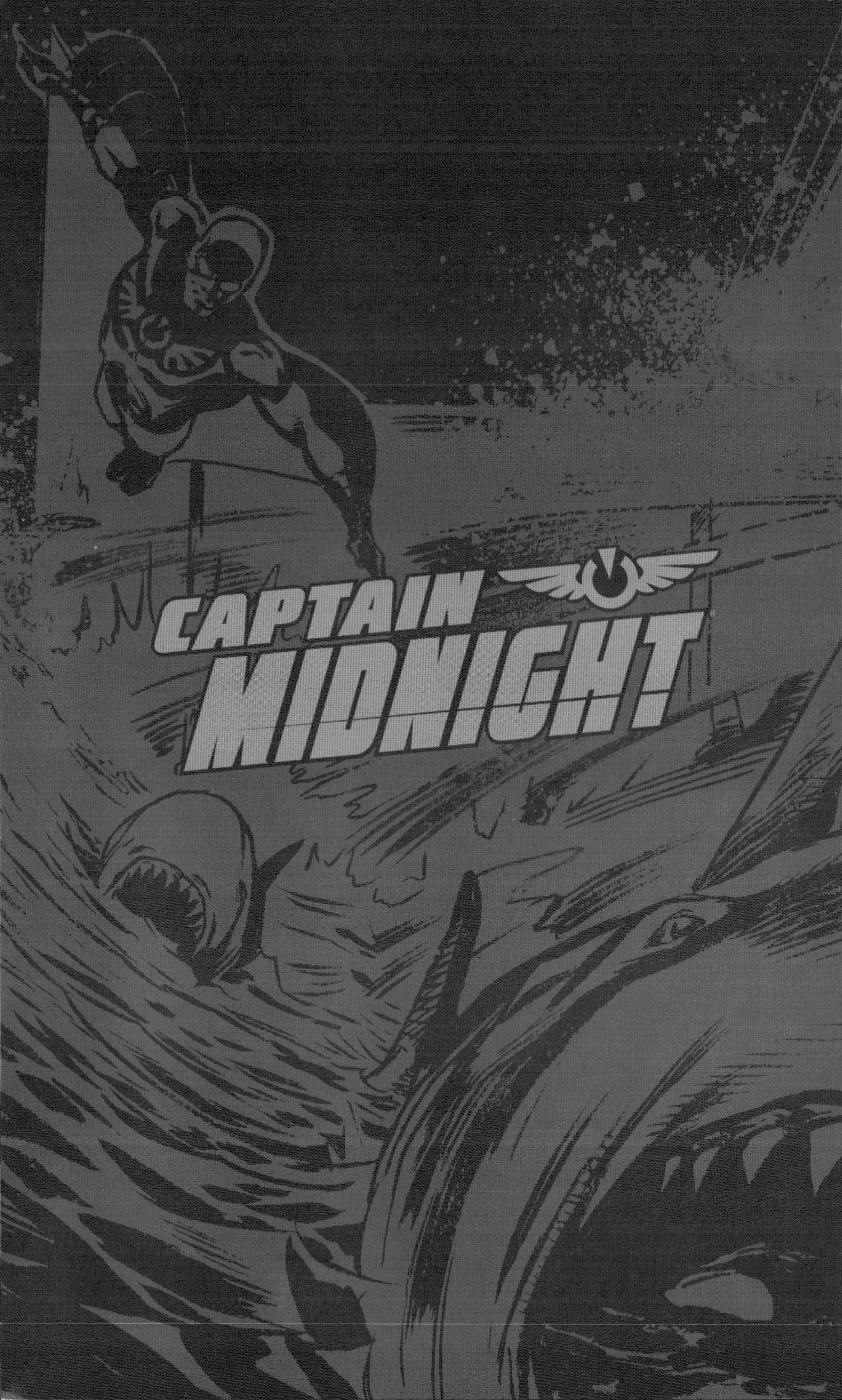
CAPTAIN
MIDNIGHT

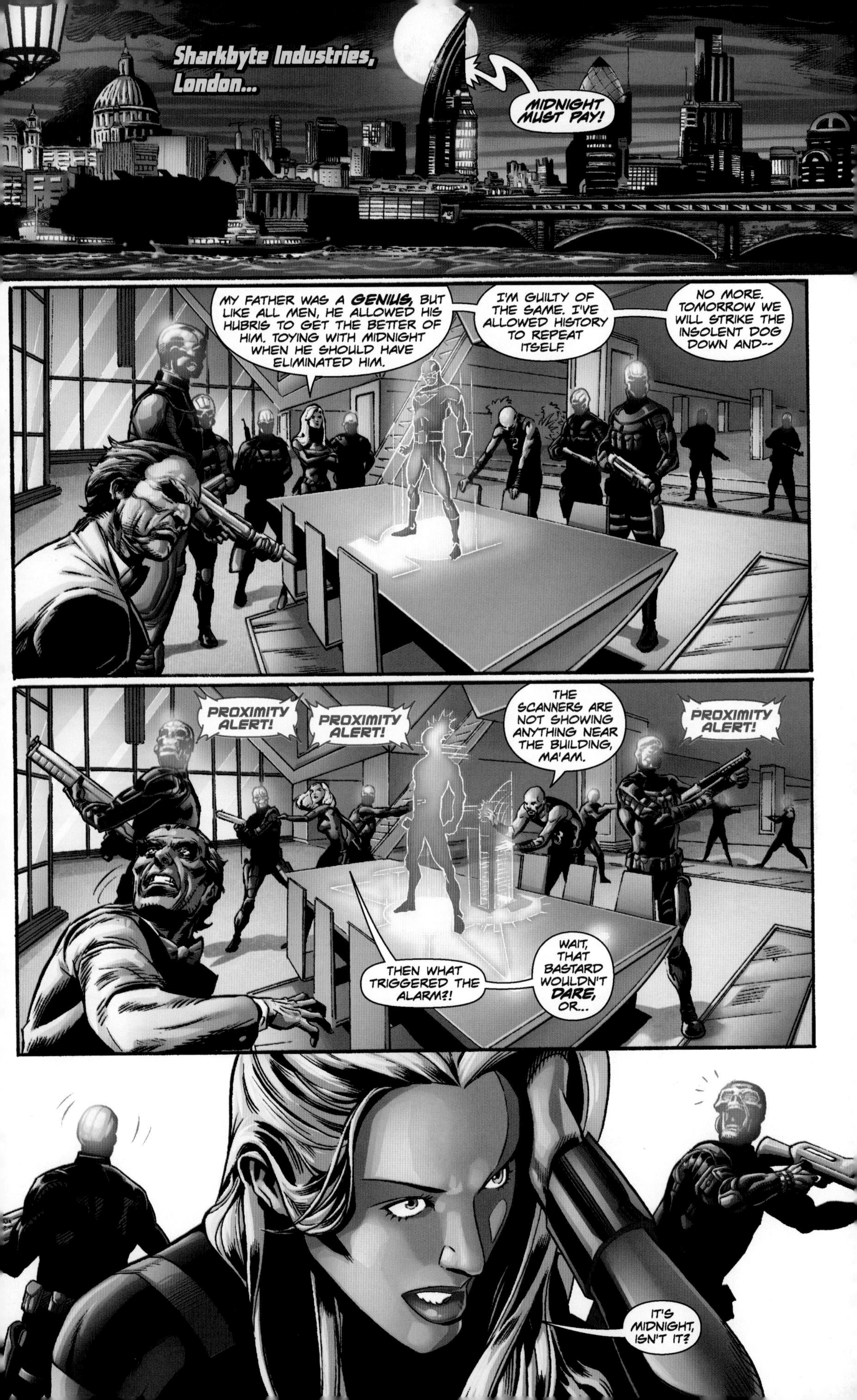
Sharkbyte Industries, London...
MIDNIGHT MUST PAY!
MY FATHER WAS A GENIUS, BUT LIKE ALL MEN, HE ALLOWED HIS HUBRIS TO GET THE BETTER OF HIM. TOYING WITH MIDNIGHT WHEN HE SHOULD HAVE ELIMINATED HIM.
I'M GUILTY OF THE SAME. I'VE ALLOWED HISTORY TO REPEAT ITSELF.
NO MORE. TOMORROW WE WILL STRIKE THE INSOLENT DOG DOWN AND--
PROXIMITY ALERT!
PROXIMITY ALERT!
THE SCANNERS ARE NOT SHOWING ANYTHING NEAR THE BUILDING, MA'AM.
PROXIMITY ALERT!
THEN WHAT TRIGGERED THE ALARM?!
WAIT, THAT BASTARD WOULDN'T DARE, OR...
IT'S MIDNIGHT, ISN'T IT?

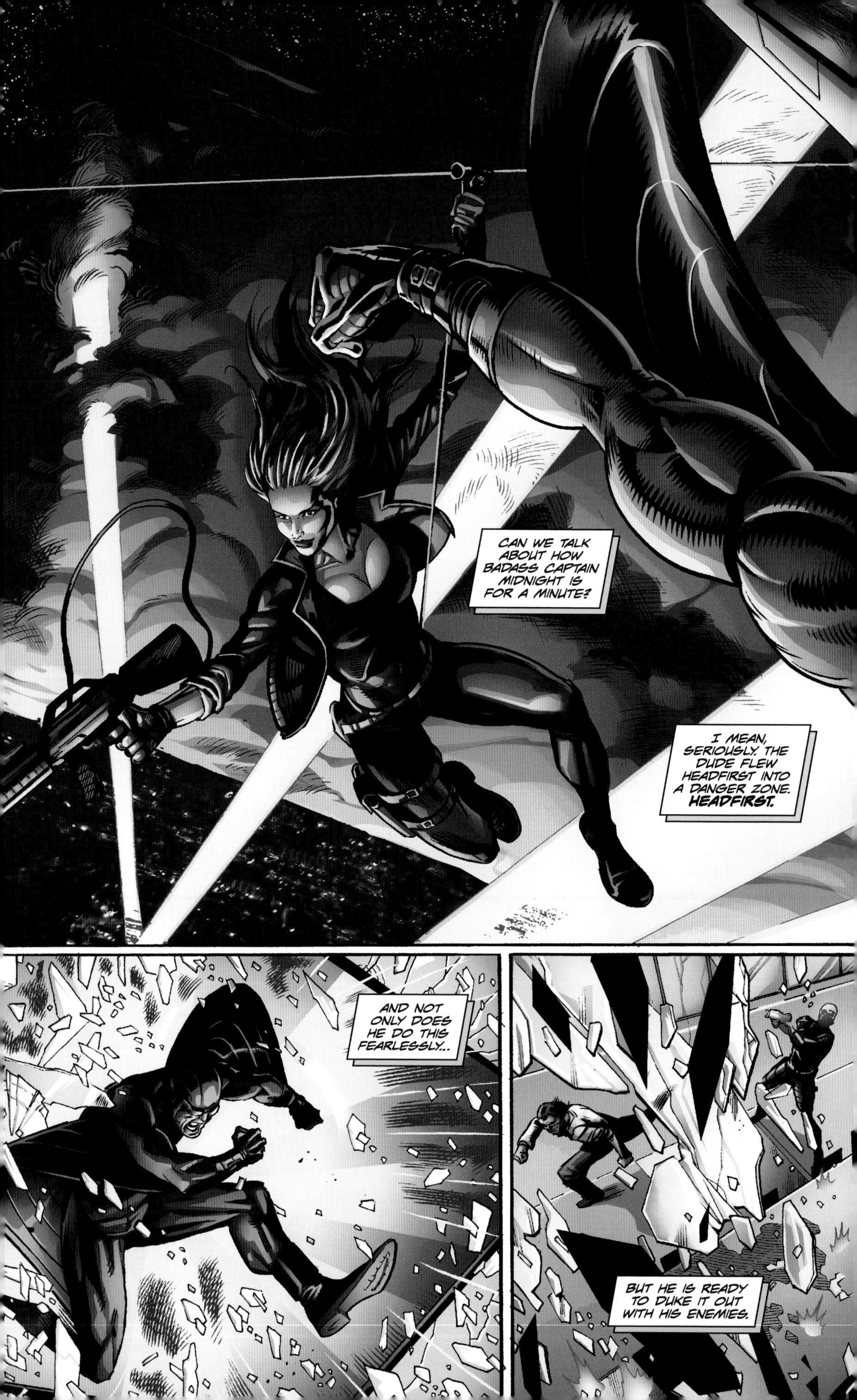
CAN WE TALK ABOUT HOW BADASS CAPTAIN MIDNIGHT IS FOR A MINUTE?
I MEAN, SERIOUSLY. THE DUDE FLEW HEADFIRST INTO A DANGER ZONE. **HEADFIRST.**
AND NOT ONLY DOES HE DO THIS FEARLESSLY...
BUT HE IS READY TO DUKE IT OUT WITH HIS ENEMIES.

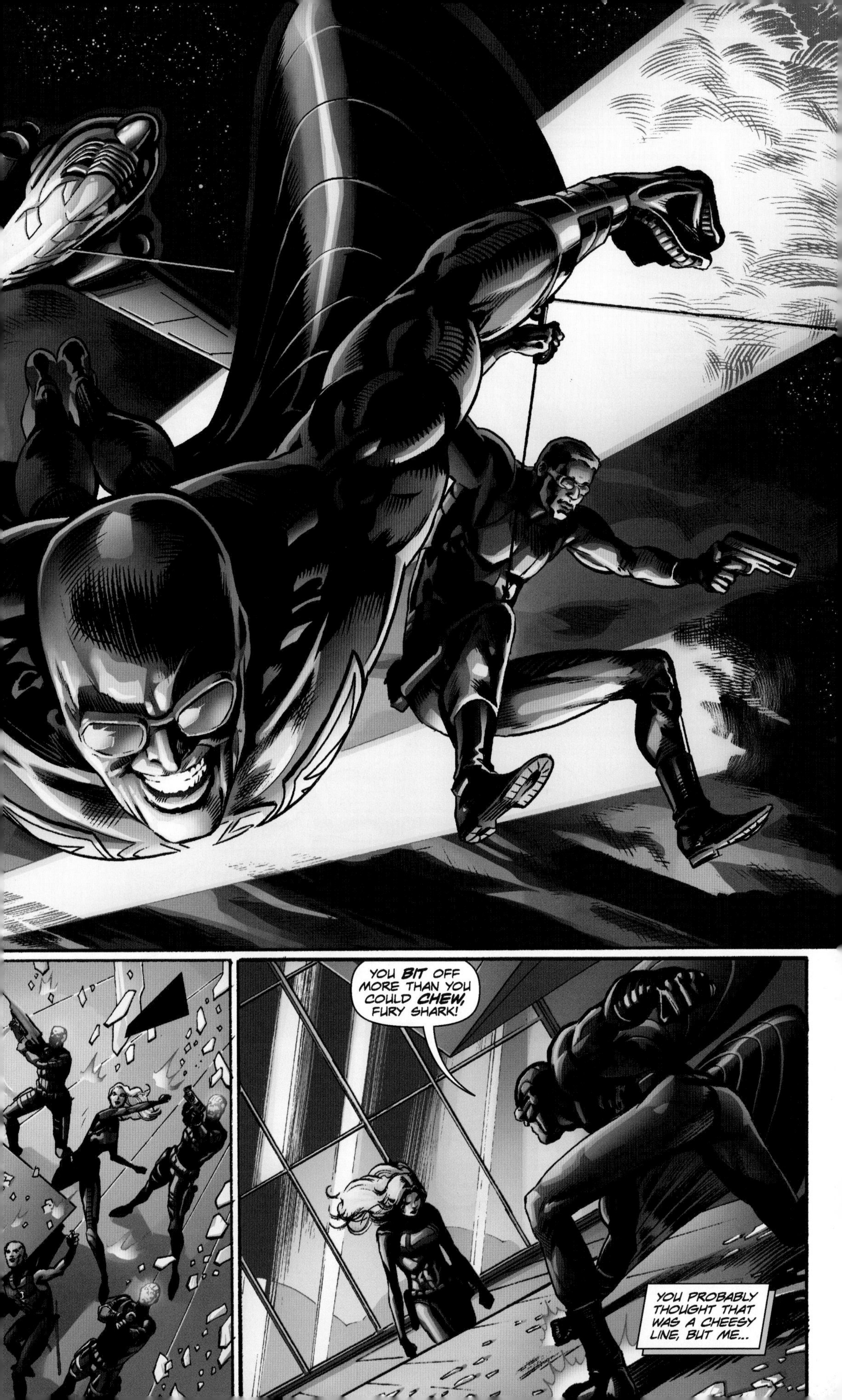
YOU BIT OFF MORE THAN YOU COULD CHEW, FURY SHARK!
YOU PROBABLY THOUGHT THAT WAS A CHEESY LINE, BUT ME...

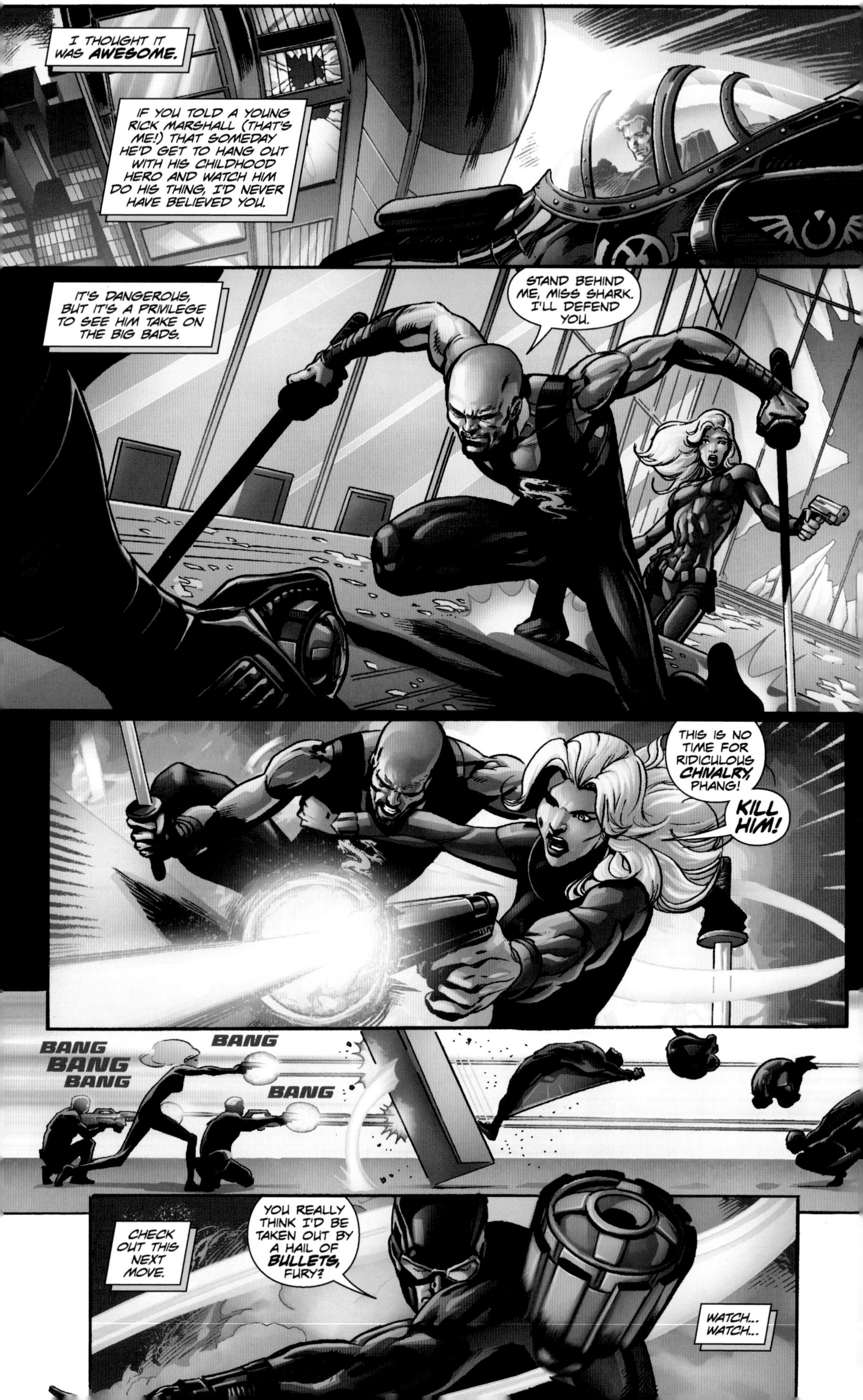

I THOUGHT IT WAS **AWESOME.**
IF YOU TOLD A YOUNG RICK MARSHALL (THAT'S ME!) THAT SOMEDAY HE'D GET TO HANG OUT WITH HIS CHILDHOOD HERO AND WATCH HIM DO HIS THING, I'D NEVER HAVE BELIEVED YOU.
IT'S DANGEROUS, BUT IT'S A PRIVILEGE TO SEE HIM TAKE ON THE BIG BADS.
STAND BEHIND ME, MISS SHARK. I'LL DEFEND YOU.
THIS IS NO TIME FOR RIDICULOUS **CHIVALRY,** PHANG!
KILL HIM!
BANG
BANG
BANG
BANG
BANG
BANG
CHECK OUT THIS NEXT MOVE.
YOU REALLY THINK I'D BE TAKEN OUT BY A HAIL OF **BULLETS,** FURY?
WATCH... WATCH...

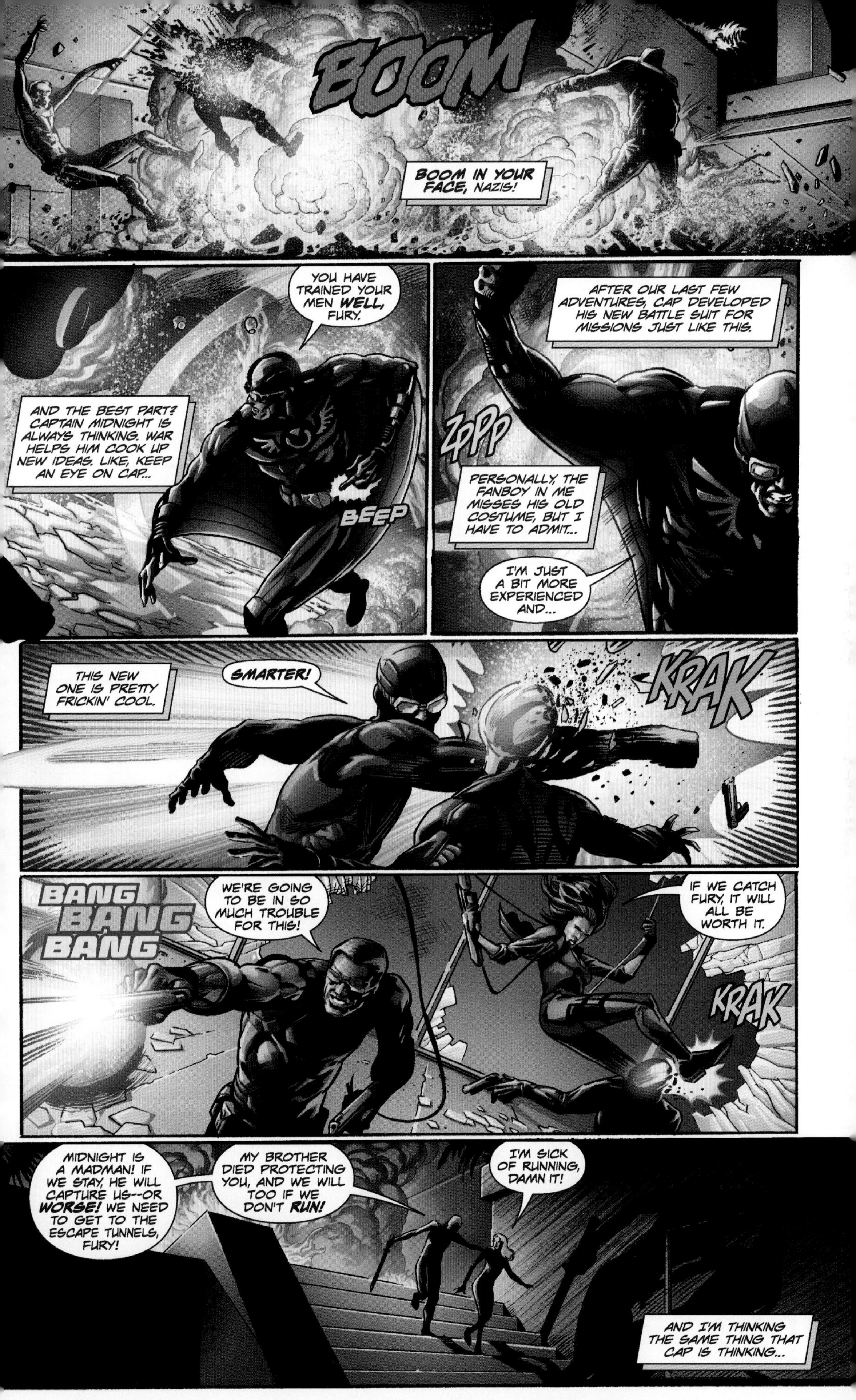
BOOM
BOOM IN YOUR FACE, NAZIS!
YOU HAVE TRAINED YOUR MEN WELL, FURY.
AND THE BEST PART? CAPTAIN MIDNIGHT IS ALWAYS THINKING. WAR HELPS HIM COOK UP NEW IDEAS. LIKE, KEEP AN EYE ON CAP...
BEEP
AFTER OUR LAST FEW ADVENTURES, CAP DEVELOPED HIS NEW BATTLE SUIT FOR MISSIONS JUST LIKE THIS.
ZPPP
PERSONALLY, THE FANBOY IN ME MISSES HIS OLD COSTUME, BUT I HAVE TO ADMIT...
I'M JUST A BIT MORE EXPERIENCED AND...
THIS NEW ONE IS PRETTY FRICKIN' COOL.
SMARTER!
KRAK
BANG BANG BANG
WE'RE GOING TO BE IN SO MUCH TROUBLE FOR THIS!
IF WE CATCH FURY, IT WILL ALL BE WORTH IT.
KRAK
MIDNIGHT IS A MADMAN! IF WE STAY, HE WILL CAPTURE US--OR WORSE! WE NEED TO GET TO THE ESCAPE TUNNELS, FURY!
MY BROTHER DIED PROTECTING YOU, AND WE WILL TOO IF WE DON'T RUN!
I'M SICK OF RUNNING, DAMN IT!
AND I'M THINKING THE SAME THING THAT CAP IS THINKING...

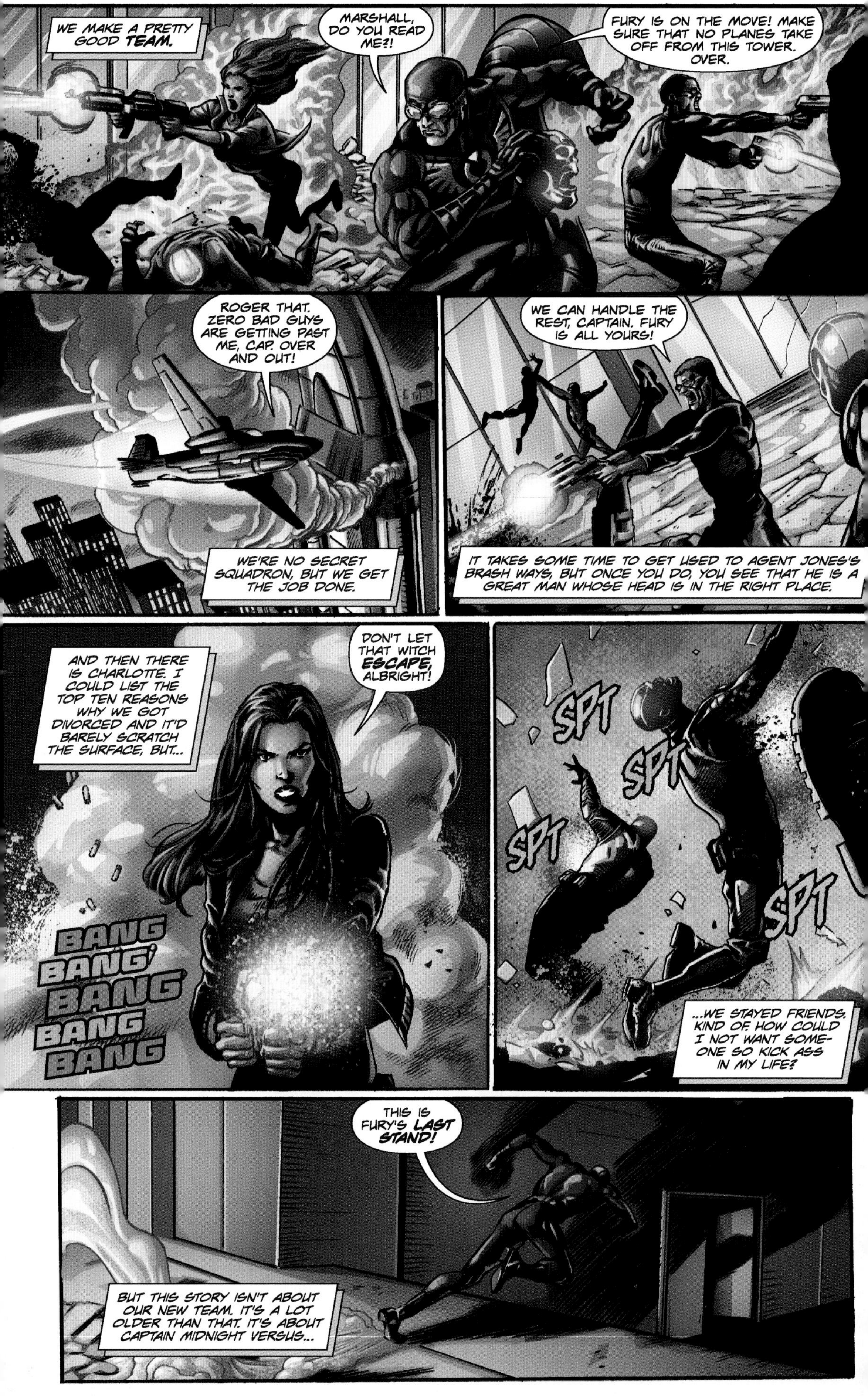

WE MAKE A PRETTY GOOD TEAM.
MARSHALL, DO YOU READ ME?!
FURY IS ON THE MOVE! MAKE SURE THAT NO PLANES TAKE OFF FROM THIS TOWER. OVER.
ROGER THAT. ZERO BAD GUYS ARE GETTING PAST ME, CAP. OVER AND OUT!
WE'RE NO SECRET SQUADRON, BUT WE GET THE JOB DONE.
WE CAN HANDLE THE REST, CAPTAIN. FURY IS ALL YOURS!
IT TAKES SOME TIME TO GET USED TO AGENT JONES'S BRASH WAYS, BUT ONCE YOU DO, YOU SEE THAT HE IS A GREAT MAN WHOSE HEAD IS IN THE RIGHT PLACE.
AND THEN THERE IS CHARLOTTE. I COULD LIST THE TOP TEN REASONS WHY WE GOT DIVORCED AND IT'D BARELY SCRATCH THE SURFACE, BUT...
DON'T LET THAT WITCH ESCAPE, ALBRIGHT!
BANG
BANG
BANG
BANG
BANG
SPT
SPT
SPT
SPT
...WE STAYED FRIENDS. KIND OF. HOW COULD I NOT WANT SOME-ONE SO KICK ASS IN MY LIFE?
THIS IS FURY'S LAST STAND!
BUT THIS STORY ISN'T ABOUT OUR NEW TEAM. IT'S A LOT OLDER THAN THAT. IT'S ABOUT CAPTAIN MIDNIGHT VERSUS...

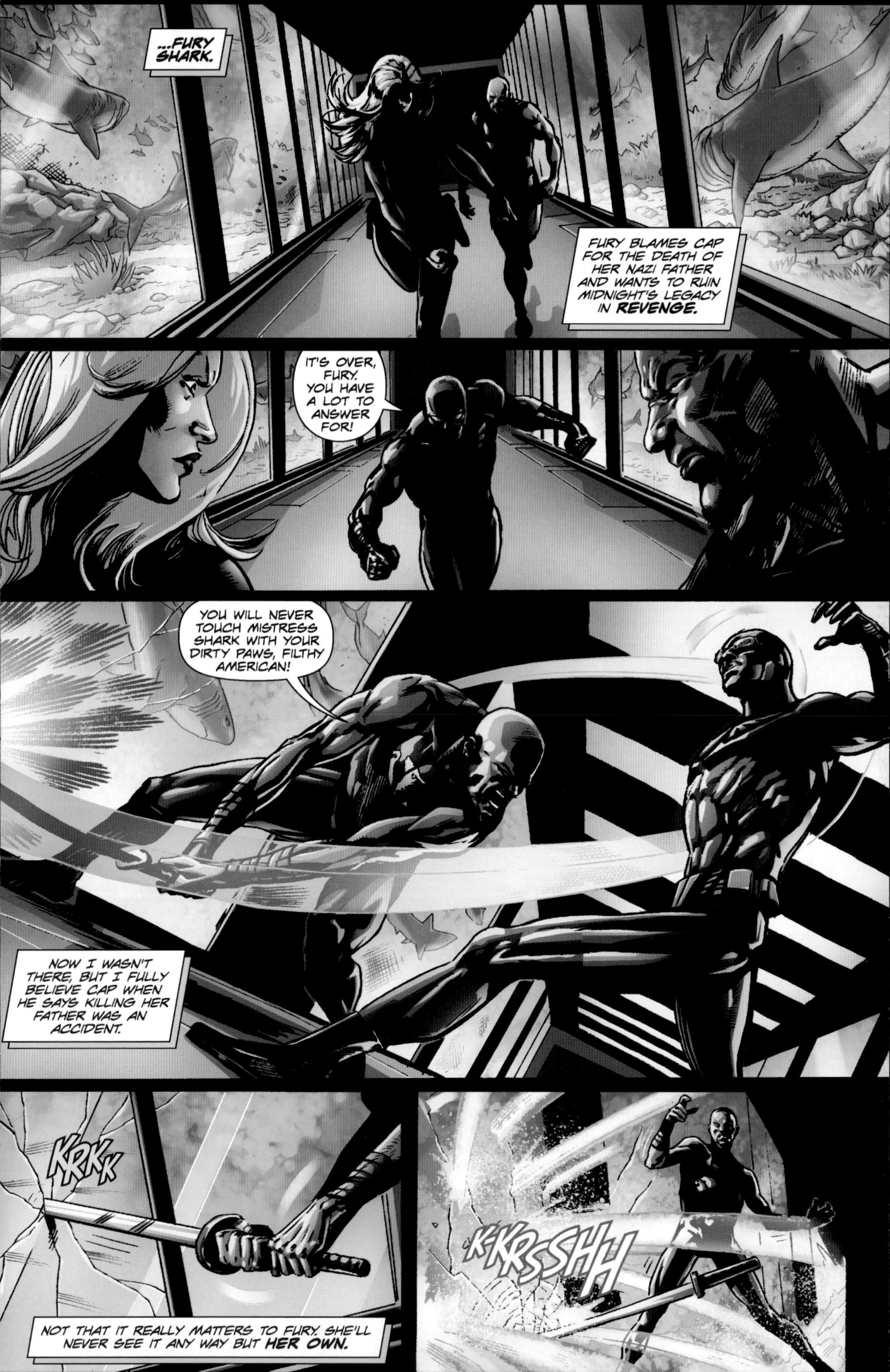
...FURY SHARK.
FURY BLAMES CAP FOR THE DEATH OF HER NAZI FATHER AND WANTS TO RUIN MIDNIGHT'S LEGACY IN REVENGE.
IT'S OVER, FURY. YOU HAVE A LOT TO ANSWER FOR!
YOU WILL NEVER TOUCH MISTRESS SHARK WITH YOUR DIRTY PAWS, FILTHY AMERICAN!
NOW I WASN'T THERE, BUT I FULLY BELIEVE CAP WHEN HE SAYS KILLING HER FATHER WAS AN ACCIDENT.
KRKK
NOT THAT IT REALLY MATTERS TO FURY. SHE'LL NEVER SEE IT ANY WAY BUT HER OWN.
K-KRSSHH

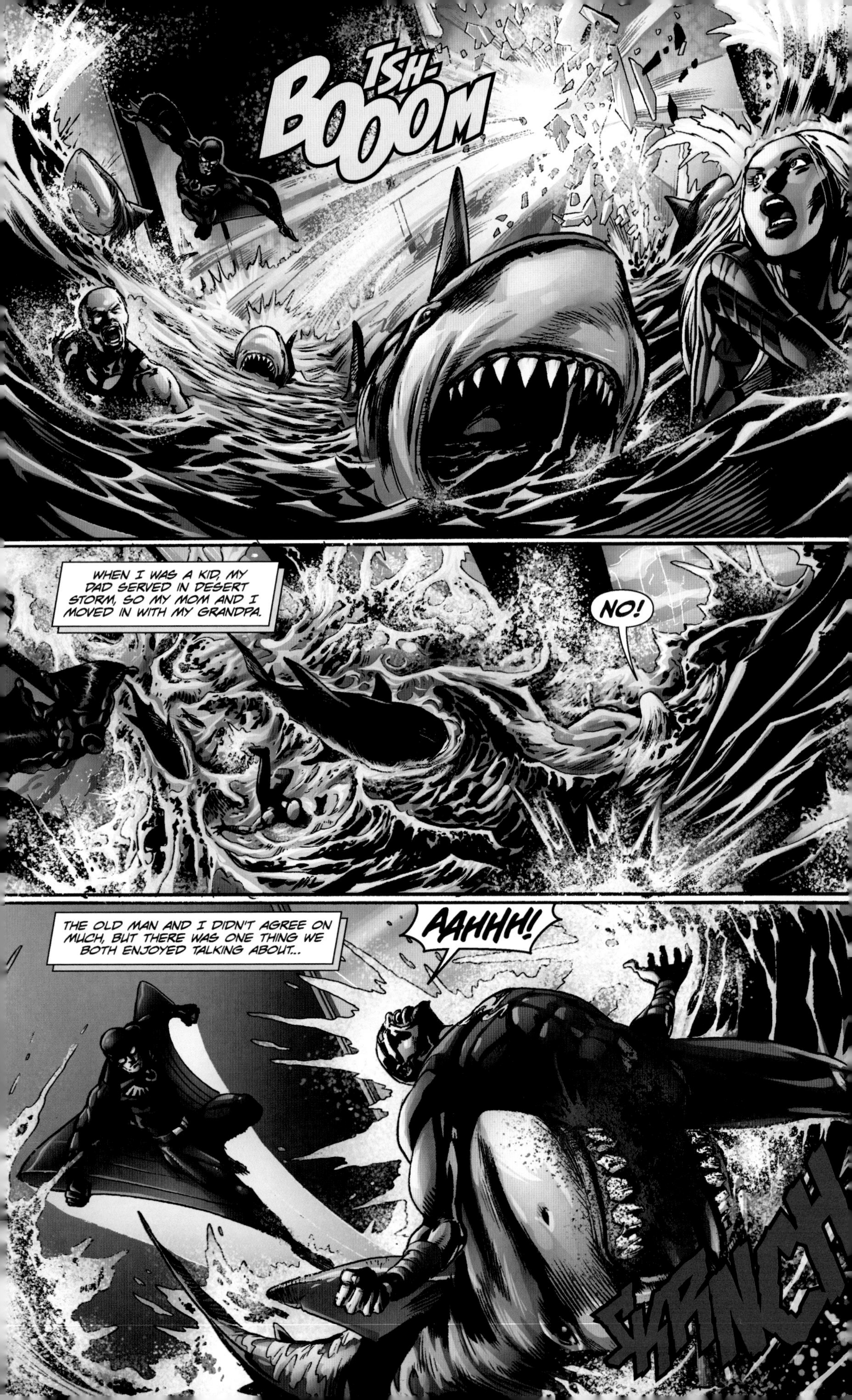
TSH-BOOOM
WHEN I WAS A KID, MY DAD SERVED IN DESERT STORM, SO MY MOM AND I MOVED IN WITH MY GRANDPA.
NO!
THE OLD MAN AND I DIDN'T AGREE ON MUCH, BUT THERE WAS ONE THING WE BOTH ENJOYED TALKING ABOUT...
AAHHH!

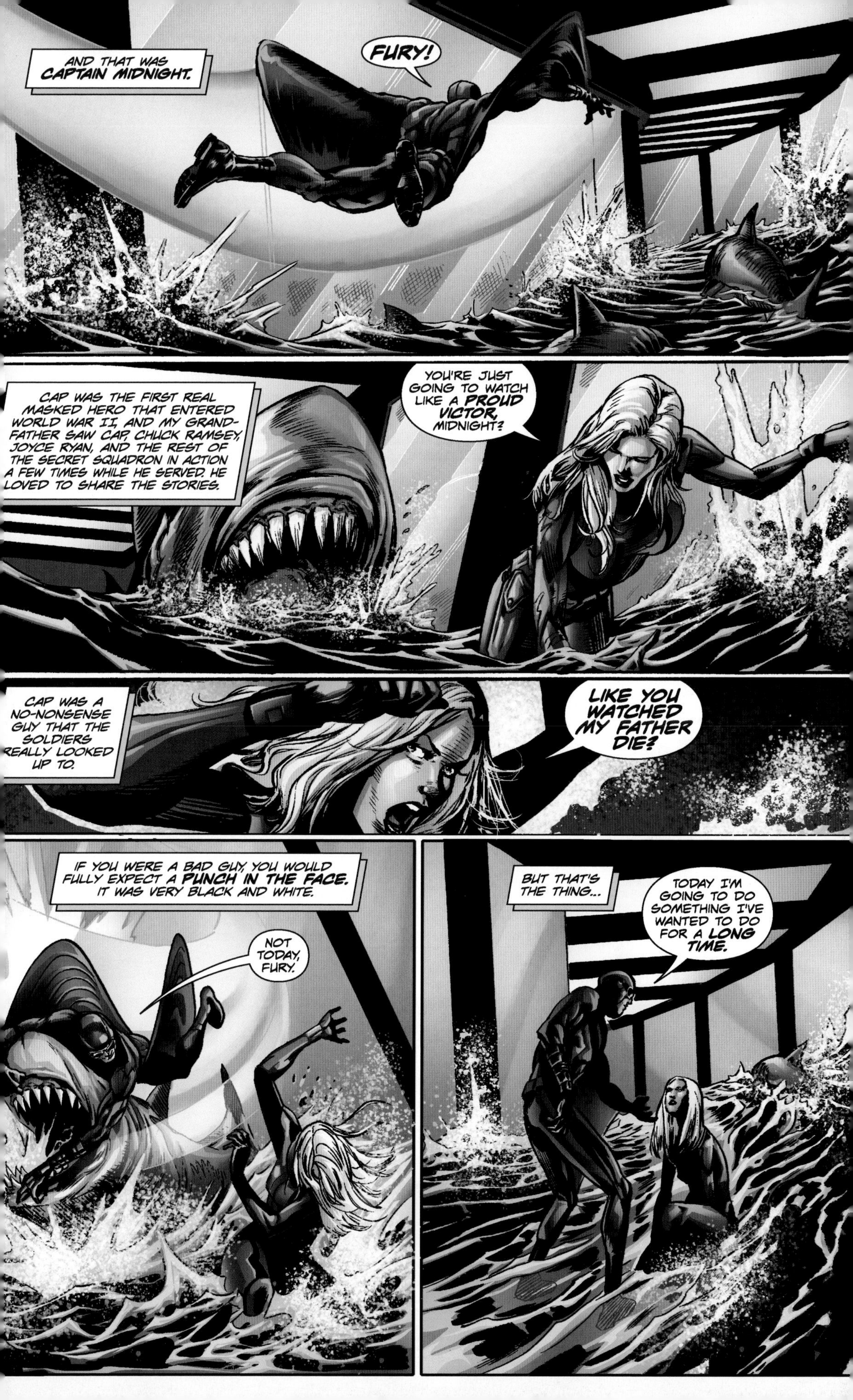
AND THAT WAS CAPTAIN MIDNIGHT.
FURY!
CAP WAS THE FIRST REAL MASKED HERO THAT ENTERED WORLD WAR II, AND MY GRAND-FATHER SAW CAP, CHUCK RAMSEY, JOYCE RYAN, AND THE REST OF THE SECRET SQUADRON IN ACTION A FEW TIMES WHILE HE SERVED. HE LOVED TO SHARE THE STORIES.
YOU'RE JUST GOING TO WATCH LIKE A PROUD VICTOR, MIDNIGHT?
CAP WAS A NO-NONSENSE GUY THAT THE SOLDIERS REALLY LOOKED UP TO.
LIKE YOU WATCHED MY FATHER DIE?
IF YOU WERE A BAD GUY, YOU WOULD FULLY EXPECT A PUNCH IN THE FACE. IT WAS VERY BLACK AND WHITE.
NOT TODAY, FURY.
BUT THAT'S THE THING...
TODAY I'M GOING TO DO SOMETHING I'VE WANTED TO DO FOR A LONG TIME.

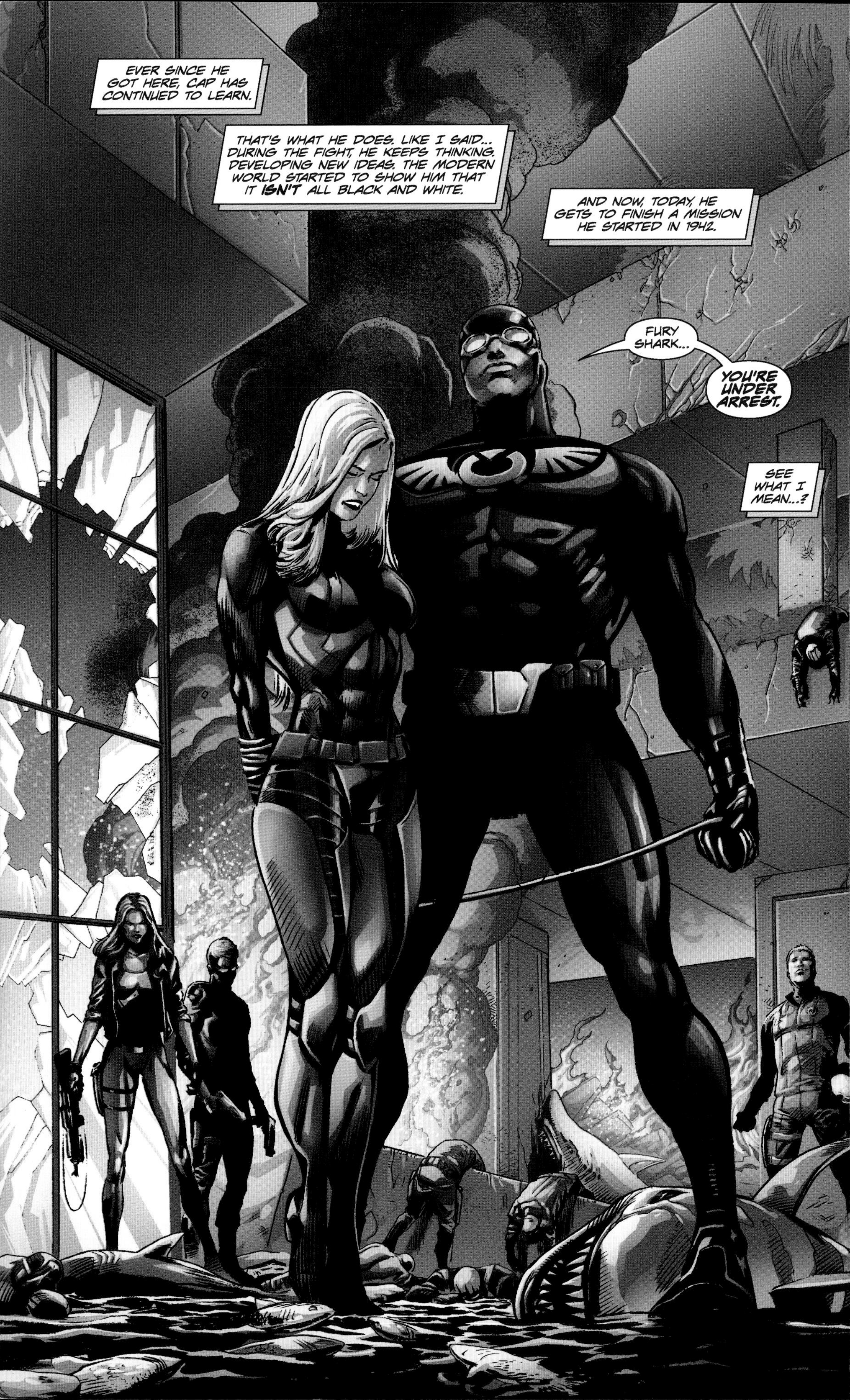
EVER SINCE HE GOT HERE, CAP HAS CONTINUED TO LEARN.
THAT'S WHAT HE DOES. LIKE I SAID... DURING THE FIGHT, HE KEEPS THINKING. DEVELOPING NEW IDEAS. THE MODERN WORLD STARTED TO SHOW HIM THAT IT ISN'T ALL BLACK AND WHITE.
AND NOW, TODAY, HE GETS TO FINISH A MISSION HE STARTED IN 1942.
FURY SHARK...
YOU'RE UNDER ARREST.
SEE WHAT I MEAN...?

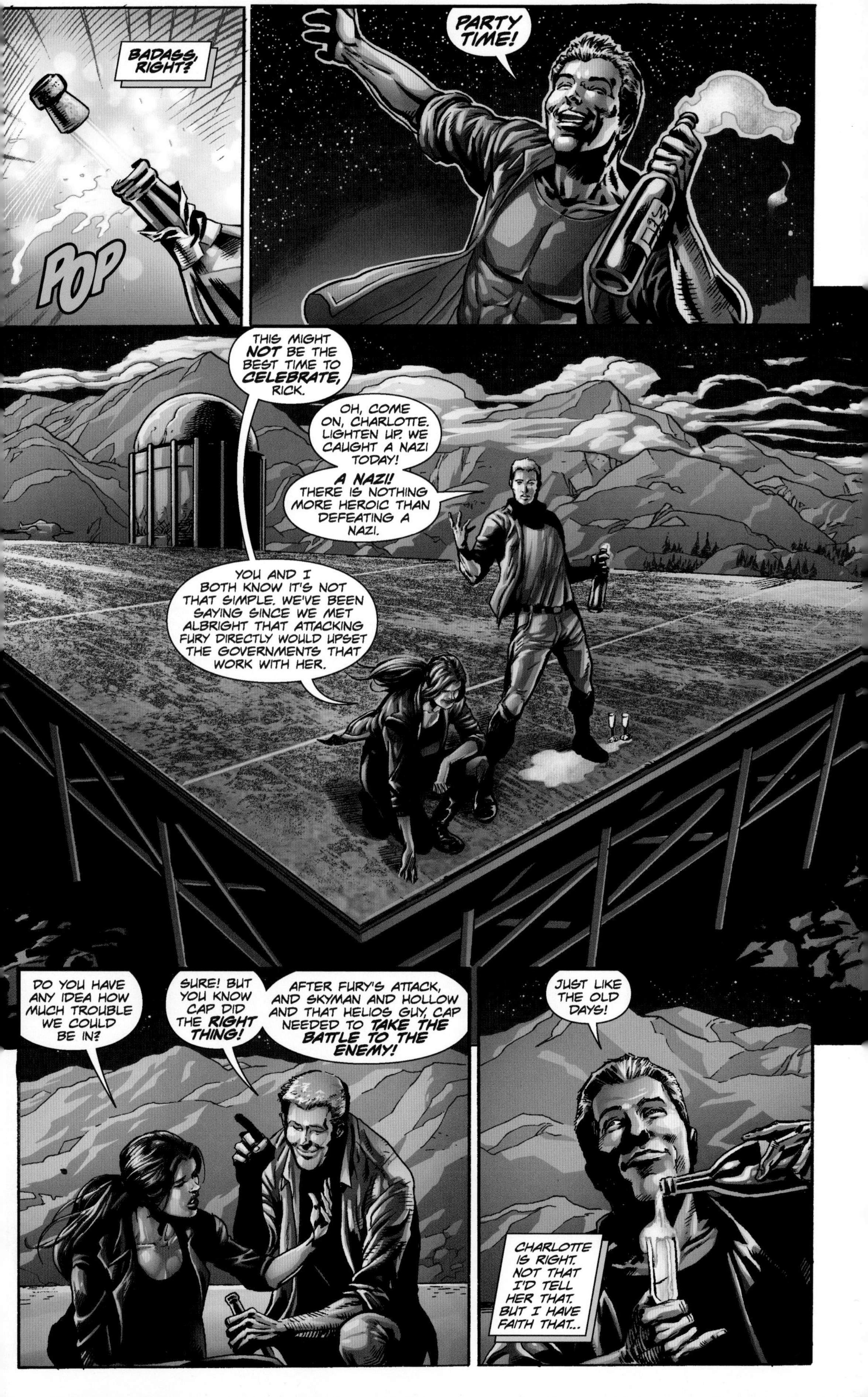
BADASS, RIGHT?
POP
PARTY TIME!
THIS MIGHT NOT BE THE BEST TIME TO CELEBRATE, RICK.
OH, COME ON, CHARLOTTE. LIGHTEN UP. WE CAUGHT A NAZI TODAY!
A NAZI! THERE IS NOTHING MORE HEROIC THAN DEFEATING A NAZI.
YOU AND I BOTH KNOW IT'S NOT THAT SIMPLE. WE'VE BEEN SAYING SINCE WE MET ALBRIGHT THAT ATTACKING FURY DIRECTLY WOULD UPSET THE GOVERNMENTS THAT WORK WITH HER.
DO YOU HAVE ANY IDEA HOW MUCH TROUBLE WE COULD BE IN?
SURE! BUT YOU KNOW CAP DID THE RIGHT THING!
AFTER FURY'S ATTACK, AND SKYMAN AND HOLLOW AND THAT HELIOS GUY, CAP NEEDED TO TAKE THE BATTLE TO THE ENEMY!
JUST LIKE THE OLD DAYS!
CHARLOTTE IS RIGHT. NOT THAT I'D TELL HER THAT. BUT I HAVE FAITH THAT...

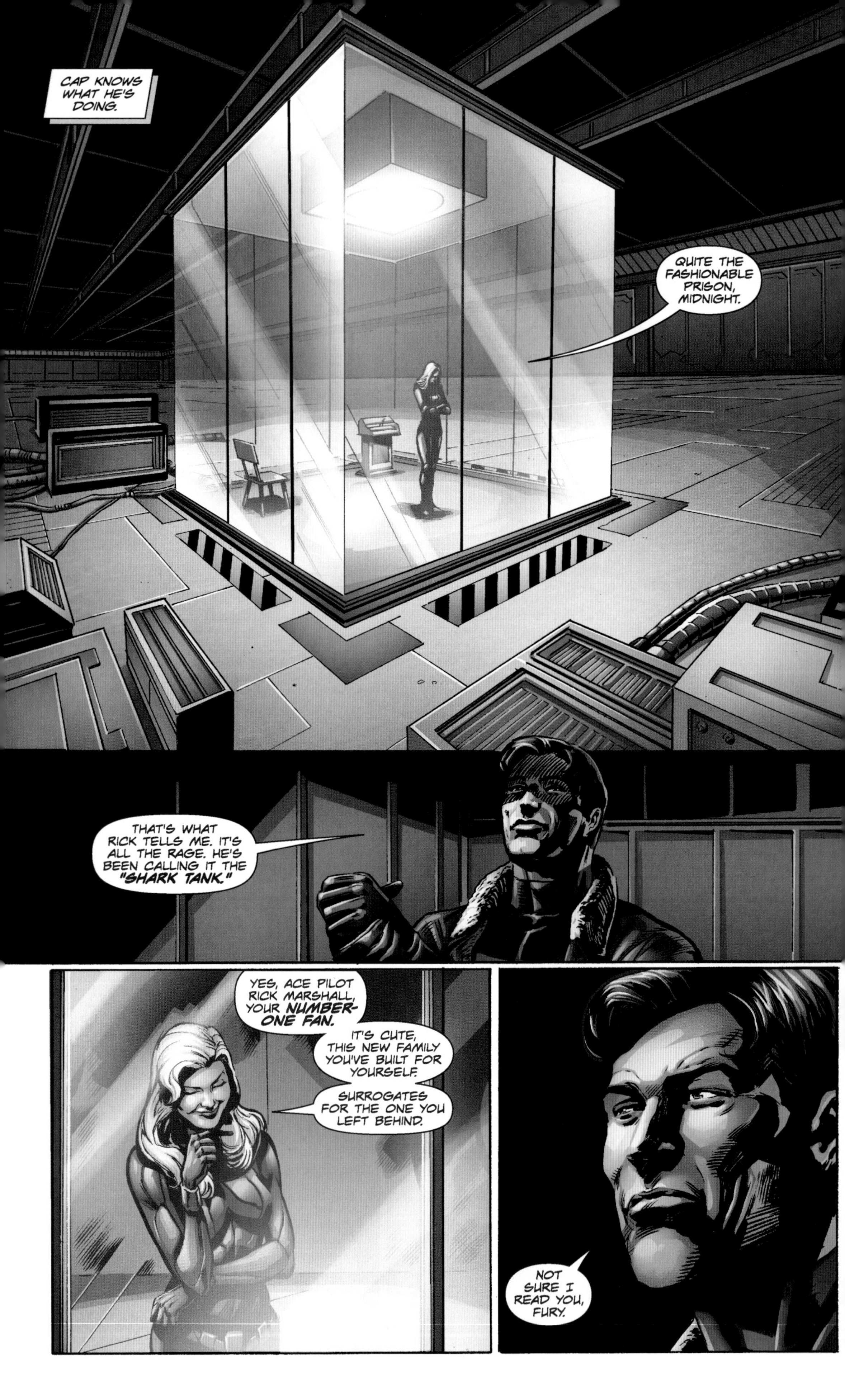
CAP KNOWS WHAT HE'S DOING.
QUITE THE FASHIONABLE PRISON, MIDNIGHT.
THAT'S WHAT RICK TELLS ME. IT'S ALL THE RAGE. HE'S BEEN CALLING IT THE "SHARK TANK."
YES, ACE PILOT RICK MARSHALL, YOUR NUMBER-ONE FAN.
IT'S CUTE, THIS NEW FAMILY YOU'VE BUILT FOR YOURSELF.
SURROGATES FOR THE ONE YOU LEFT BEHIND.
NOT SURE I READ YOU, FURY.

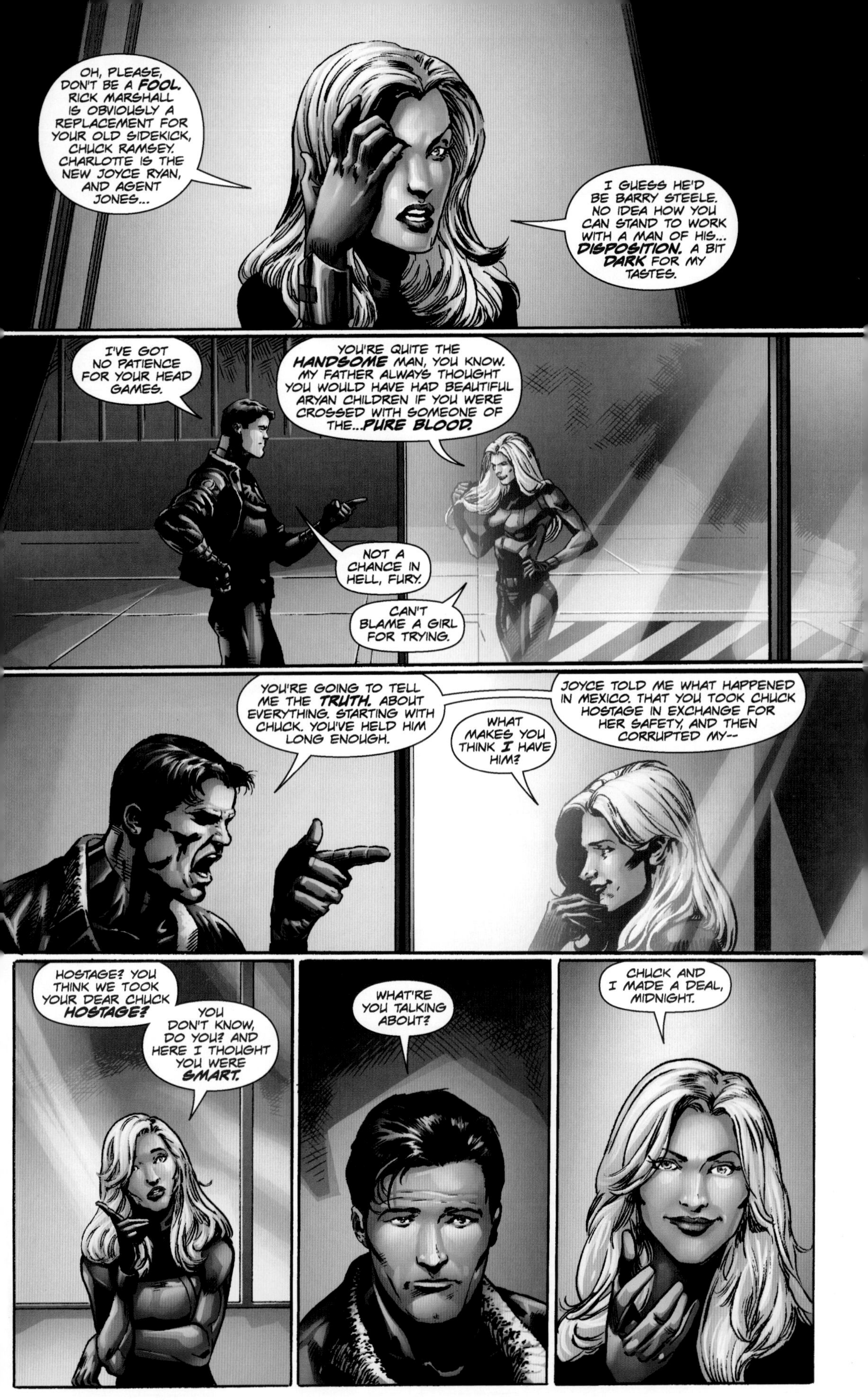
OH, PLEASE, DON'T BE A FOOL. RICK MARSHALL IS OBVIOUSLY A REPLACEMENT FOR YOUR OLD SIDEKICK, CHUCK RAMSEY. CHARLOTTE IS THE NEW JOYCE RYAN, AND AGENT JONES...
I GUESS HE'D BE BARRY STEELE. NO IDEA HOW YOU CAN STAND TO WORK WITH A MAN OF HIS... DISPOSITION. A BIT DARK FOR MY TASTES.
I'VE GOT NO PATIENCE FOR YOUR HEAD GAMES.
YOU'RE QUITE THE HANDSOME MAN, YOU KNOW. MY FATHER ALWAYS THOUGHT YOU WOULD HAVE HAD BEAUTIFUL ARYAN CHILDREN IF YOU WERE CROSSED WITH SOMEONE OF THE...PURE BLOOD.
NOT A CHANCE IN HELL, FURY.
CAN'T BLAME A GIRL FOR TRYING.
YOU'RE GOING TO TELL ME THE TRUTH. ABOUT EVERYTHING. STARTING WITH CHUCK. YOU'VE HELD HIM LONG ENOUGH.
WHAT MAKES YOU THINK I HAVE HIM?
JOYCE TOLD ME WHAT HAPPENED IN MEXICO. THAT YOU TOOK CHUCK HOSTAGE IN EXCHANGE FOR HER SAFETY, AND THEN CORRUPTED MY--
HOSTAGE? YOU THINK WE TOOK YOUR DEAR CHUCK HOSTAGE?
YOU DON'T KNOW, DO YOU? AND HERE I THOUGHT YOU WERE SMART.
WHAT'RE YOU TALKING ABOUT?
CHUCK AND I MADE A DEAL, MIDNIGHT.

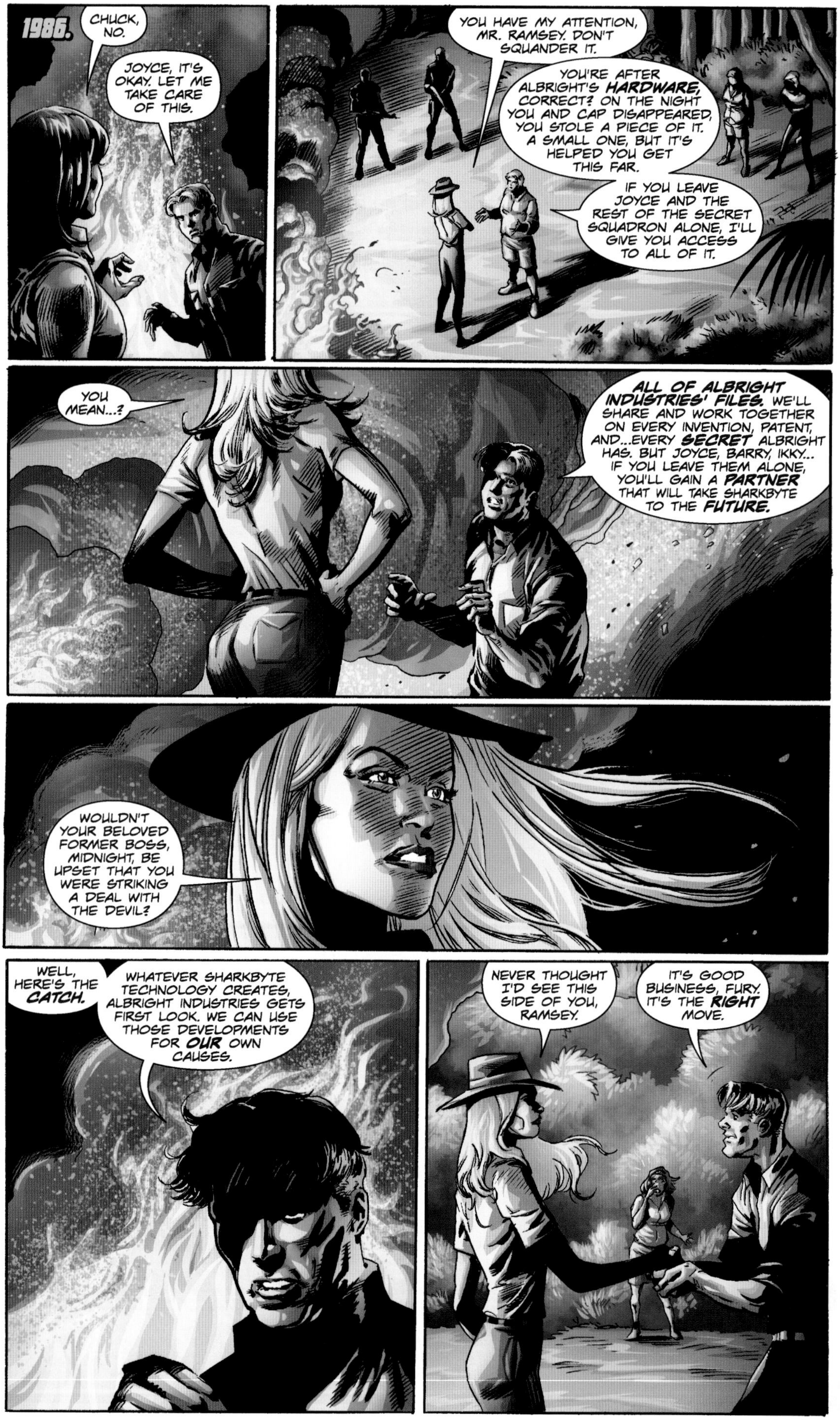
1986.
CHUCK, NO.
JOYCE, IT'S OKAY. LET ME TAKE CARE OF THIS.
YOU HAVE MY ATTENTION, MR. RAMSEY. DON'T SQUANDER IT.
YOU'RE AFTER ALBRIGHT'S HARDWARE, CORRECT? ON THE NIGHT YOU AND CAP DISAPPEARED, YOU STOLE A PIECE OF IT. A SMALL ONE, BUT IT'S HELPED YOU GET THIS FAR.
IF YOU LEAVE JOYCE AND THE REST OF THE SECRET SQUADRON ALONE, I'LL GIVE YOU ACCESS TO ALL OF IT.
YOU MEAN...?
ALL OF ALBRIGHT INDUSTRIES' FILES. WE'LL SHARE AND WORK TOGETHER ON EVERY INVENTION, PATENT, AND...EVERY SECRET ALBRIGHT HAS. BUT JOYCE, BARRY, IKKY... IF YOU LEAVE THEM ALONE, YOU'LL GAIN A PARTNER THAT WILL TAKE SHARKBYTE TO THE FUTURE.
WOULDN'T YOUR BELOVED FORMER BOSS, MIDNIGHT, BE UPSET THAT YOU WERE STRIKING A DEAL WITH THE DEVIL?
WELL, HERE'S THE CATCH.
WHATEVER SHARKBYTE TECHNOLOGY CREATES, ALBRIGHT INDUSTRIES GETS FIRST LOOK. WE CAN USE THOSE DEVELOPMENTS FOR OUR OWN CAUSES.
NEVER THOUGHT I'D SEE THIS SIDE OF YOU, RAMSEY.
IT'S GOOD BUSINESS, FURY. IT'S THE RIGHT MOVE.

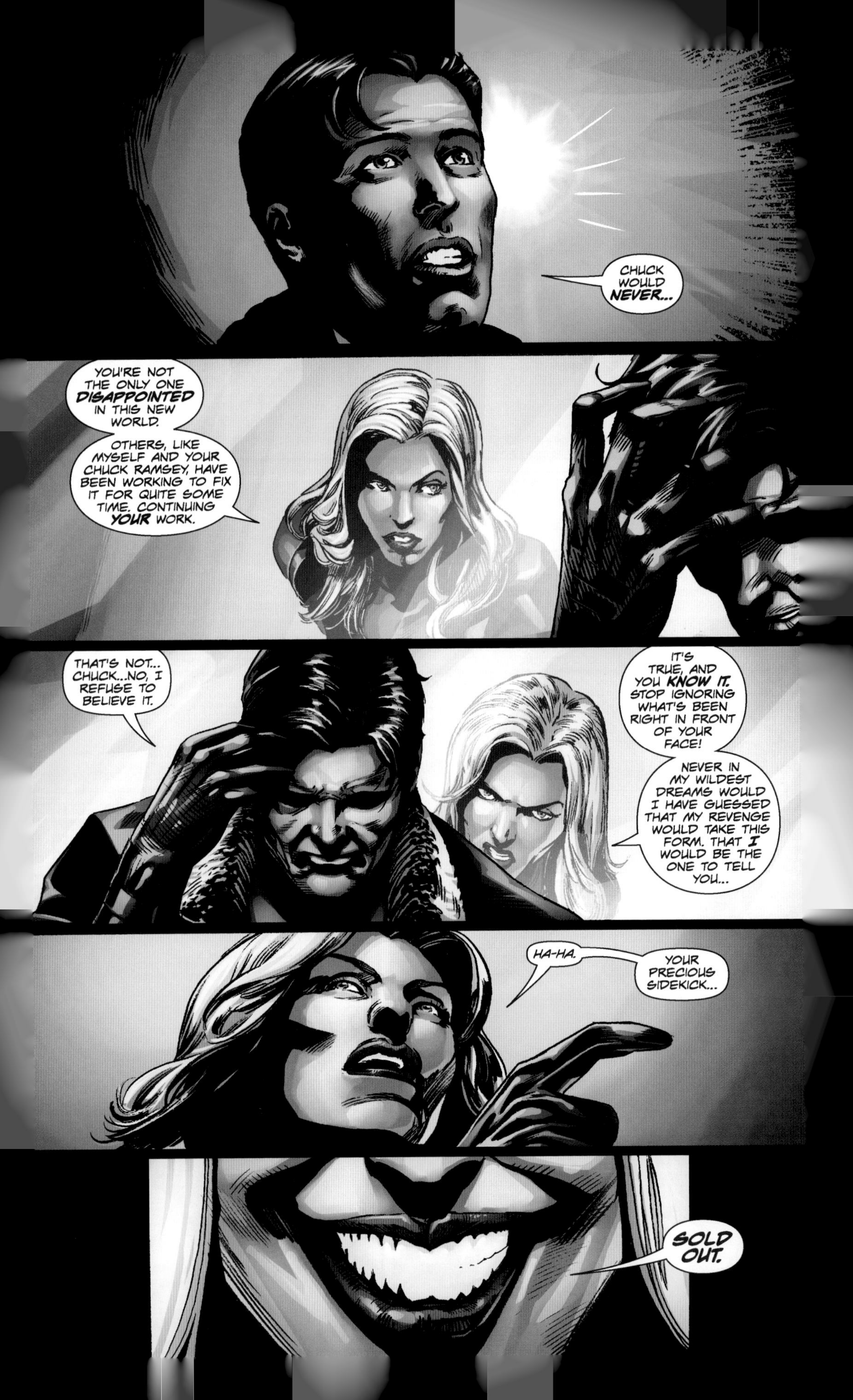
CHUCK WOULD NEVER...
YOU'RE NOT THE ONLY ONE DISAPPOINTED IN THIS NEW WORLD.
OTHERS, LIKE MYSELF AND YOUR CHUCK RAMSEY, HAVE BEEN WORKING TO FIX IT FOR QUITE SOME TIME. CONTINUING YOUR WORK.
THAT'S NOT... CHUCK...NO, I REFUSE TO BELIEVE IT.
IT'S TRUE, AND YOU KNOW IT. STOP IGNORING WHAT'S BEEN RIGHT IN FRONT OF YOUR FACE!
NEVER IN MY WILDEST DREAMS WOULD I HAVE GUESSED THAT MY REVENGE WOULD TAKE THIS FORM. THAT I WOULD BE THE ONE TO TELL YOU...
HA-HA.
YOUR PRECIOUS SIDEKICK...
SOLD OUT.

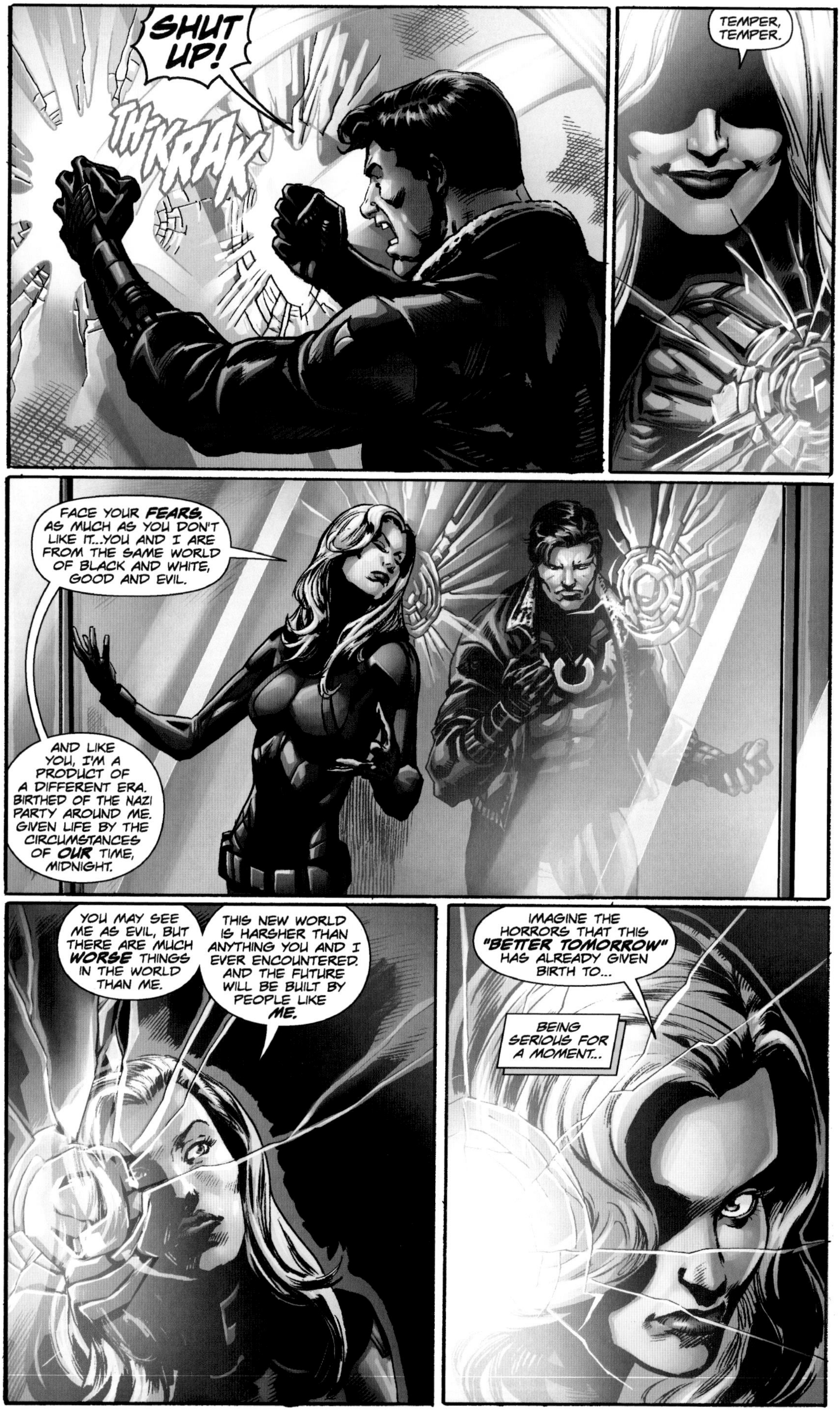
SHUT UP!
THKRAK
TEMPER, TEMPER.
FACE YOUR FEARS. AS MUCH AS YOU DON'T LIKE IT...YOU AND I ARE FROM THE SAME WORLD OF BLACK AND WHITE, GOOD AND EVIL.
AND LIKE YOU, I'M A PRODUCT OF A DIFFERENT ERA. BIRTHED OF THE NAZI PARTY AROUND ME. GIVEN LIFE BY THE CIRCUMSTANCES OF OUR TIME, MIDNIGHT.
YOU MAY SEE ME AS EVIL, BUT THERE ARE MUCH WORSE THINGS IN THE WORLD THAN ME.
THIS NEW WORLD IS HARSHER THAN ANYTHING YOU AND I EVER ENCOUNTERED. AND THE FUTURE WILL BE BUILT BY PEOPLE LIKE ME.
BEING SERIOUS FOR A MOMENT...
IMAGINE THE HORRORS THAT THIS "BETTER TOMORROW" HAS ALREADY GIVEN BIRTH TO...

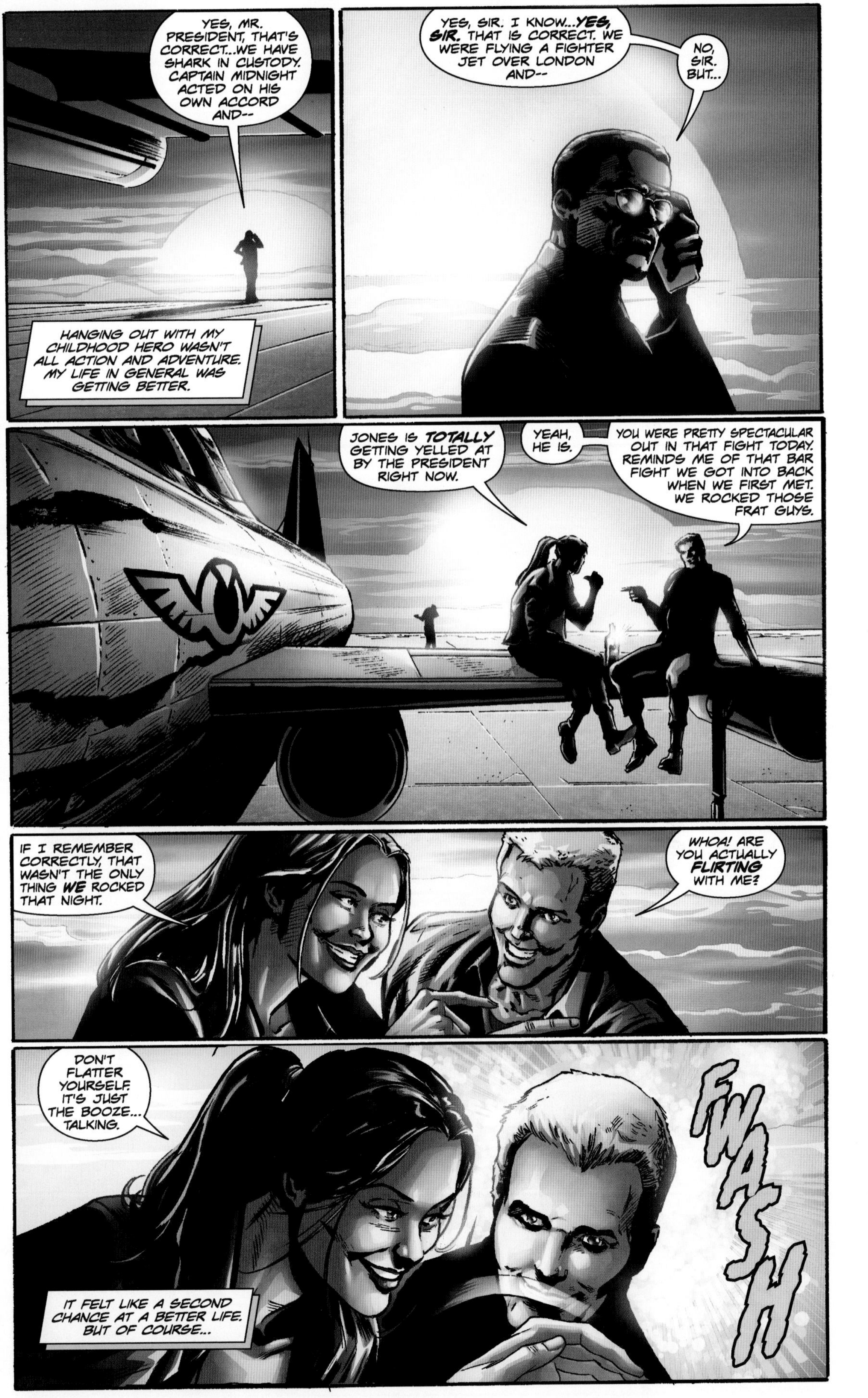
YES, MR. PRESIDENT, THAT'S CORRECT...WE HAVE SHARK IN CUSTODY. CAPTAIN MIDNIGHT ACTED ON HIS OWN ACCORD AND--
HANGING OUT WITH MY CHILDHOOD HERO WASN'T ALL ACTION AND ADVENTURE. MY LIFE IN GENERAL WAS GETTING BETTER.
YES, SIR. I KNOW...YES, SIR. THAT IS CORRECT. WE WERE FLYING A FIGHTER JET OVER LONDON AND--
NO, SIR. BUT...
JONES IS TOTALLY GETTING YELLED AT BY THE PRESIDENT RIGHT NOW.
YEAH, HE IS.
YOU WERE PRETTY SPECTACULAR OUT IN THAT FIGHT TODAY. REMINDS ME OF THAT BAR FIGHT WE GOT INTO BACK WHEN WE FIRST MET. WE ROCKED THOSE FRAT GUYS.
IF I REMEMBER CORRECTLY, THAT WASN'T THE ONLY THING WE ROCKED THAT NIGHT.
WHOA! ARE YOU ACTUALLY FLIRTING WITH ME?
DON'T FLATTER YOURSELF. IT'S JUST THE BOOZE... TALKING.
FWASH
IT FELT LIKE A SECOND CHANCE AT A BETTER LIFE. BUT OF COURSE...

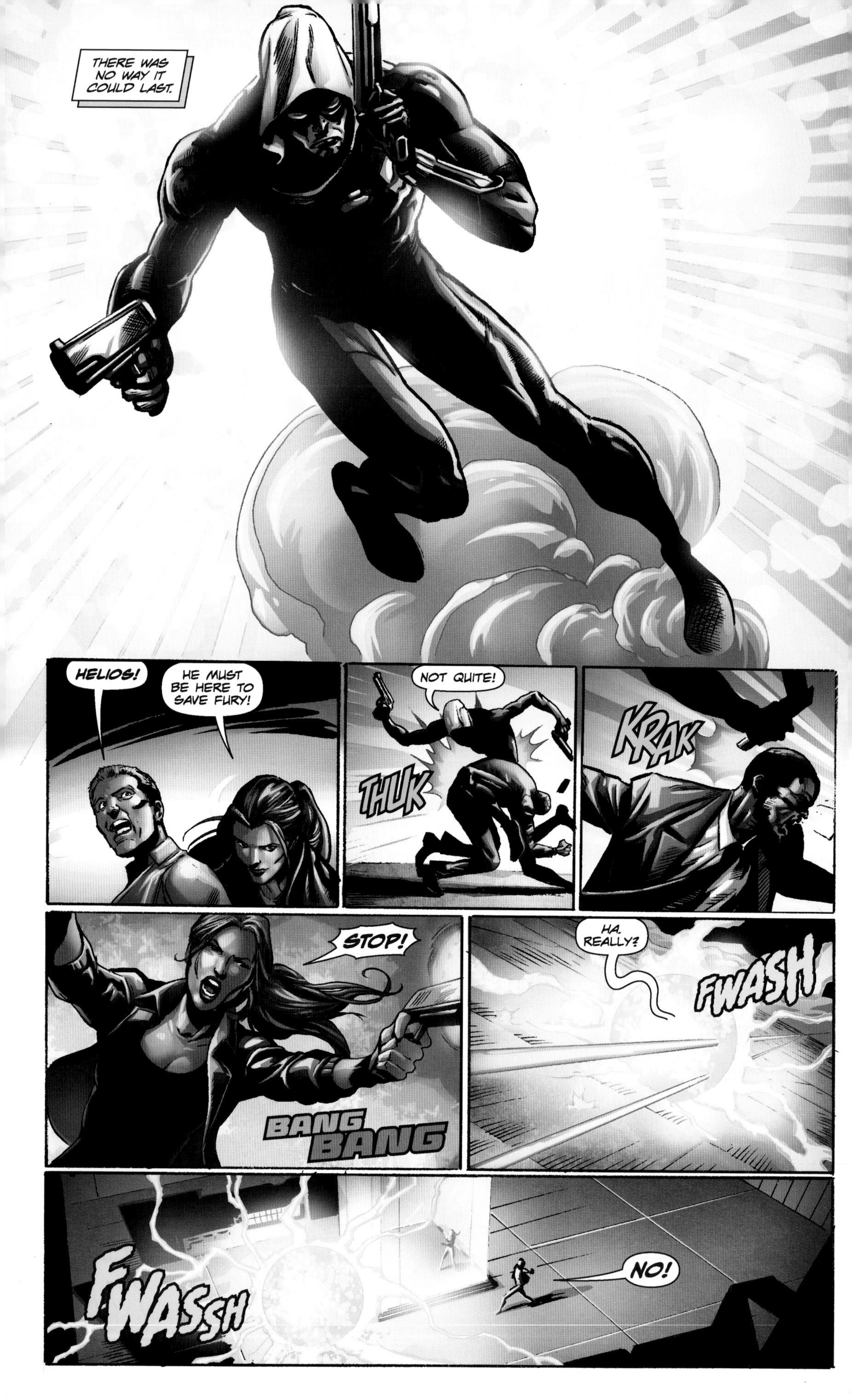
THERE WAS NO WAY IT COULD LAST.
HELIOS!
HE MUST BE HERE TO SAVE FURY!
NOT QUITE!
THUK
KRAK
STOP!
BANG BANG
HA. REALLY?
FWASH
FWASSH
NO!

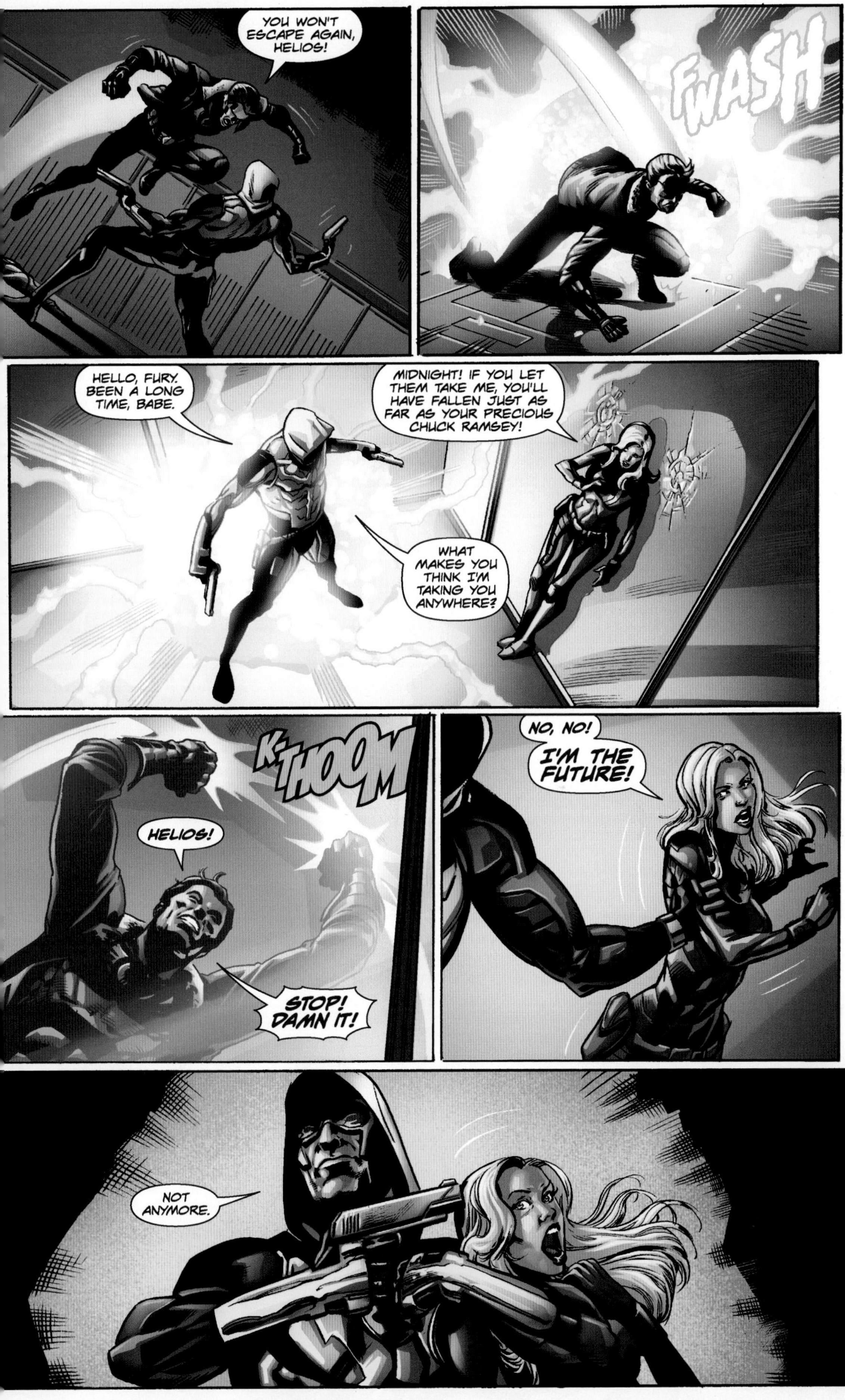
YOU WON'T ESCAPE AGAIN, HELIOS!
FWASH
HELLO, FURY. BEEN A LONG TIME, BABE.
MIDNIGHT! IF YOU LET THEM TAKE ME, YOU'LL HAVE FALLEN JUST AS FAR AS YOUR PRECIOUS CHUCK RAMSEY!
WHAT MAKES YOU THINK I'M TAKING YOU ANYWHERE?
K-THOOM
HELIOS!
STOP! DAMN IT!
NO, NO!
I'M THE FUTURE!
NOT ANYMORE.

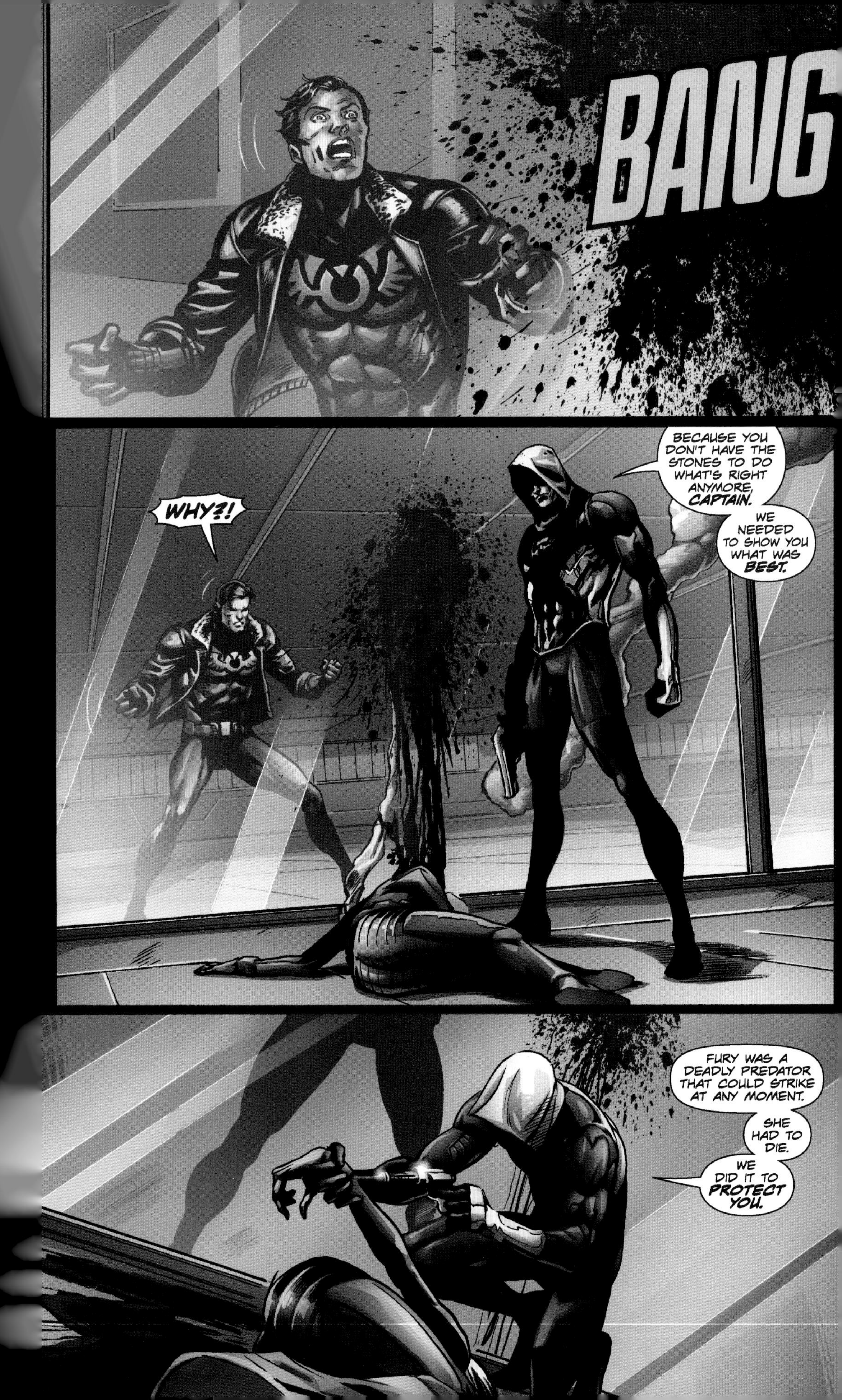

BANG
WHY?!
BECAUSE YOU DON'T HAVE THE STONES TO DO WHAT'S RIGHT ANYMORE, CAPTAIN.
WE NEEDED TO SHOW YOU WHAT WAS BEST.
FURY WAS A DEADLY PREDATOR THAT COULD STRIKE AT ANY MOMENT.
SHE HAD TO DIE.
WE DID IT TO PROTECT YOU.

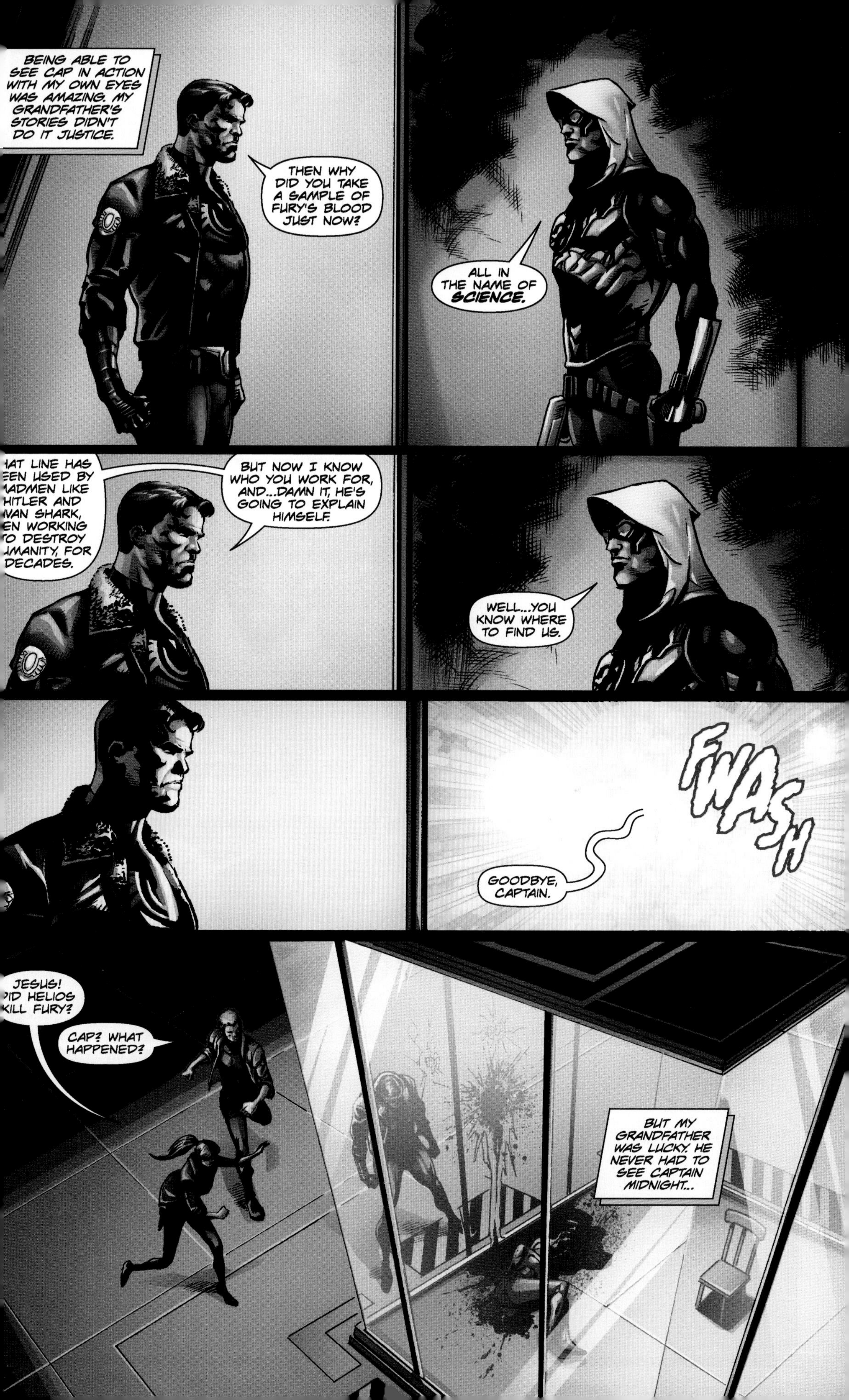
BEING ABLE TO SEE CAP IN ACTION WITH MY OWN EYES WAS AMAZING. MY GRANDFATHER'S STORIES DIDN'T DO IT JUSTICE.
THEN WHY DID YOU TAKE A SAMPLE OF FURY'S BLOOD JUST NOW?
ALL IN THE NAME OF SCIENCE.
HAT LINE HAS EEN USED BY ADMEN LIKE HITLER AND VAN SHARK, EN WORKING TO DESTROY UMANITY, FOR DECADES.
BUT NOW I KNOW WHO YOU WORK FOR, AND...DAMN IT, HE'S GOING TO EXPLAIN HIMSELF.
WELL...YOU KNOW WHERE TO FIND US.
FWASH
GOODBYE, CAPTAIN.
JESUS! ID HELIOS KILL FURY?
CAP? WHAT HAPPENED?
BUT MY GRANDFATHER WAS LUCKY. HE NEVER HAD TO SEE CAPTAIN MIDNIGHT...

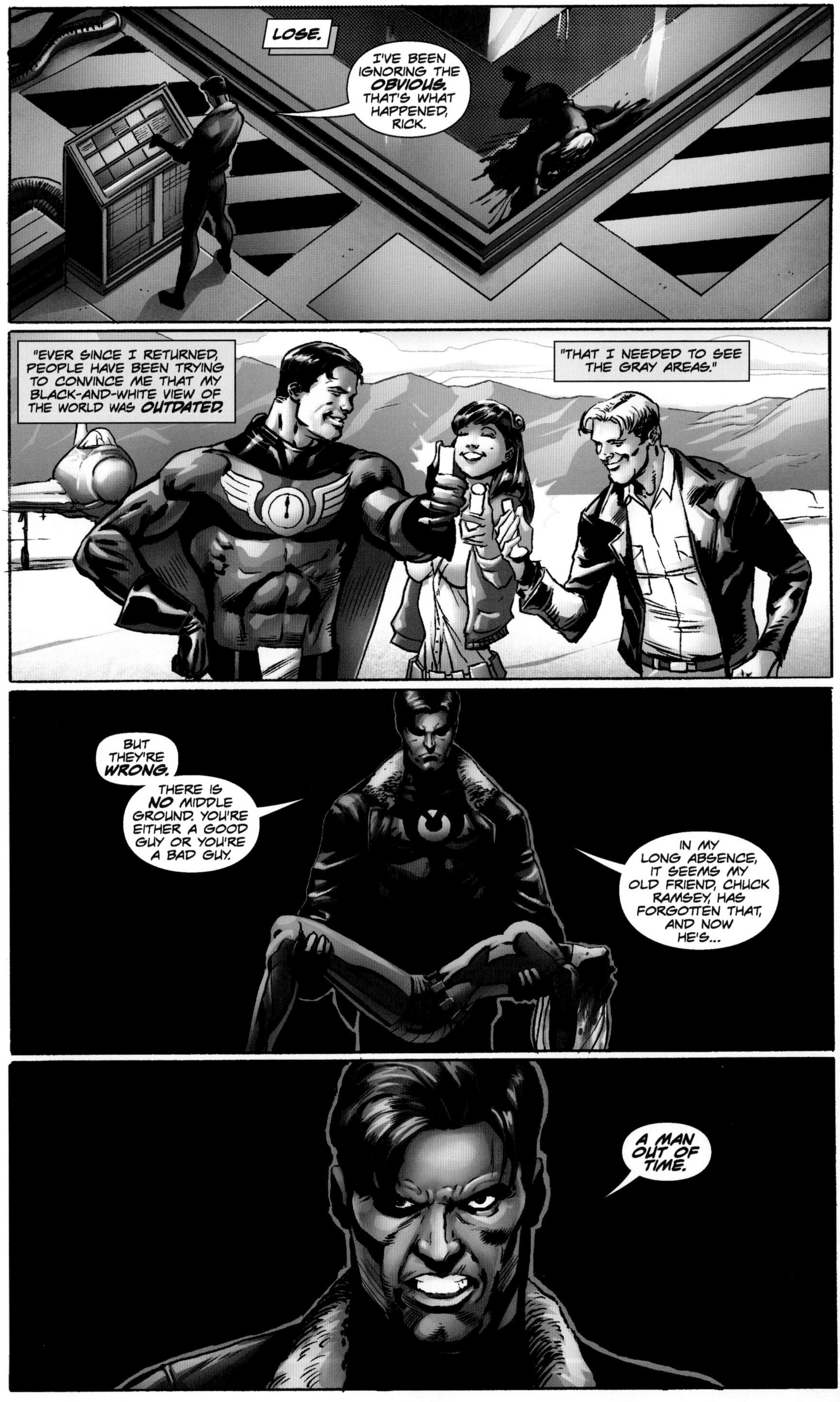
LOSE.
I'VE BEEN IGNORING THE OBVIOUS. THAT'S WHAT HAPPENED, RICK.
"EVER SINCE I RETURNED, PEOPLE HAVE BEEN TRYING TO CONVINCE ME THAT MY BLACK-AND-WHITE VIEW OF THE WORLD WAS OUTDATED.
"THAT I NEEDED TO SEE THE GRAY AREAS."
BUT THEY'RE WRONG.
THERE IS NO MIDDLE GROUND. YOU'RE EITHER A GOOD GUY OR YOU'RE A BAD GUY.
IN MY LONG ABSENCE, IT SEEMS MY OLD FRIEND, CHUCK RAMSEY, HAS FORGOTTEN THAT, AND NOW HE'S...
A MAN OUT OF TIME.

CHAPTER 3

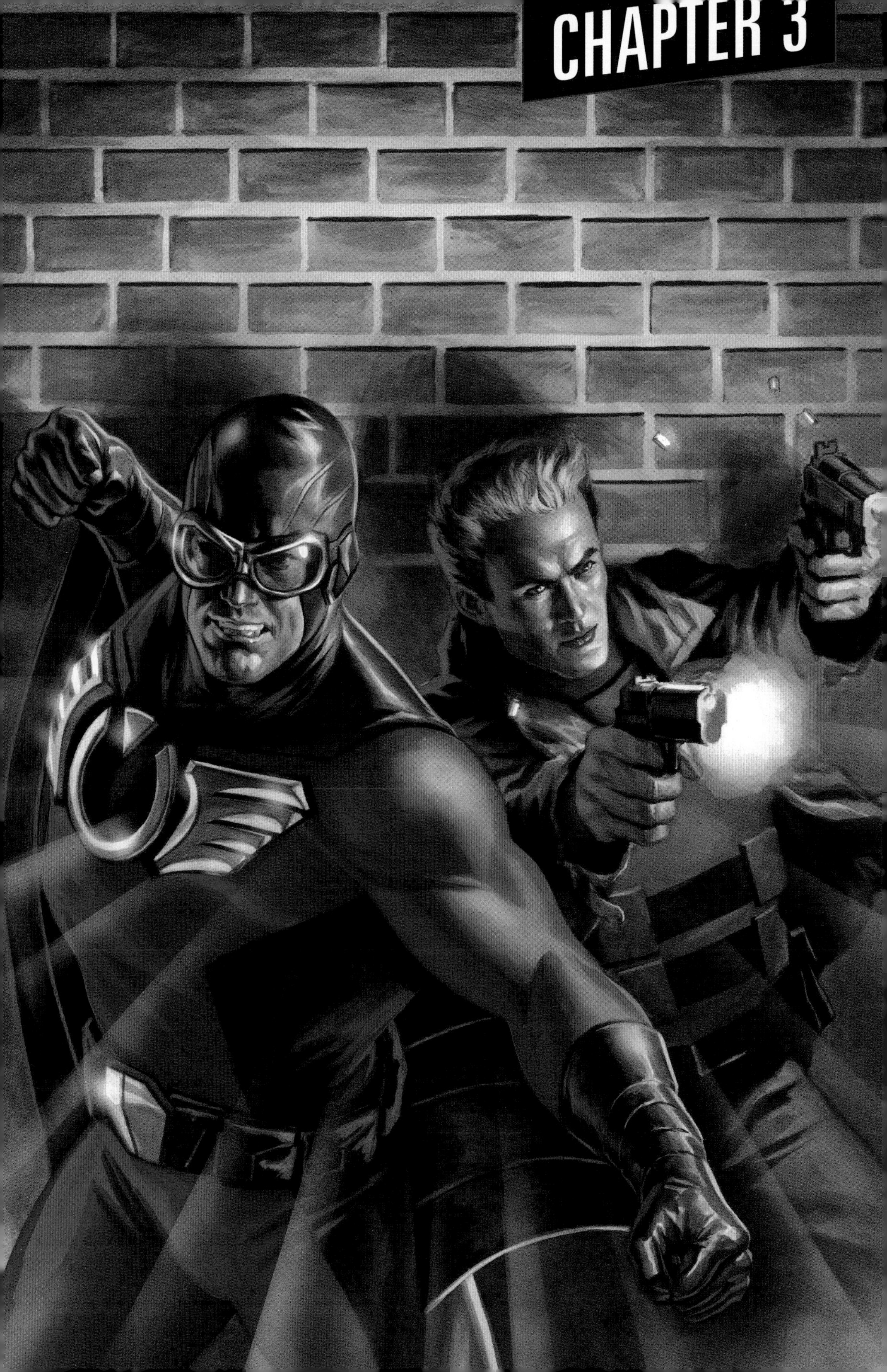

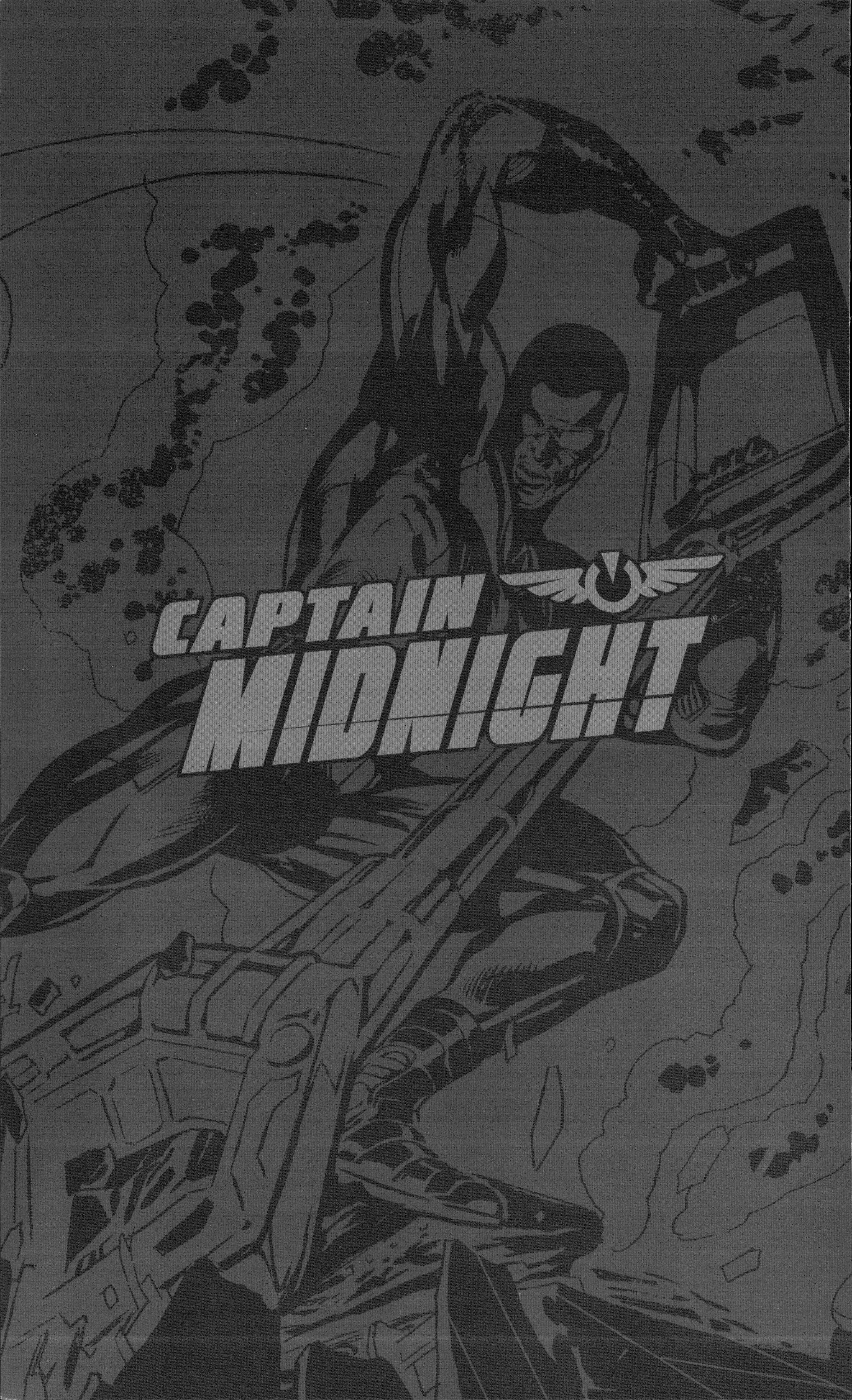
CAPTAIN
MIDNIGHT

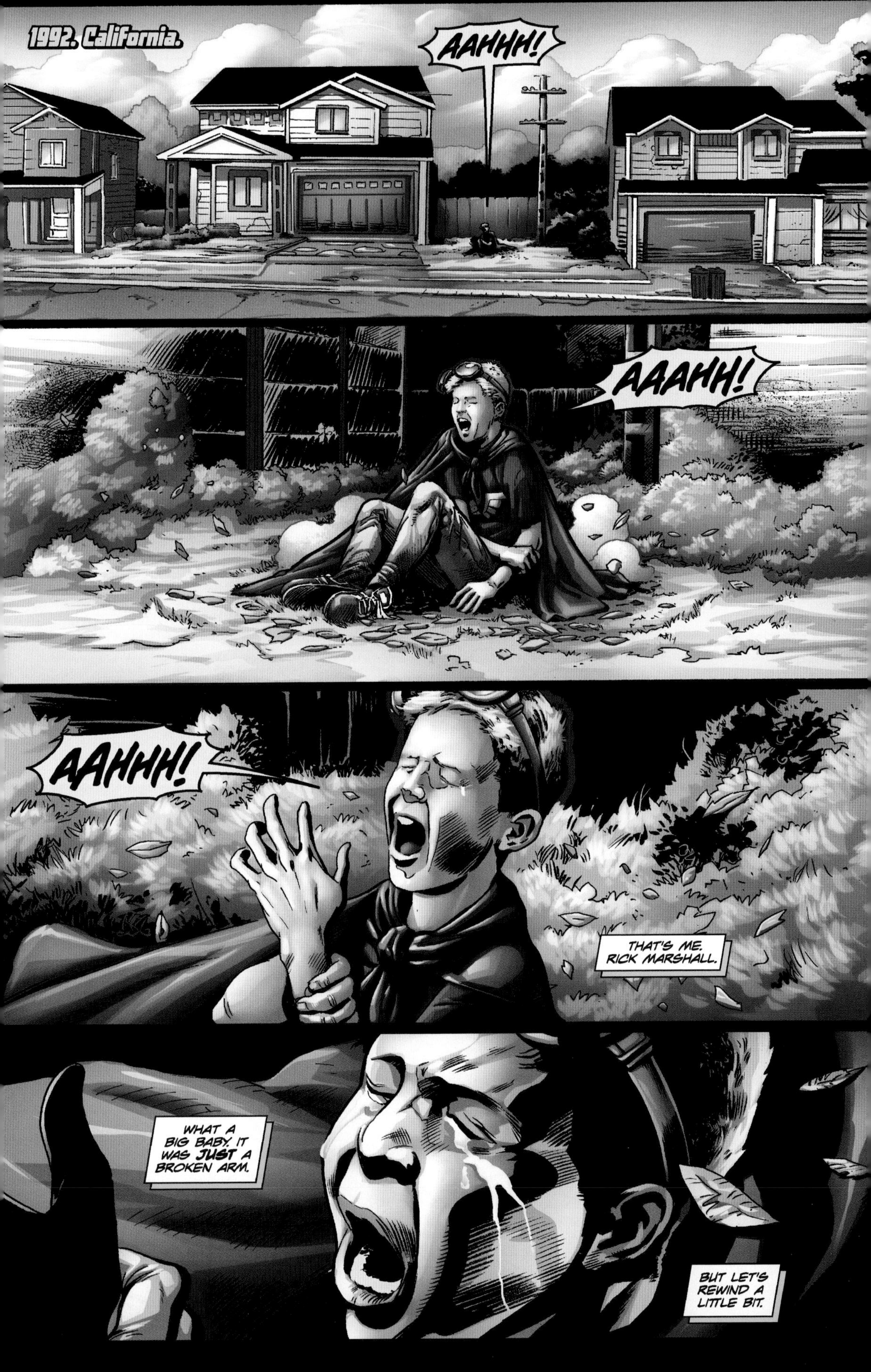
1992. California.
AAHHH!
AAAHH!
AAHHH!
THAT'S ME. RICK MARSHALL.
WHAT A BIG BABY. IT WAS JUST A BROKEN ARM.
BUT LET'S REWIND A LITTLE BIT.

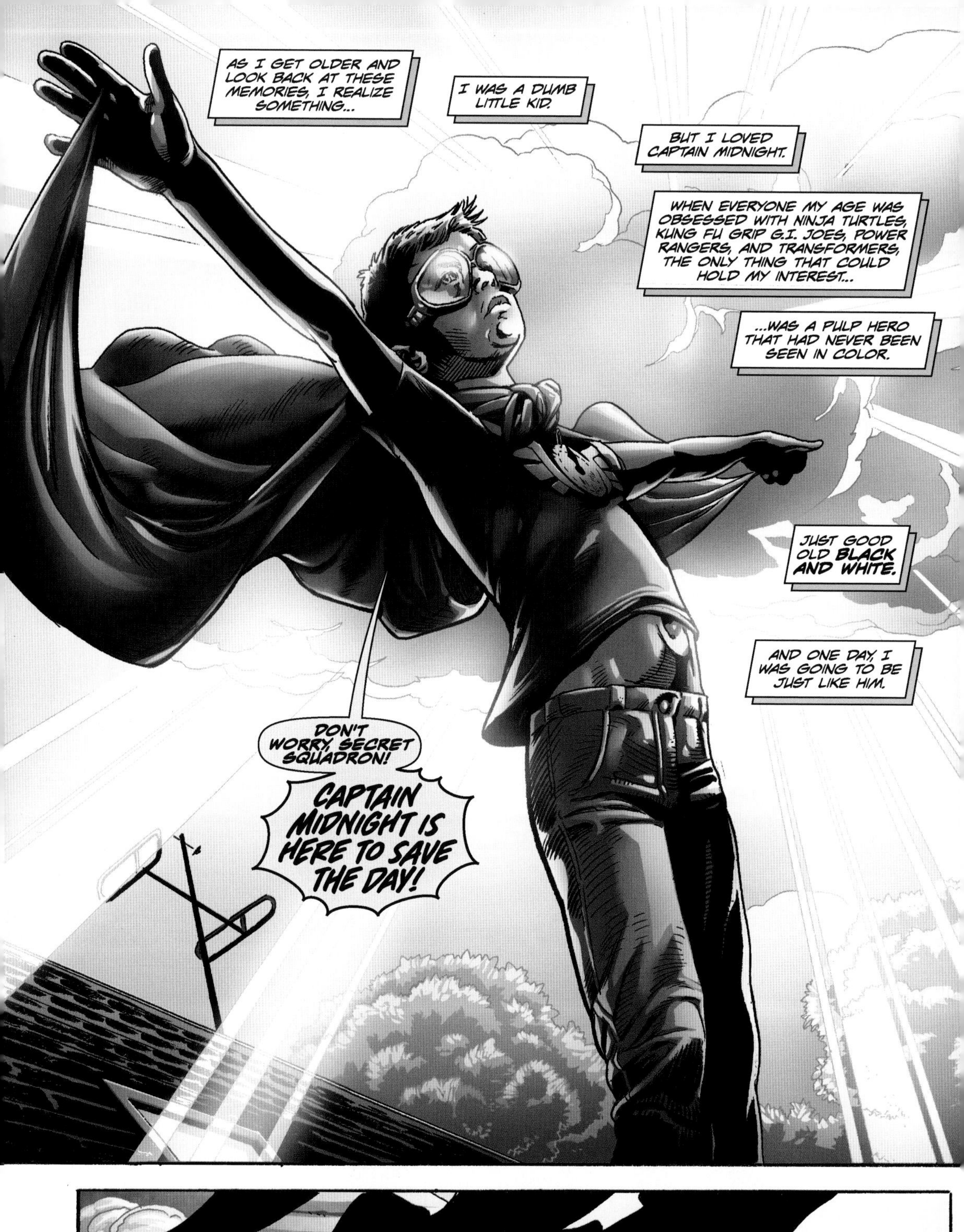
AS I GET OLDER AND LOOK BACK AT THESE MEMORIES, I REALIZE SOMETHING...
I WAS A DUMB LITTLE KID.
BUT I LOVED CAPTAIN MIDNIGHT.
WHEN EVERYONE MY AGE WAS OBSESSED WITH NINJA TURTLES, KUNG FU GRIP G.I. JOES, POWER RANGERS, AND TRANSFORMERS, THE ONLY THING THAT COULD HOLD MY INTEREST...
...WAS A PULP HERO THAT HAD NEVER BEEN SEEN IN COLOR.
JUST GOOD OLD BLACK AND WHITE.
AND ONE DAY, I WAS GOING TO BE JUST LIKE HIM.
DON'T WORRY, SECRET SQUADRON!
CAPTAIN MIDNIGHT IS HERE TO SAVE THE DAY!

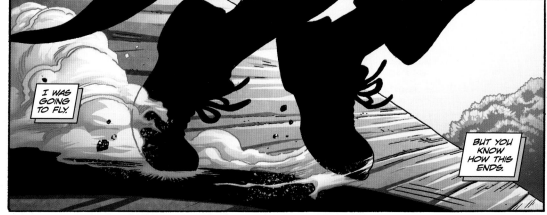

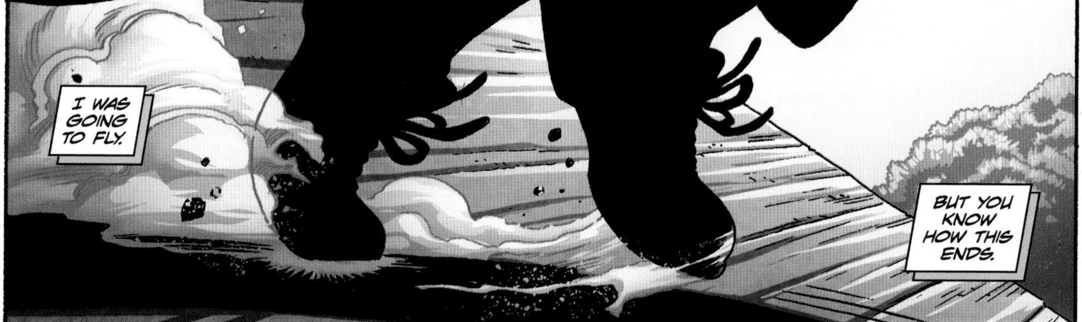
I WAS GOING TO FLY.
BUT YOU KNOW HOW THIS ENDS.

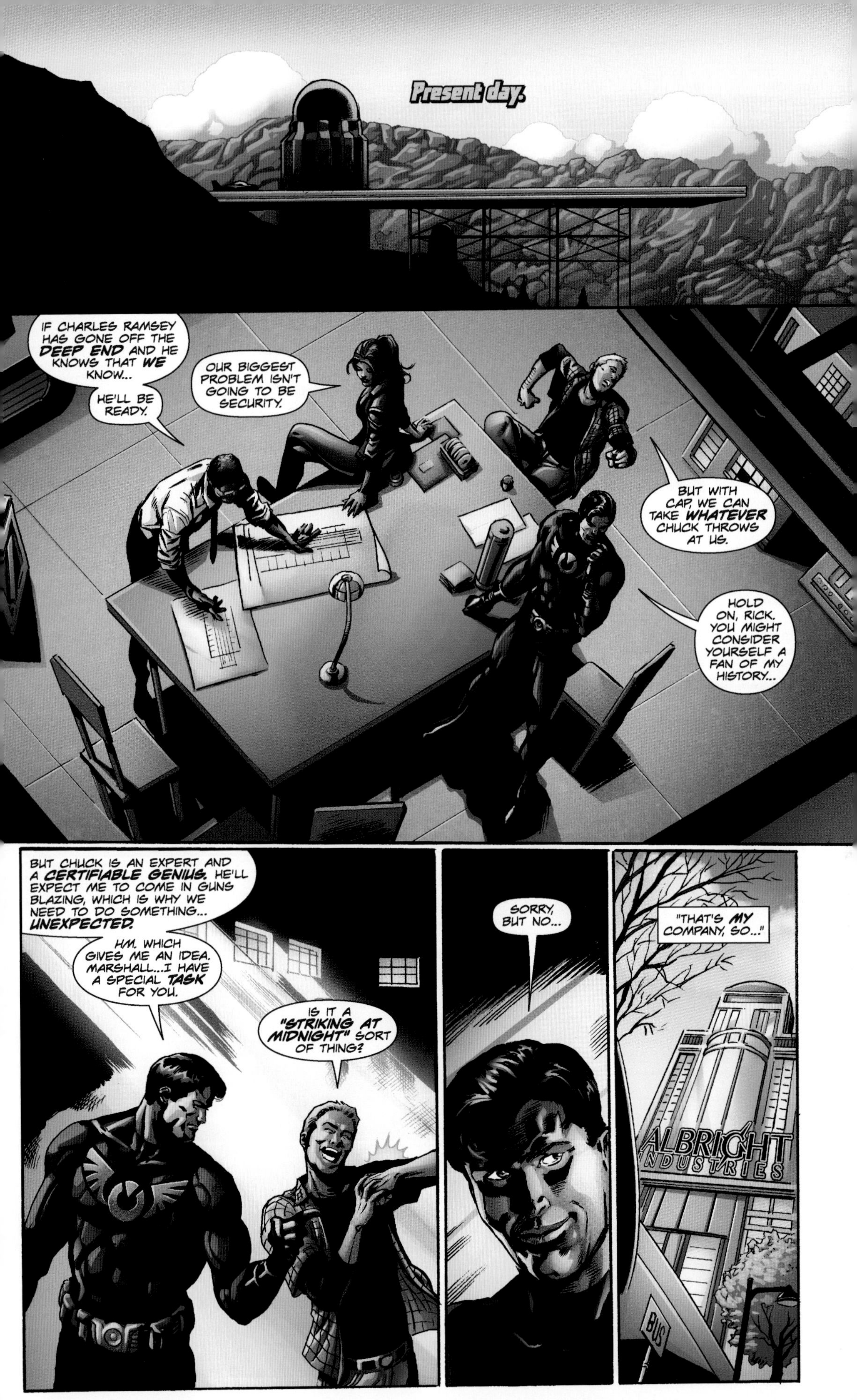
Present day.
IF CHARLES RAMSEY HAS GONE OFF THE DEEP END AND HE KNOWS THAT WE KNOW...
HE'LL BE READY.
OUR BIGGEST PROBLEM ISN'T GOING TO BE SECURITY.
BUT WITH CAP, WE CAN TAKE WHATEVER CHUCK THROWS AT US.
HOLD ON, RICK. YOU MIGHT CONSIDER YOURSELF A FAN OF MY HISTORY...
BUT CHUCK IS AN EXPERT AND A CERTIFIABLE GENIUS. HE'LL EXPECT ME TO COME IN GUNS BLAZING, WHICH IS WHY WE NEED TO DO SOMETHING... UNEXPECTED.
HM. WHICH GIVES ME AN IDEA. MARSHALL...I HAVE A SPECIAL TASK FOR YOU.
IS IT A "STRIKING AT MIDNIGHT" SORT OF THING?
SORRY, BUT NO...
"THAT'S MY COMPANY, SO..."
ALBRIGHT INDUSTRIES
BUS

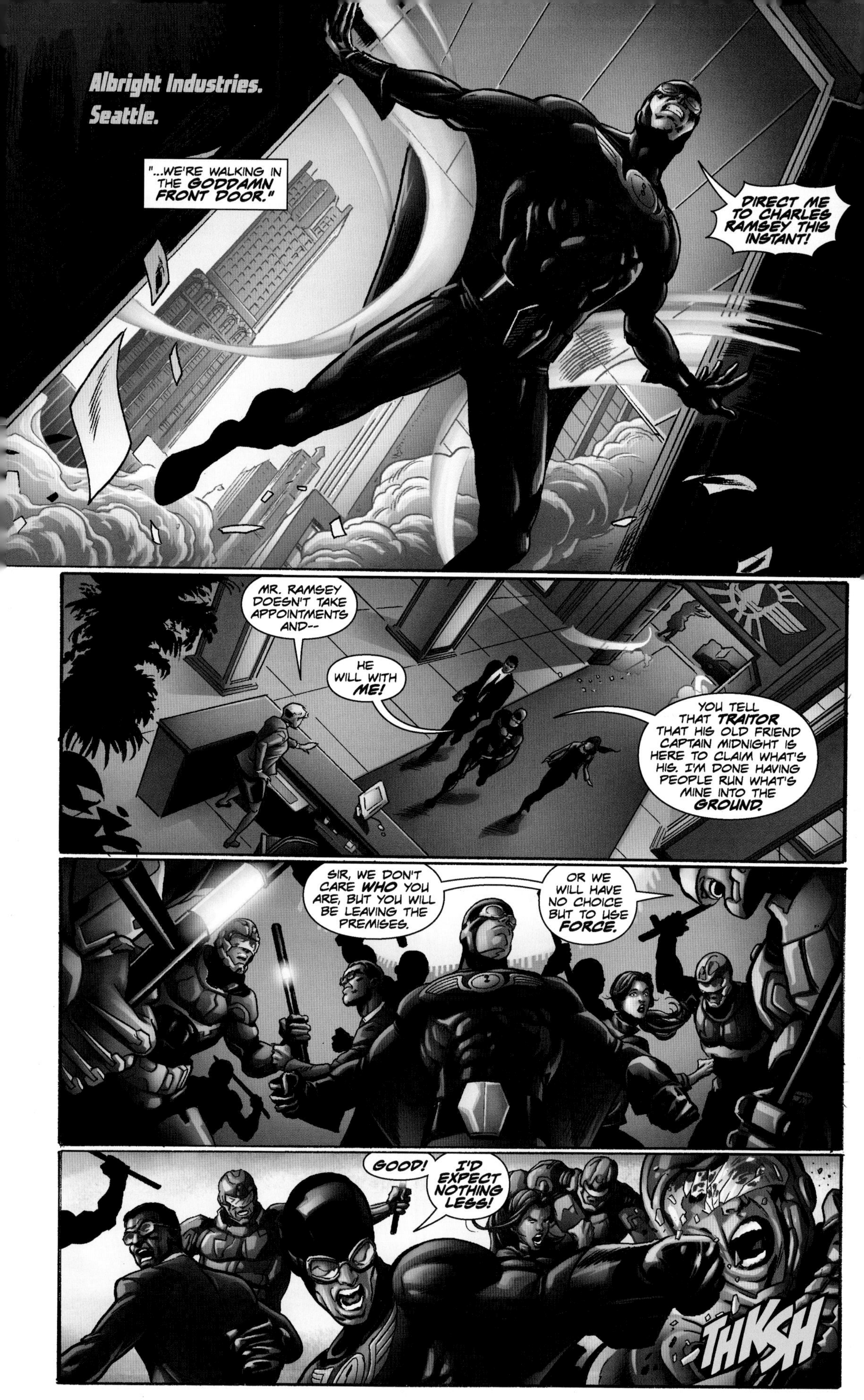

Albright Industries.
Seattle.
"...WE'RE WALKING IN THE GODDAMN FRONT DOOR."
DIRECT ME TO CHARLES RAMSEY THIS INSTANT!
MR. RAMSEY DOESN'T TAKE APPOINTMENTS AND--
HE WILL WITH ME!
YOU TELL THAT TRAITOR THAT HIS OLD FRIEND CAPTAIN MIDNIGHT IS HERE TO CLAIM WHAT'S HIS. I'M DONE HAVING PEOPLE RUN WHAT'S MINE INTO THE GROUND.
SIR, WE DON'T CARE WHO YOU ARE, BUT YOU WILL BE LEAVING THE PREMISES.
OR WE WILL HAVE NO CHOICE BUT TO USE FORCE.
GOOD!
I'D EXPECT NOTHING LESS!
THKSH

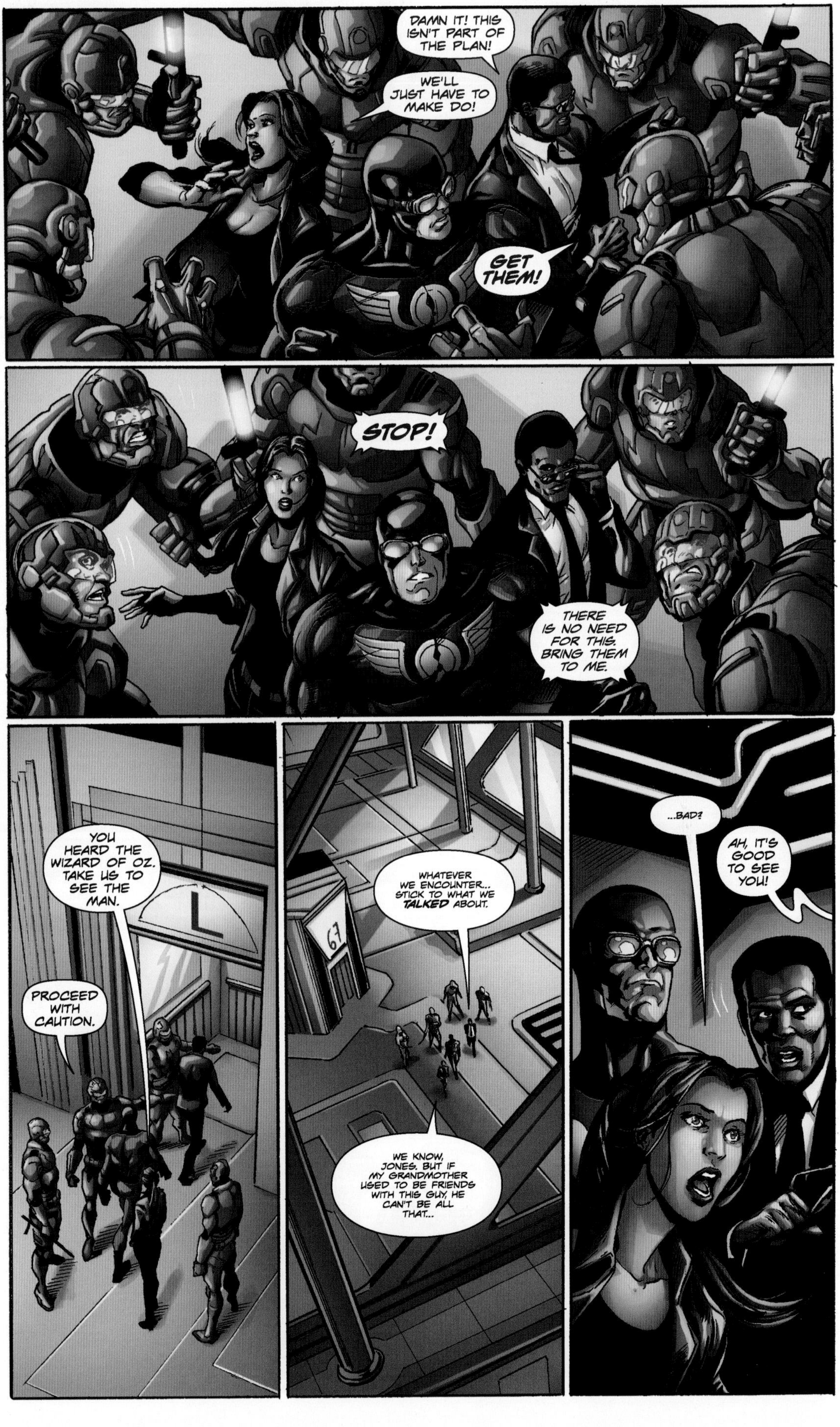
DAMN IT! THIS ISN'T PART OF THE PLAN!
WE'LL JUST HAVE TO MAKE DO!
GET THEM!
STOP!
THERE IS NO NEED FOR THIS. BRING THEM TO ME.
YOU HEARD THE WIZARD OF OZ. TAKE US TO SEE THE MAN.
PROCEED WITH CAUTION.
L
WHATEVER WE ENCOUNTER... STICK TO WHAT WE TALKED ABOUT.
67
WE KNOW, JONES. BUT IF MY GRANDMOTHER USED TO BE FRIENDS WITH THIS GUY, HE CAN'T BE ALL THAT...
...BAD?
AH, IT'S GOOD TO SEE YOU!

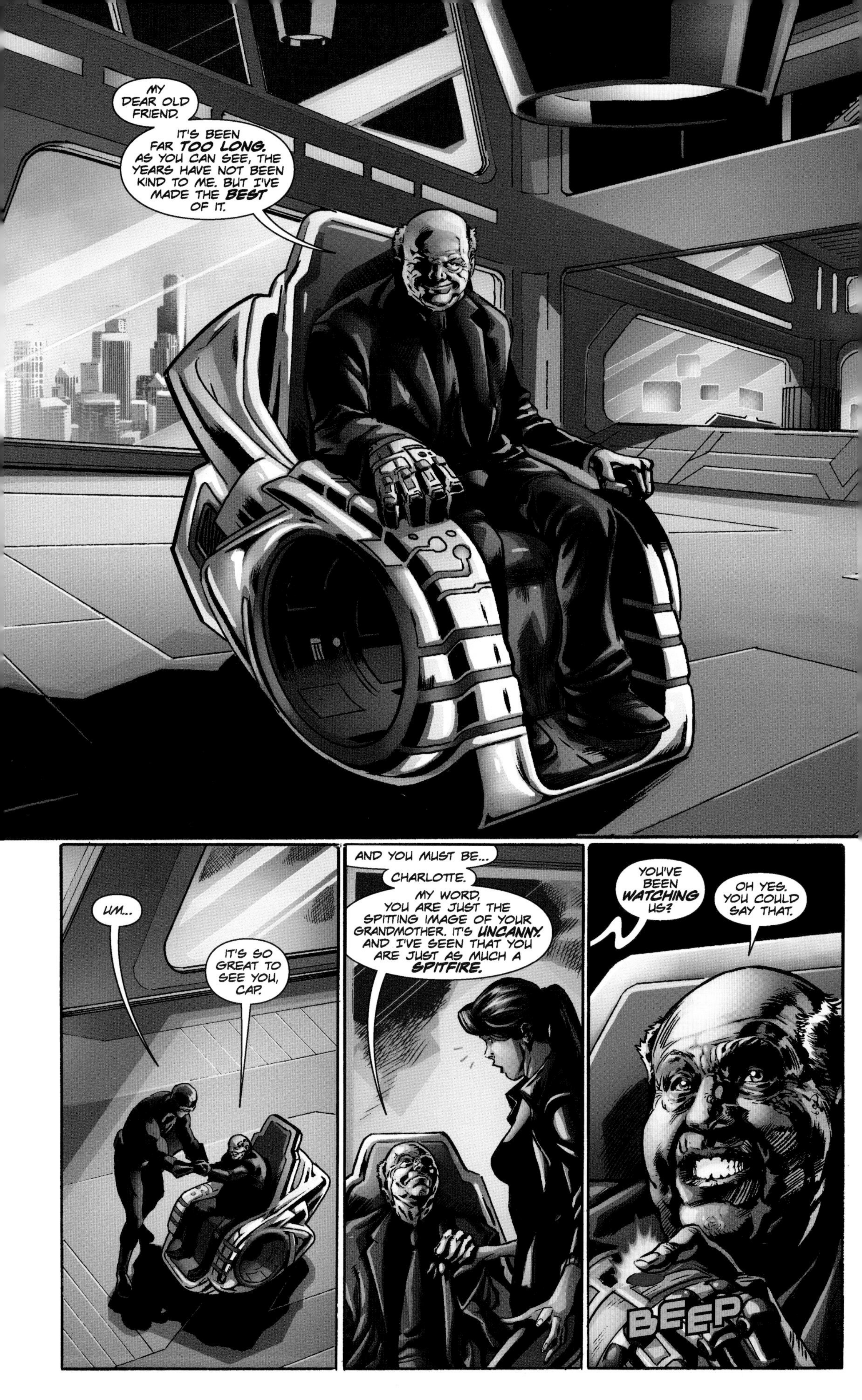
MY DEAR OLD FRIEND.
IT'S BEEN FAR TOO LONG. AS YOU CAN SEE, THE YEARS HAVE NOT BEEN KIND TO ME. BUT I'VE MADE THE BEST OF IT.
UM...
IT'S SO GREAT TO SEE YOU, CAP.
AND YOU MUST BE...
CHARLOTTE.
MY WORD, YOU ARE JUST THE SPITTING IMAGE OF YOUR GRANDMOTHER. IT'S UNCANNY. AND I'VE SEEN THAT YOU ARE JUST AS MUCH A SPITFIRE.
YOU'VE BEEN WATCHING US?
OH YES. YOU COULD SAY THAT.
BEEP

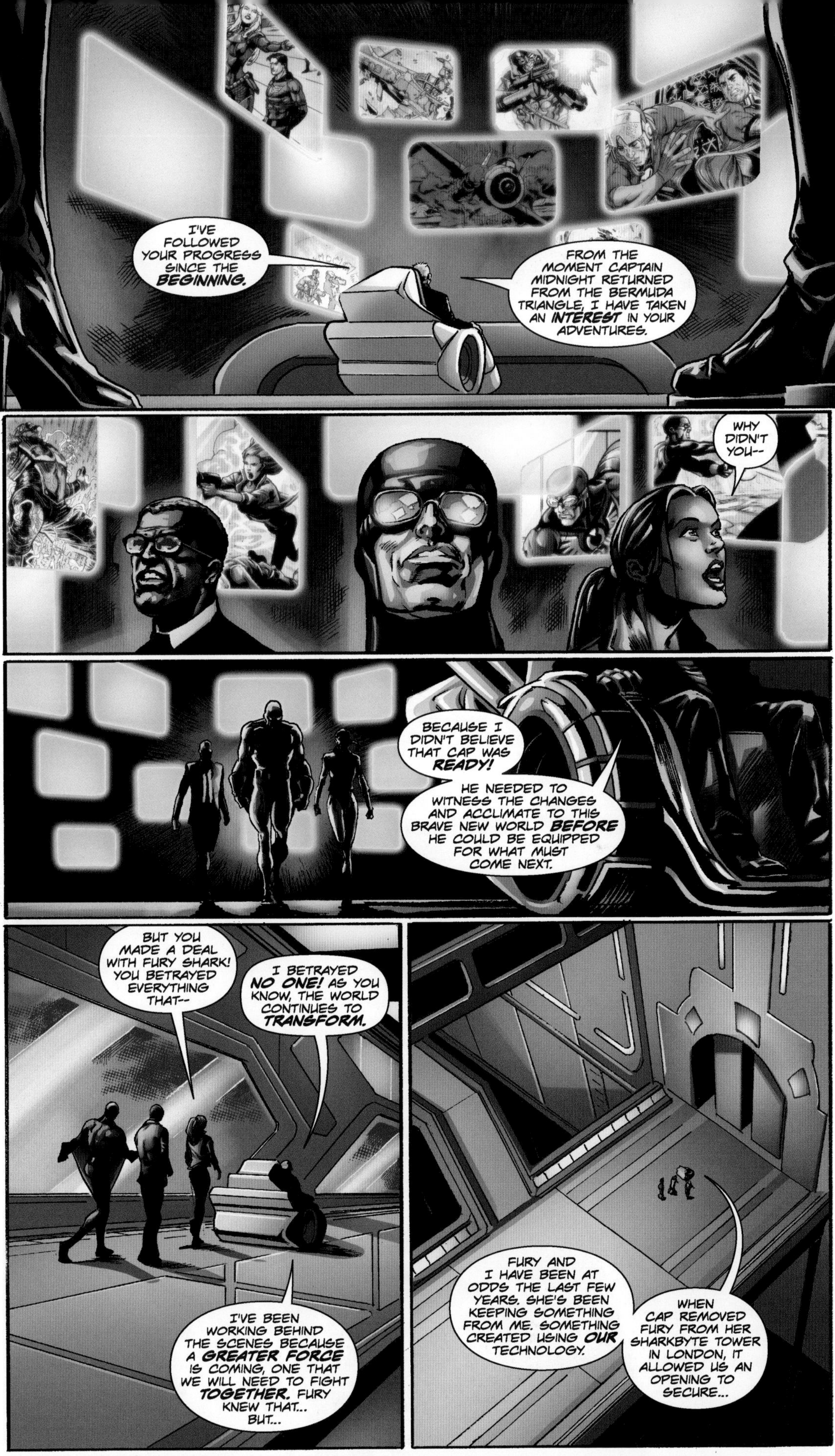
I'VE FOLLOWED YOUR PROGRESS SINCE THE BEGINNING.
FROM THE MOMENT CAPTAIN MIDNIGHT RETURNED FROM THE BERMUDA TRIANGLE, I HAVE TAKEN AN INTEREST IN YOUR ADVENTURES.
WHY DIDN'T YOU--
BECAUSE I DIDN'T BELIEVE THAT CAP WAS READY!
HE NEEDED TO WITNESS THE CHANGES AND ACCLIMATE TO THIS BRAVE NEW WORLD BEFORE HE COULD BE EQUIPPED FOR WHAT MUST COME NEXT.
BUT YOU MADE A DEAL WITH FURY SHARK! YOU BETRAYED EVERYTHING THAT--
I BETRAYED NO ONE! AS YOU KNOW, THE WORLD CONTINUES TO TRANSFORM.
I'VE BEEN WORKING BEHIND THE SCENES BECAUSE A GREATER FORCE IS COMING, ONE THAT WE WILL NEED TO FIGHT TOGETHER. FURY KNEW THAT... BUT...
FURY AND I HAVE BEEN AT ODDS THE LAST FEW YEARS. SHE'S BEEN KEEPING SOMETHING FROM ME. SOMETHING CREATED USING OUR TECHNOLOGY.
WHEN CAP REMOVED FURY FROM HER SHARKBYTE TOWER IN LONDON, IT ALLOWED US AN OPENING TO SECURE...

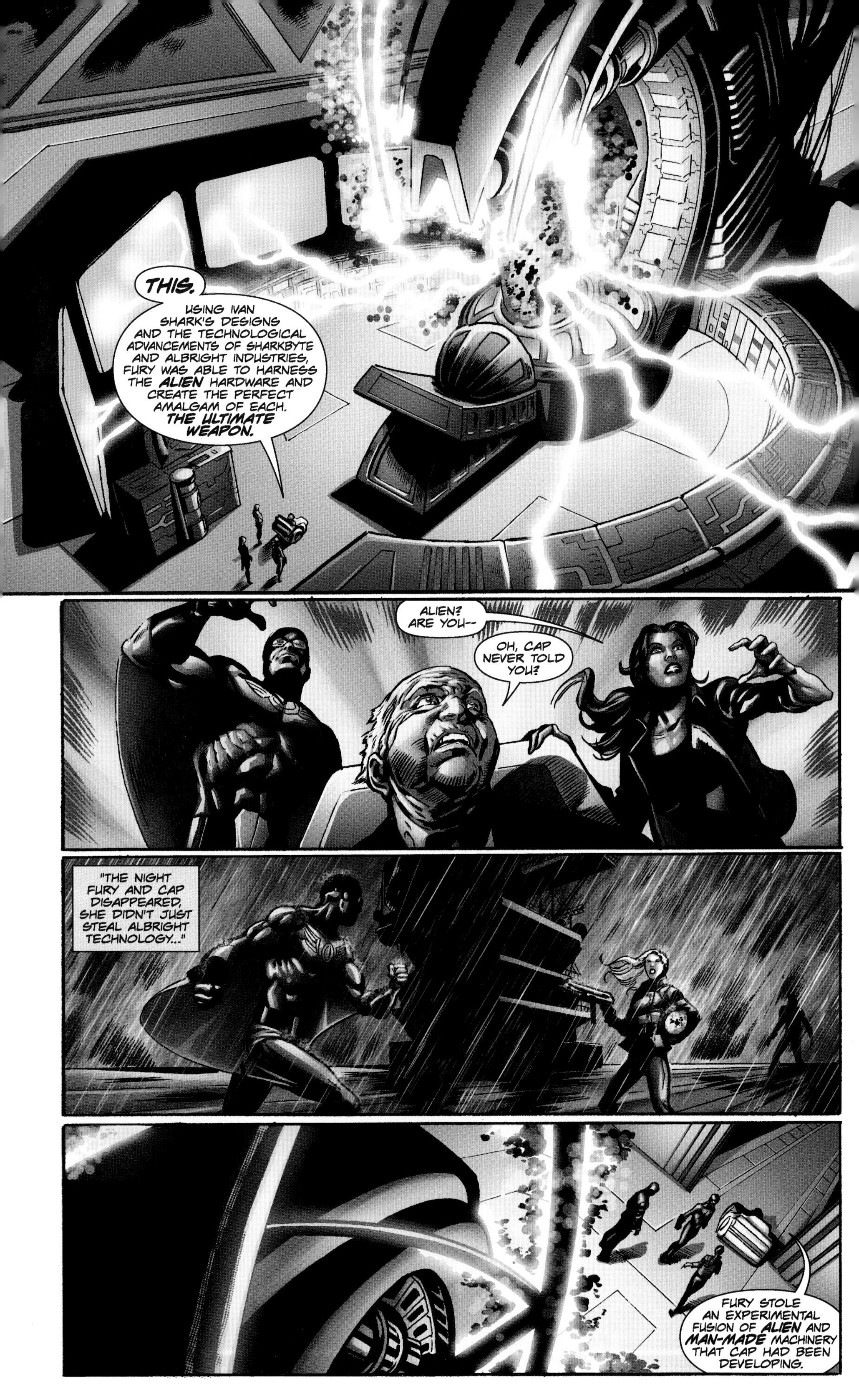
THIS.
USING IVAN SHARK'S DESIGNS AND THE TECHNOLOGICAL ADVANCEMENTS OF SHARKBYTE AND ALBRIGHT INDUSTRIES, FURY WAS ABLE TO HARNESS THE ALIEN HARDWARE AND CREATE THE PERFECT AMALGAM OF EACH. THE ULTIMATE WEAPON.
ALIEN? ARE YOU--
OH, CAP NEVER TOLD YOU?
"THE NIGHT FURY AND CAP DISAPPEARED, SHE DIDN'T JUST STEAL ALBRIGHT TECHNOLOGY..."
FURY STOLE AN EXPERIMENTAL FUSION OF ALIEN AND MAN-MADE MACHINERY THAT CAP HAD BEEN DEVELOPING.

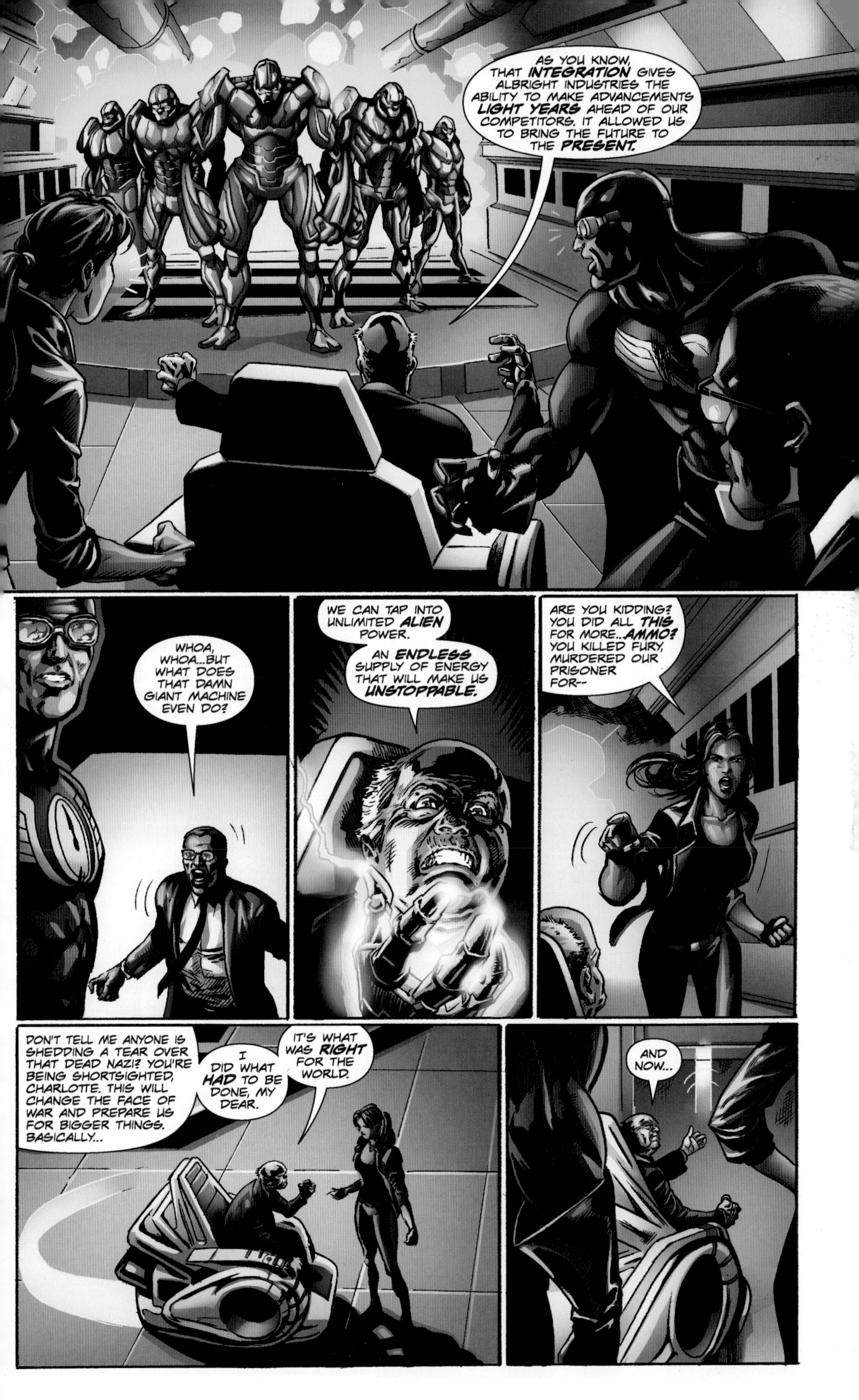
AS YOU KNOW, THAT INTEGRATION GIVES ALBRIGHT INDUSTRIES THE ABILITY TO MAKE ADVANCEMENTS LIGHT YEARS AHEAD OF OUR COMPETITORS. IT ALLOWED US TO BRING THE FUTURE TO THE PRESENT.
WHOA, WHOA...BUT WHAT DOES THAT DAMN GIANT MACHINE EVEN DO?
WE CAN TAP INTO UNLIMITED ALIEN POWER.
AN ENDLESS SUPPLY OF ENERGY THAT WILL MAKE US UNSTOPPABLE.
ARE YOU KIDDING? YOU DID ALL THIS FOR MORE...AMMO? YOU KILLED FURY, MURDERED OUR PRISONER FOR--
DON'T TELL ME ANYONE IS SHEDDING A TEAR OVER THAT DEAD NAZI? YOU'RE BEING SHORTSIGHTED, CHARLOTTE. THIS WILL CHANGE THE FACE OF WAR AND PREPARE US FOR BIGGER THINGS. BASICALLY...
I DID WHAT HAD TO BE DONE, MY DEAR.
IT'S WHAT WAS RIGHT FOR THE WORLD.
AND NOW...

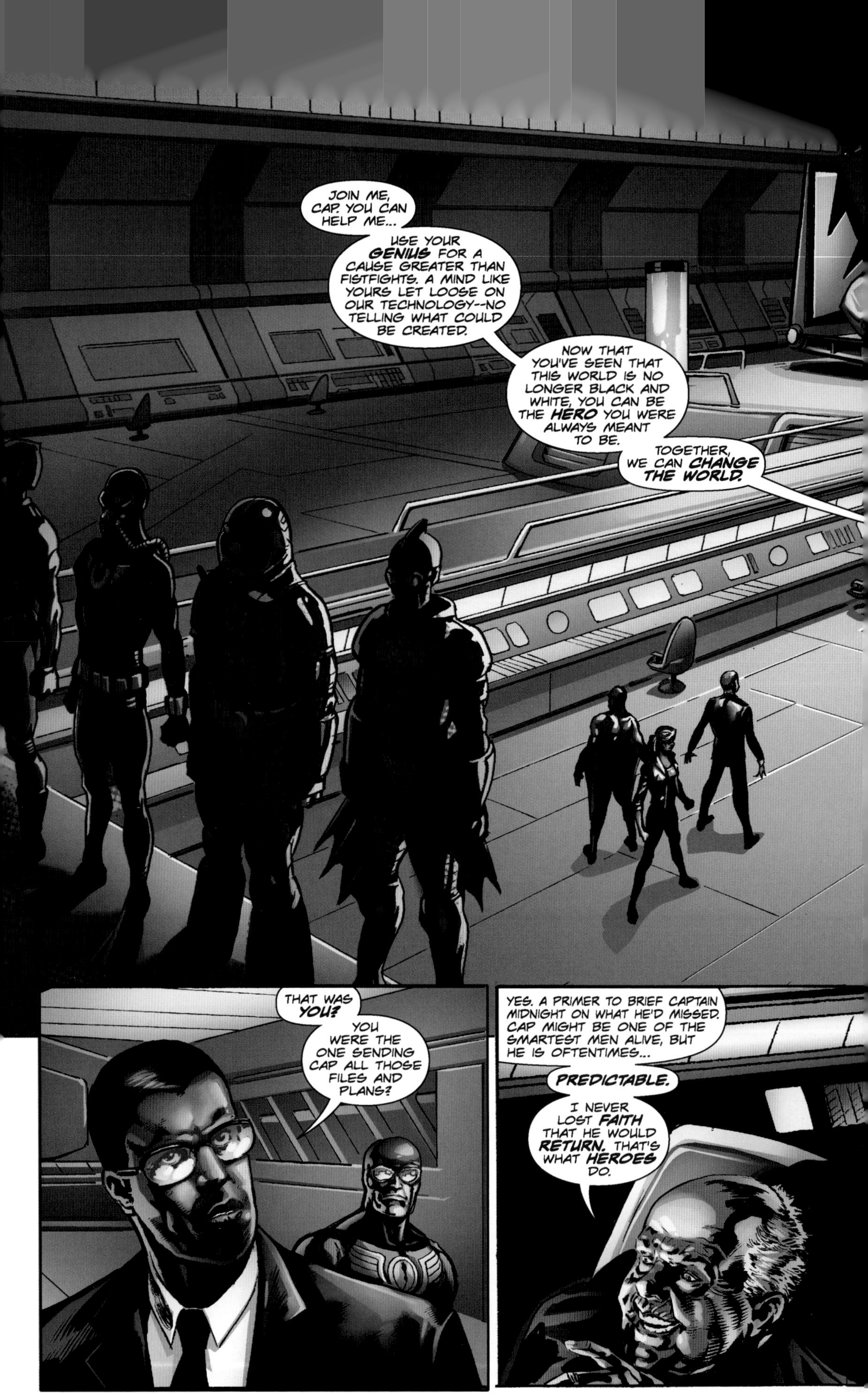
JOIN ME, CAP. YOU CAN HELP ME...
USE YOUR GENIUS FOR A CAUSE GREATER THAN FISTFIGHTS. A MIND LIKE YOURS LET LOOSE ON OUR TECHNOLOGY--NO TELLING WHAT COULD BE CREATED.
NOW THAT YOU'VE SEEN THAT THIS WORLD IS NO LONGER BLACK AND WHITE, YOU CAN BE THE HERO YOU WERE ALWAYS MEANT TO BE.
TOGETHER, WE CAN CHANGE THE WORLD.
THAT WAS YOU?
YOU WERE THE ONE SENDING CAP ALL THOSE FILES AND PLANS?
YES. A PRIMER TO BRIEF CAPTAIN MIDNIGHT ON WHAT HE'D MISSED. CAP MIGHT BE ONE OF THE SMARTEST MEN ALIVE, BUT HE IS OFTENTIMES...
PREDICTABLE.
I NEVER LOST FAITH THAT HE WOULD RETURN. THAT'S WHAT HEROES DO.

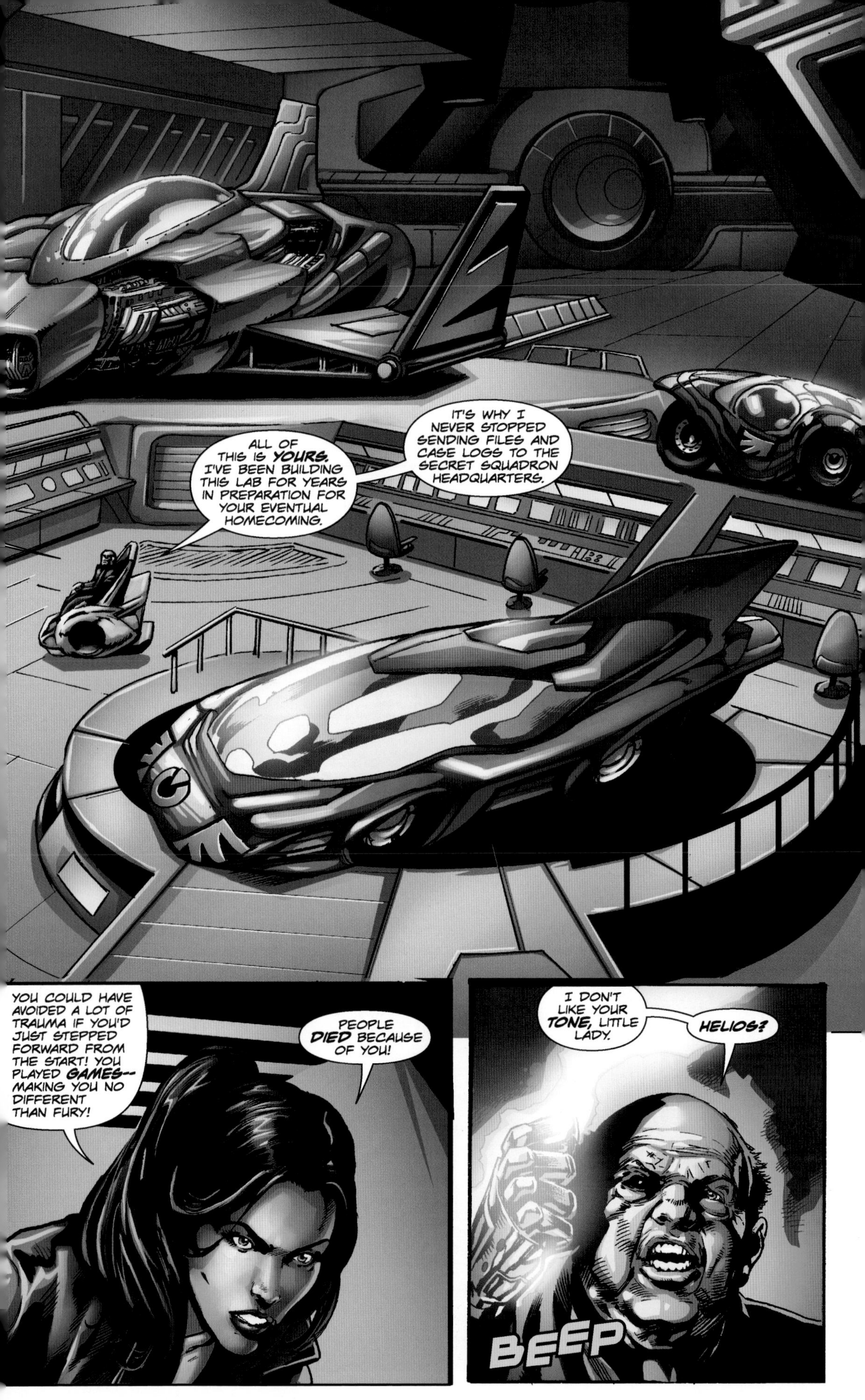
ALL OF THIS IS YOURS. I'VE BEEN BUILDING THIS LAB FOR YEARS IN PREPARATION FOR YOUR EVENTUAL HOMECOMING.
IT'S WHY I NEVER STOPPED SENDING FILES AND CASE LOGS TO THE SECRET SQUADRON HEADQUARTERS.
YOU COULD HAVE AVOIDED A LOT OF TRAUMA IF YOU'D JUST STEPPED FORWARD FROM THE START! YOU PLAYED GAMES-- MAKING YOU NO DIFFERENT THAN FURY!
PEOPLE DIED BECAUSE OF YOU!
I DON'T LIKE YOUR TONE, LITTLE LADY.
HELIOS?
BEEP

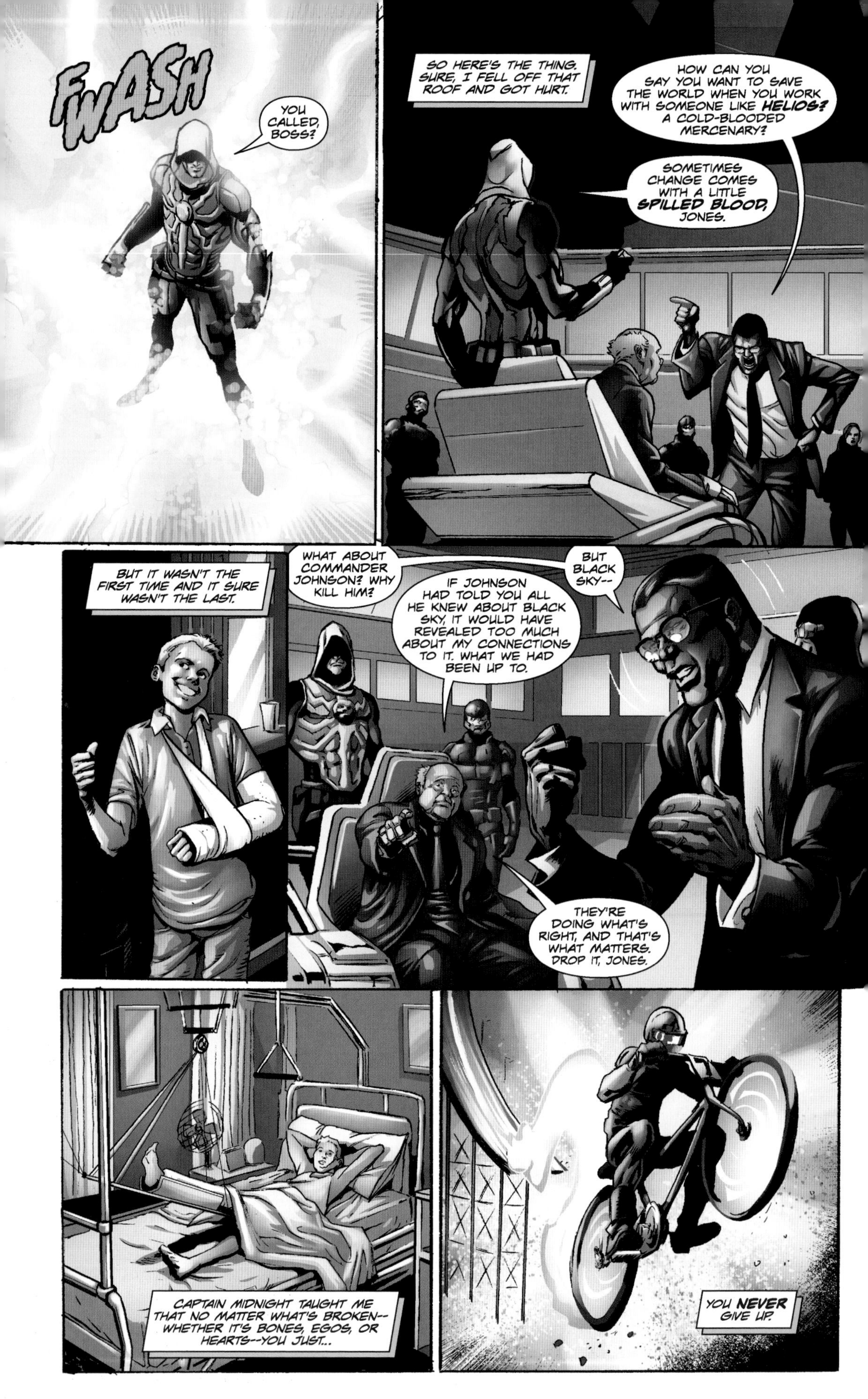
FWASH
YOU CALLED, BOSS?
SO HERE'S THE THING. SURE, I FELL OFF THAT ROOF AND GOT HURT.
HOW CAN YOU SAY YOU WANT TO SAVE THE WORLD WHEN YOU WORK WITH SOMEONE LIKE HELIOS? A COLD-BLOODED MERCENARY?
SOMETIMES CHANGE COMES WITH A LITTLE SPILLED BLOOD, JONES.
BUT IT WASN'T THE FIRST TIME AND IT SURE WASN'T THE LAST.
WHAT ABOUT COMMANDER JOHNSON? WHY KILL HIM?
IF JOHNSON HAD TOLD YOU ALL HE KNEW ABOUT BLACK SKY, IT WOULD HAVE REVEALED TOO MUCH ABOUT MY CONNECTIONS TO IT. WHAT WE HAD BEEN UP TO.
BUT BLACK SKY--
THEY'RE DOING WHAT'S RIGHT, AND THAT'S WHAT MATTERS. DROP IT, JONES.
CAPTAIN MIDNIGHT TAUGHT ME THAT NO MATTER WHAT'S BROKEN--WHETHER IT'S BONES, EGOS, OR HEARTS--YOU JUST...
YOU NEVER GIVE UP.

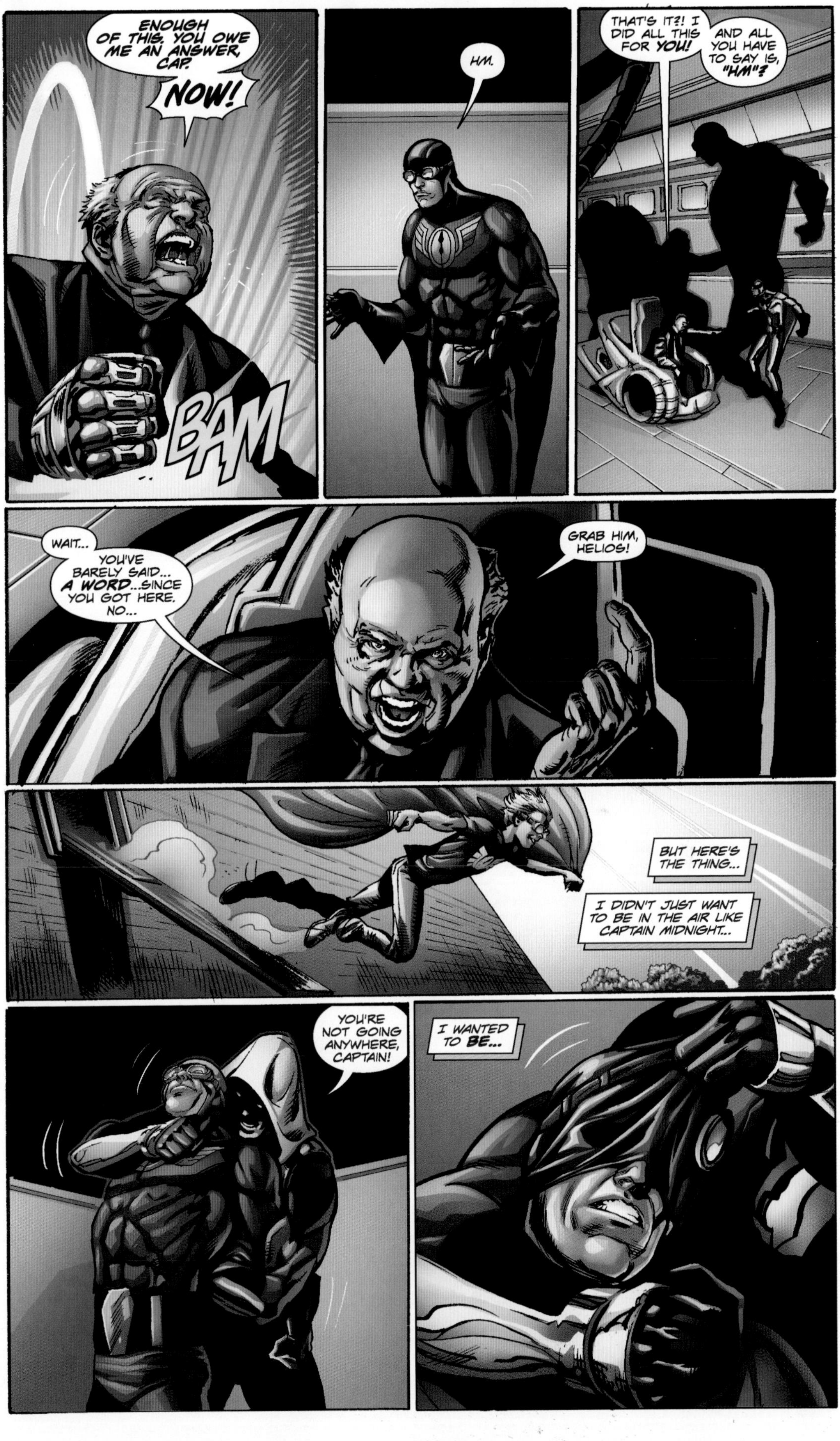
ENOUGH OF THIS. YOU OWE ME AN ANSWER, CAP.
NOW!
BAM
HM.
THAT'S IT?! I DID ALL THIS FOR YOU!
AND ALL YOU HAVE TO SAY IS, "HM"?
WAIT... YOU'VE BARELY SAID... A WORD...SINCE YOU GOT HERE. NO...
GRAB HIM, HELIOS!
BUT HERE'S THE THING...
I DIDN'T JUST WANT TO BE IN THE AIR LIKE CAPTAIN MIDNIGHT...
YOU'RE NOT GOING ANYWHERE, CAPTAIN!
I WANTED TO BE...

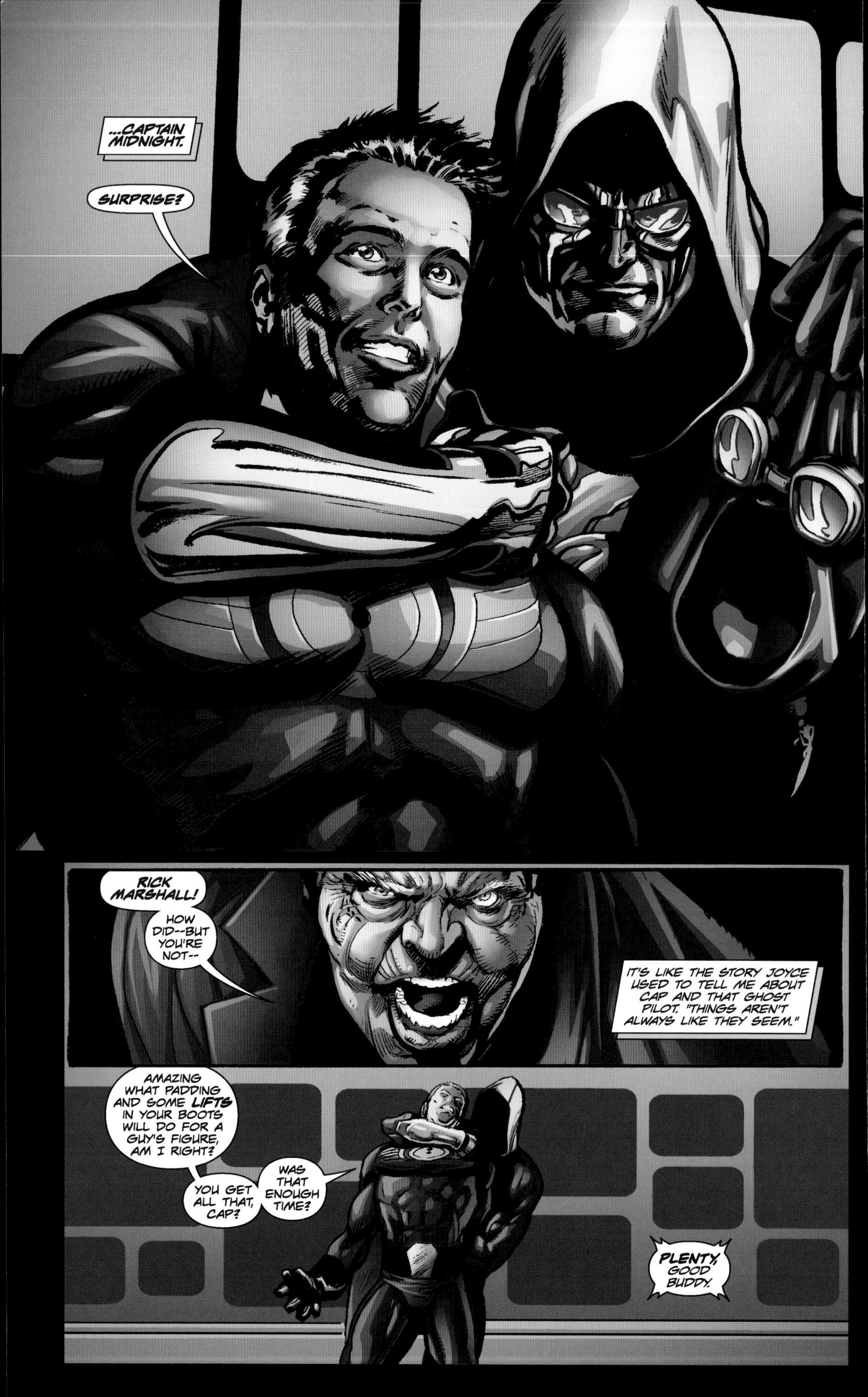
...CAPTAIN MIDNIGHT.
SURPRISE?
RICK MARSHALL!
HOW DID--BUT YOU'RE NOT--
IT'S LIKE THE STORY JOYCE USED TO TELL ME ABOUT CAP AND THAT GHOST PILOT. "THINGS AREN'T ALWAYS LIKE THEY SEEM."
AMAZING WHAT PADDING AND SOME LIFTS IN YOUR BOOTS WILL DO FOR A GUY'S FIGURE, AM I RIGHT?
YOU GET ALL THAT, CAP?
WAS THAT ENOUGH TIME?
PLENTY, GOOD BUDDY.

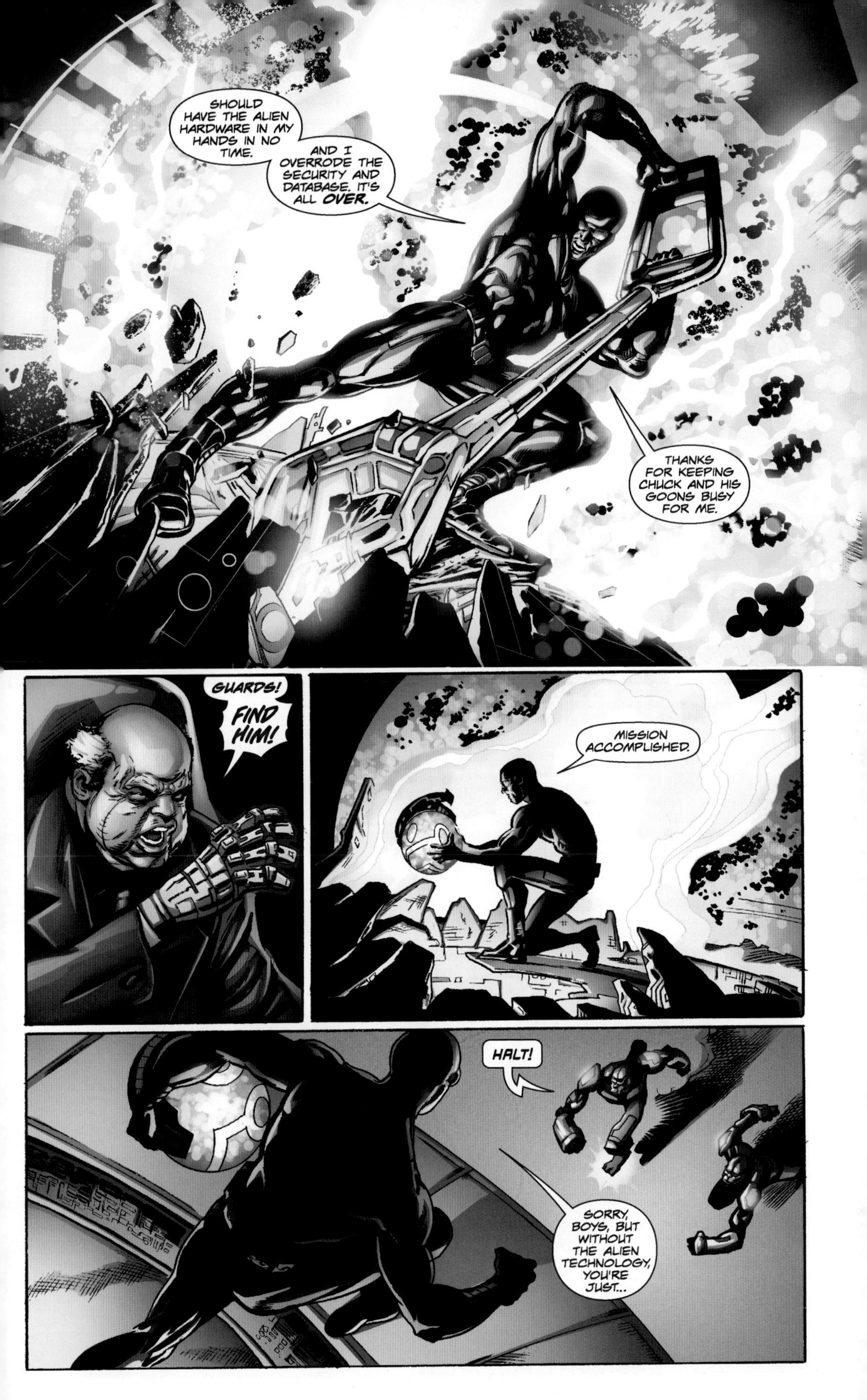
SHOULD HAVE THE ALIEN HARDWARE IN MY HANDS IN NO TIME.
AND I OVERRODE THE SECURITY AND DATABASE. IT'S ALL **OVER.**
THANKS FOR KEEPING CHUCK AND HIS GOONS BUSY FOR ME.
GUARDS! FIND HIM!
MISSION ACCOMPLISHED.
HALT!
SORRY, BOYS, BUT WITHOUT THE ALIEN TECHNOLOGY, YOU'RE JUST...

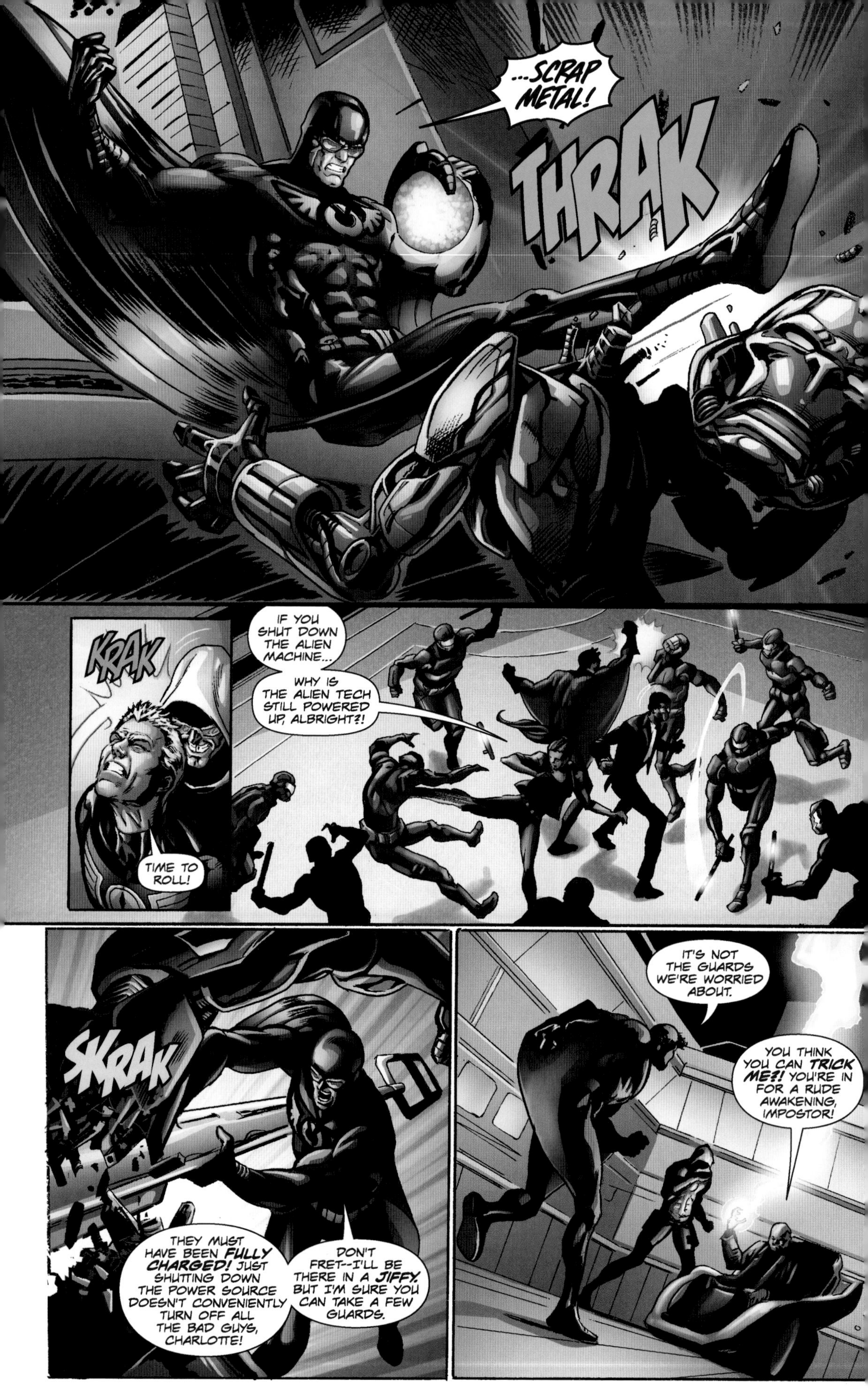
...SCRAP METAL!
THRAK
KRAK
IF YOU SHUT DOWN THE ALIEN MACHINE...
WHY IS THE ALIEN TECH STILL POWERED UP, ALBRIGHT?!
TIME TO ROLL!
SKRAK
THEY MUST HAVE BEEN FULLY CHARGED! JUST SHUTTING DOWN THE POWER SOURCE DOESN'T CONVENIENTLY TURN OFF ALL THE BAD GUYS, CHARLOTTE!
DON'T FRET--I'LL BE THERE IN A JIFFY. BUT I'M SURE YOU CAN TAKE A FEW GUARDS.
IT'S NOT THE GUARDS WE'RE WORRIED ABOUT.
YOU THINK YOU CAN TRICK ME?! YOU'RE IN FOR A RUDE AWAKENING, IMPOSTOR!

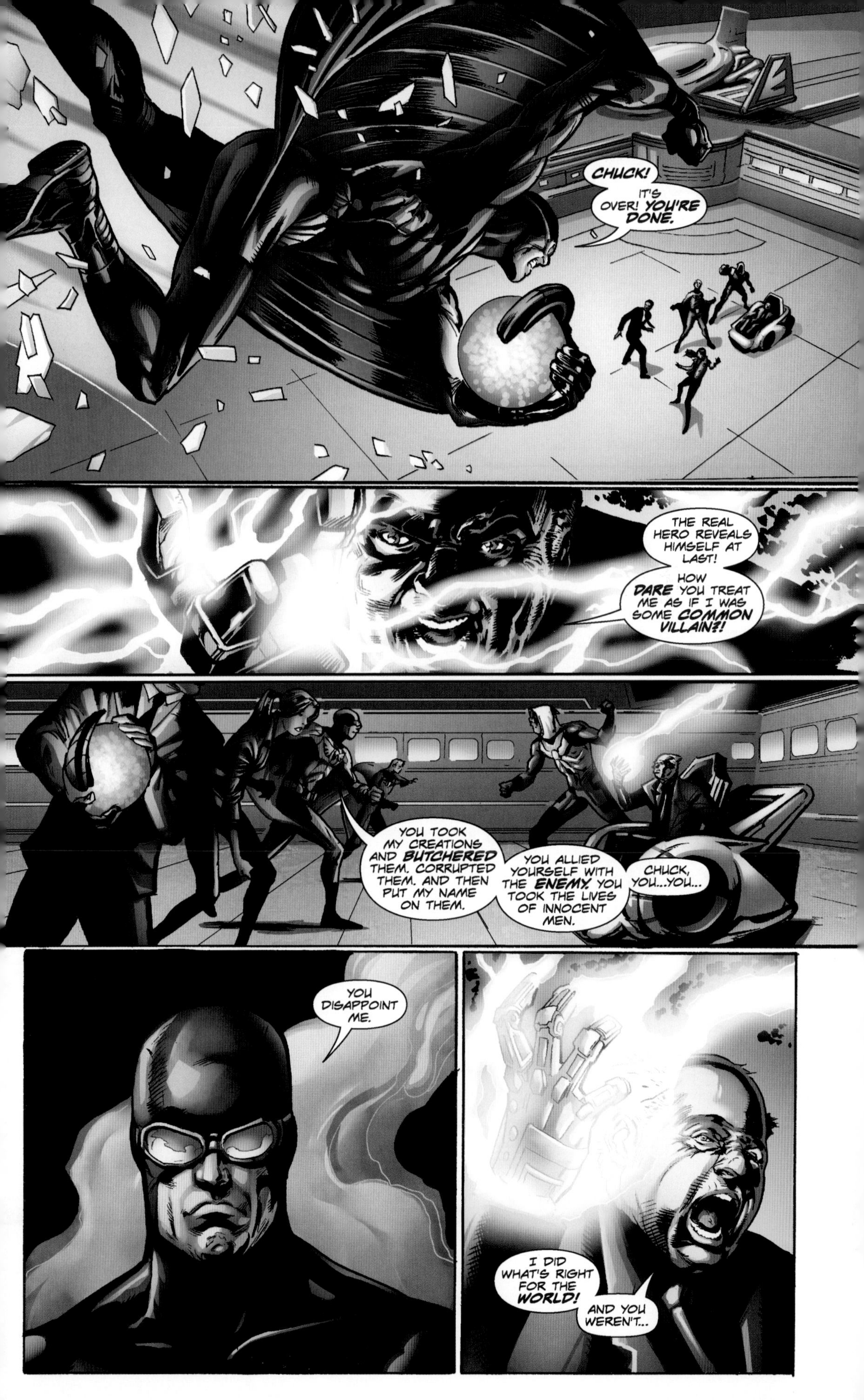
CHUCK!
IT'S OVER! YOU'RE DONE.
THE REAL HERO REVEALS HIMSELF AT LAST!
HOW DARE YOU TREAT ME AS IF I WAS SOME COMMON VILLAIN?!
YOU TOOK MY CREATIONS AND BUTCHERED THEM. CORRUPTED THEM. AND THEN PUT MY NAME ON THEM.
YOU ALLIED YOURSELF WITH THE ENEMY. YOU TOOK THE LIVES OF INNOCENT MEN.
CHUCK, YOU...YOU...
YOU DISAPPOINT ME.
I DID WHAT'S RIGHT FOR THE WORLD!
AND YOU WEREN'T...

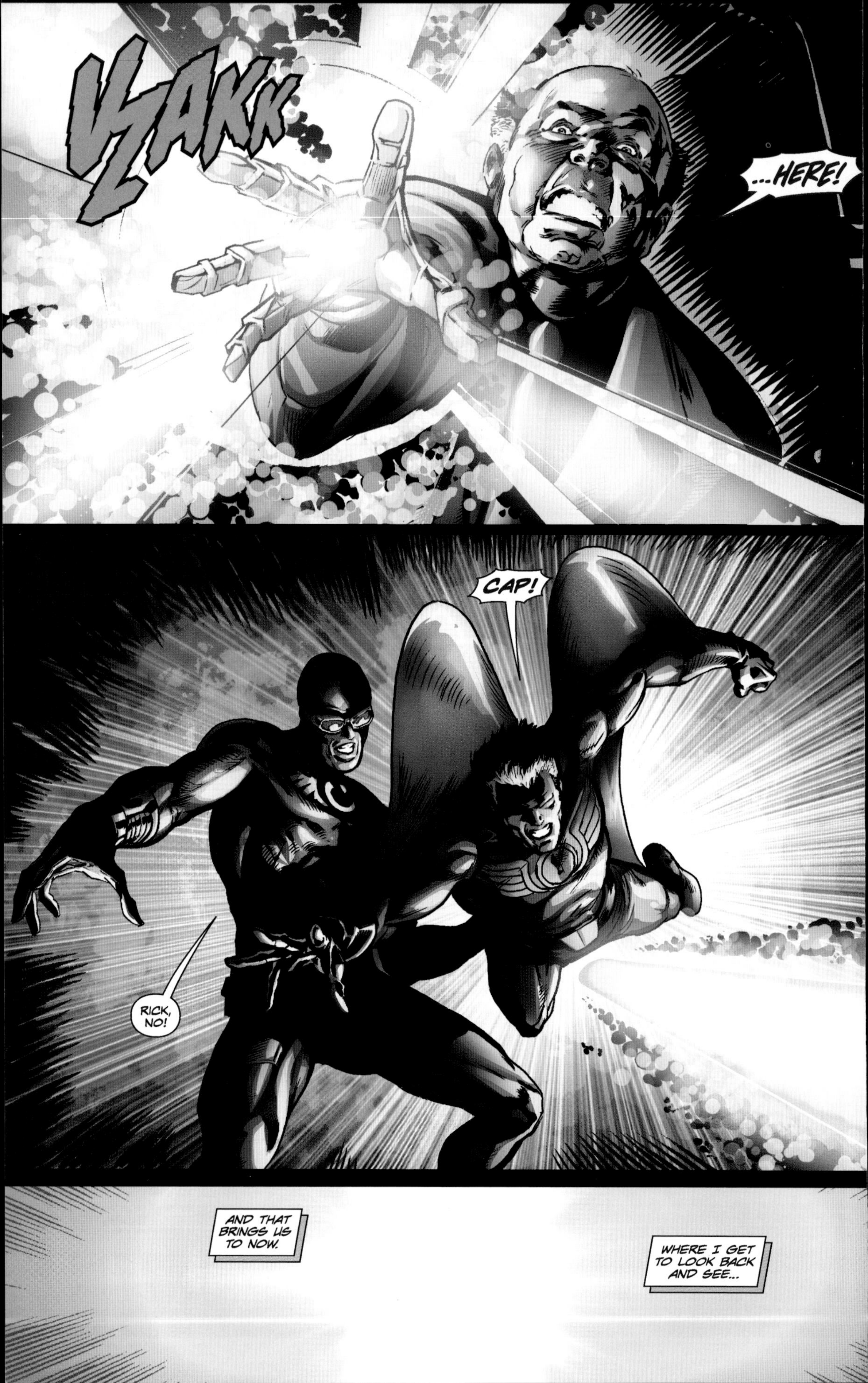
VZAKK
...HERE!
CAP!
RICK, NO!
AND THAT BRINGS US TO NOW.
WHERE I GET TO LOOK BACK AND SEE...

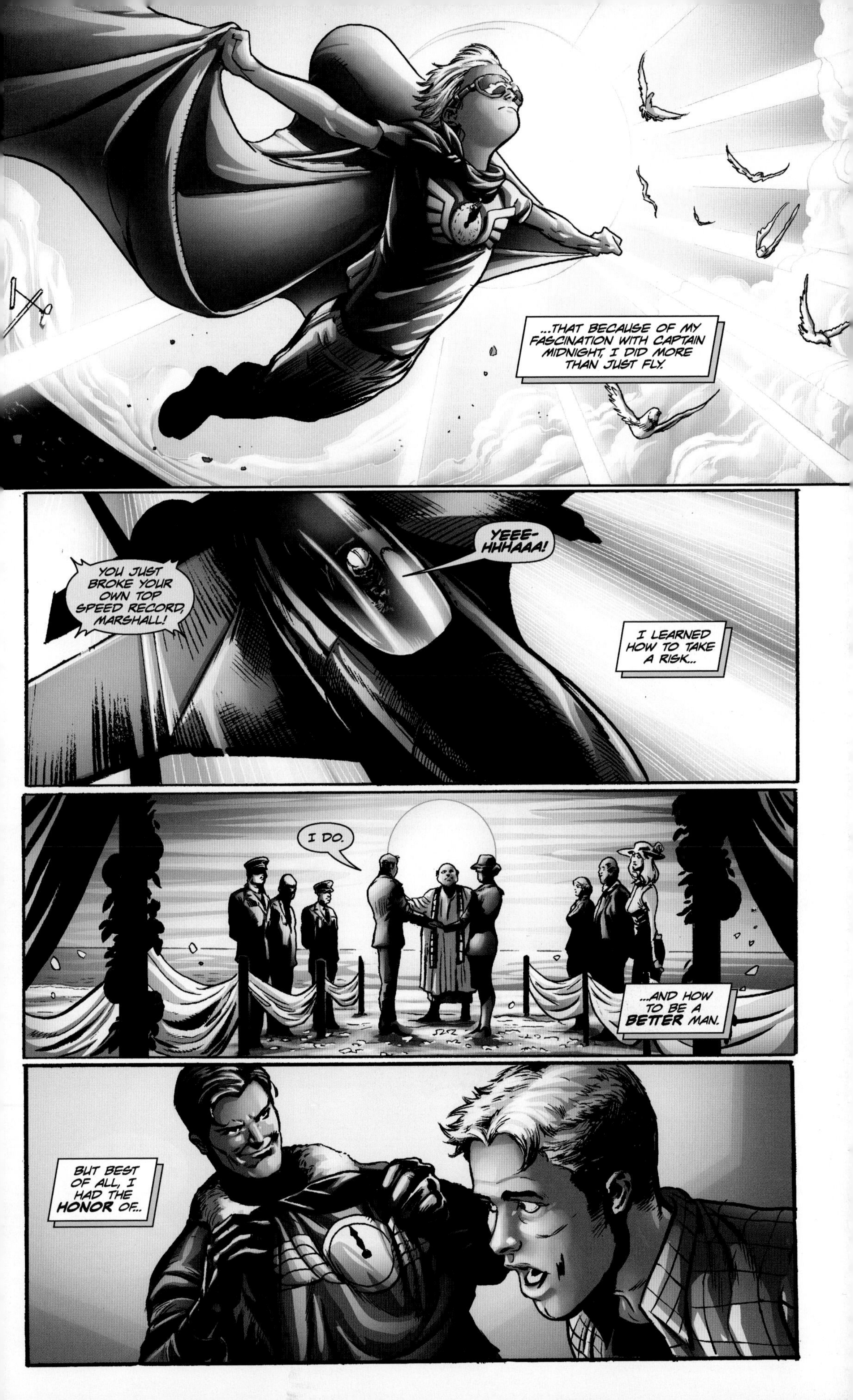
...THAT BECAUSE OF MY FASCINATION WITH CAPTAIN MIDNIGHT, I DID MORE THAN JUST FLY.
YOU JUST BROKE YOUR OWN TOP SPEED RECORD, MARSHALL!
YEEE-HHHAAA!
I LEARNED HOW TO TAKE A RISK...
I DO.
...AND HOW TO BE A BETTER MAN.
BUT BEST OF ALL, I HAD THE HONOR OF...

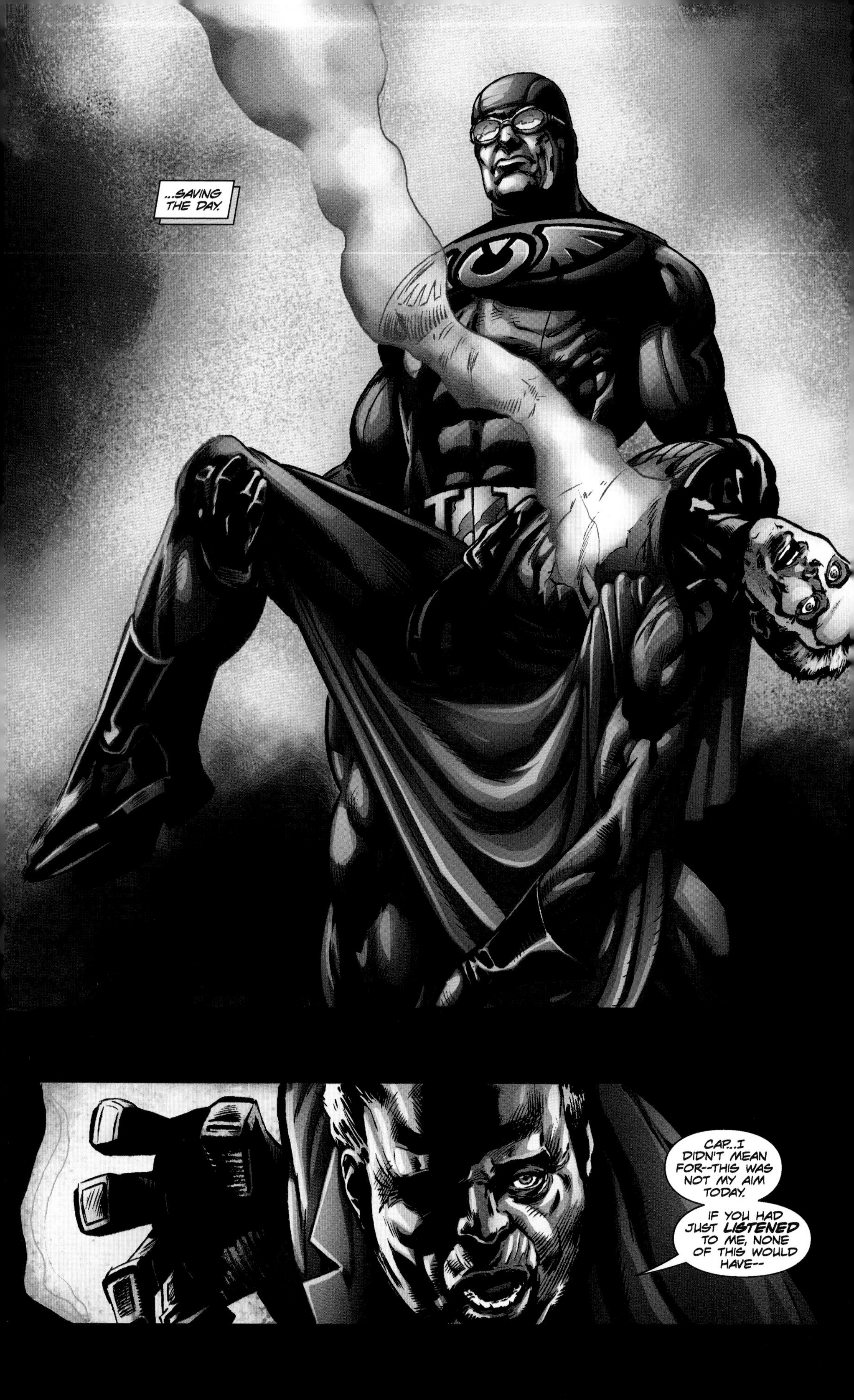
...SAVING THE DAY.
CAP...I DIDN'T MEAN FOR--THIS WAS NOT MY AIM TODAY.
IF YOU HAD JUST LISTENED TO ME, NONE OF THIS WOULD HAVE--

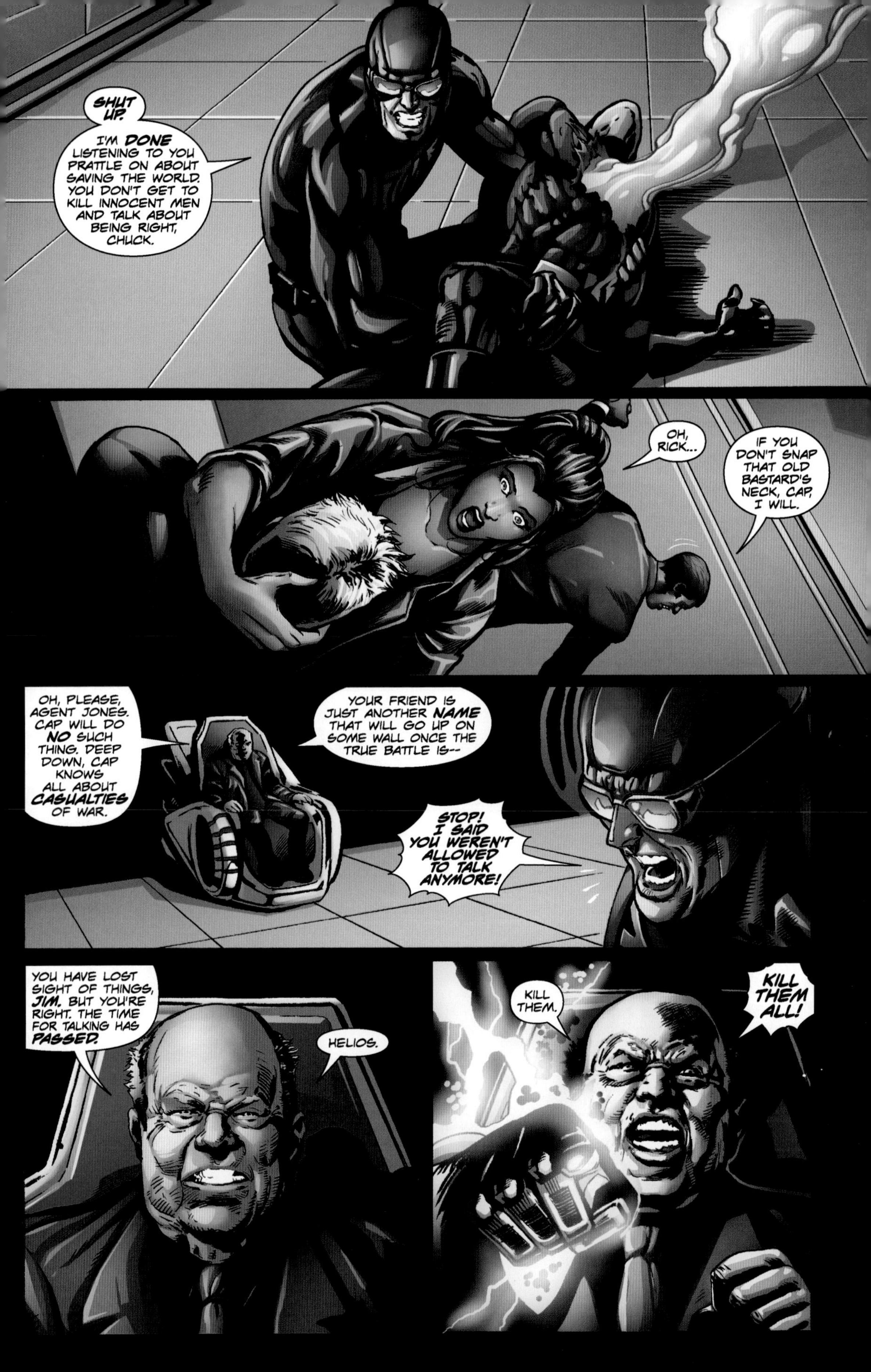
SHUT UP.
I'M DONE LISTENING TO YOU PRATTLE ON ABOUT SAVING THE WORLD. YOU DON'T GET TO KILL INNOCENT MEN AND TALK ABOUT BEING RIGHT, CHUCK.
OH, RICK...
IF YOU DON'T SNAP THAT OLD BASTARD'S NECK, CAP, I WILL.
OH, PLEASE, AGENT JONES. CAP WILL DO NO SUCH THING. DEEP DOWN, CAP KNOWS ALL ABOUT CASUALTIES OF WAR.
YOUR FRIEND IS JUST ANOTHER NAME THAT WILL GO UP ON SOME WALL ONCE THE TRUE BATTLE IS--
STOP! I SAID YOU WEREN'T ALLOWED TO TALK ANYMORE!
YOU HAVE LOST SIGHT OF THINGS, JIM. BUT YOU'RE RIGHT. THE TIME FOR TALKING HAS PASSED.
HELIOS.
KILL THEM.
KILL THEM ALL!

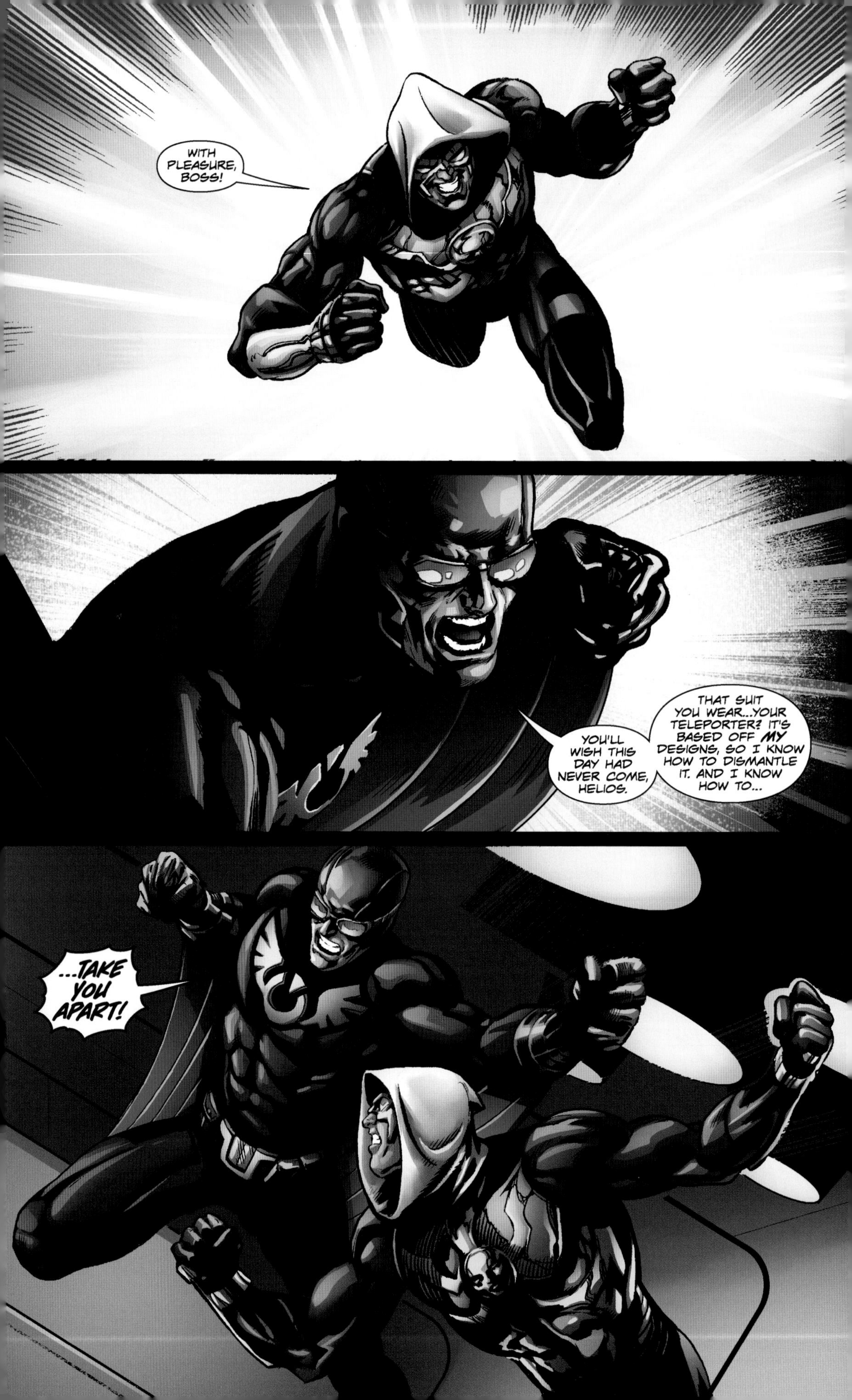
WITH PLEASURE, BOSS!
YOU'LL WISH THIS DAY HAD NEVER COME, HELIOS.
THAT SUIT YOU WEAR...YOUR TELEPORTER? IT'S BASED OFF MY DESIGNS, SO I KNOW HOW TO DISMANTLE IT. AND I KNOW HOW TO...
...TAKE YOU APART!

CHAPTER 4

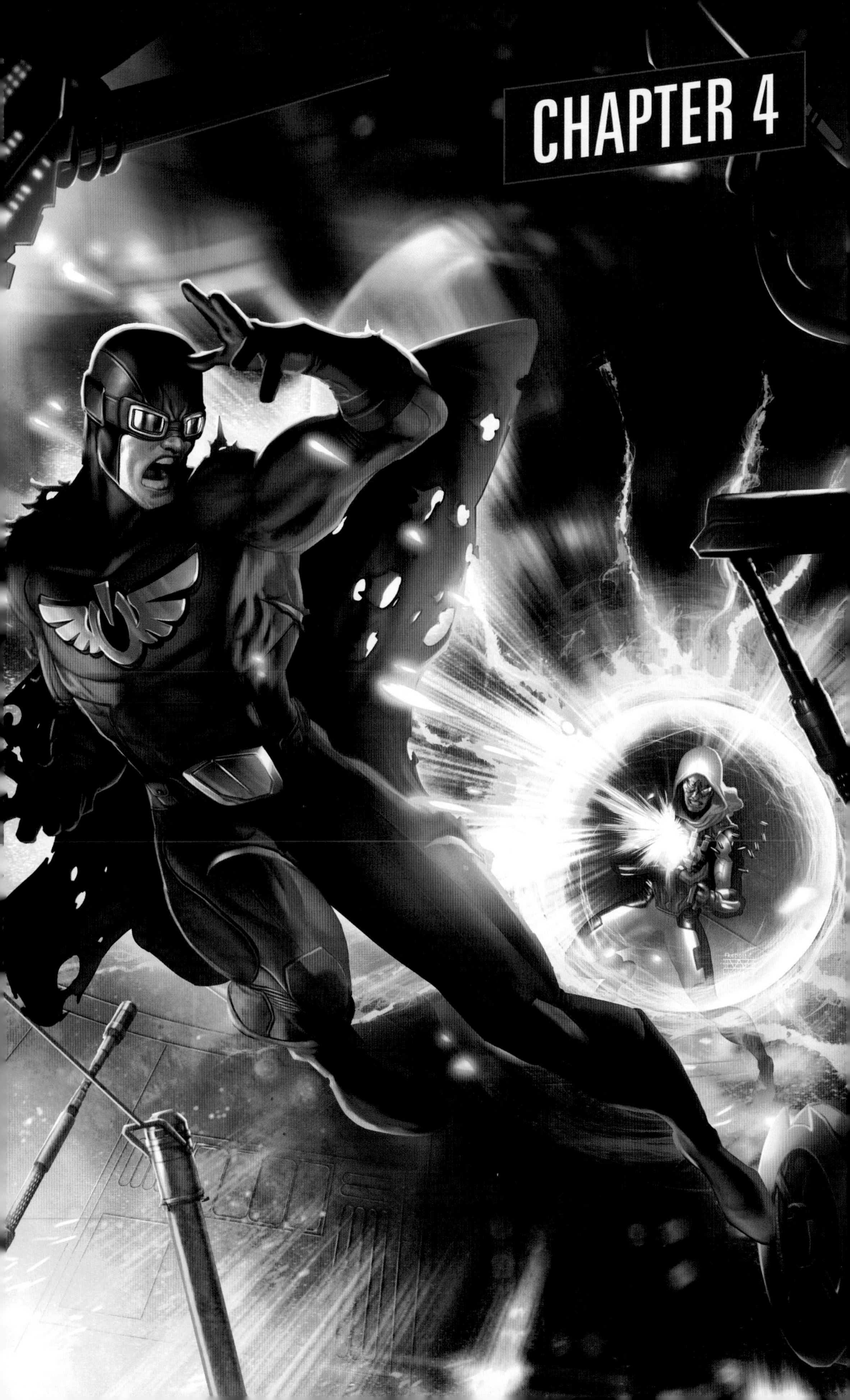

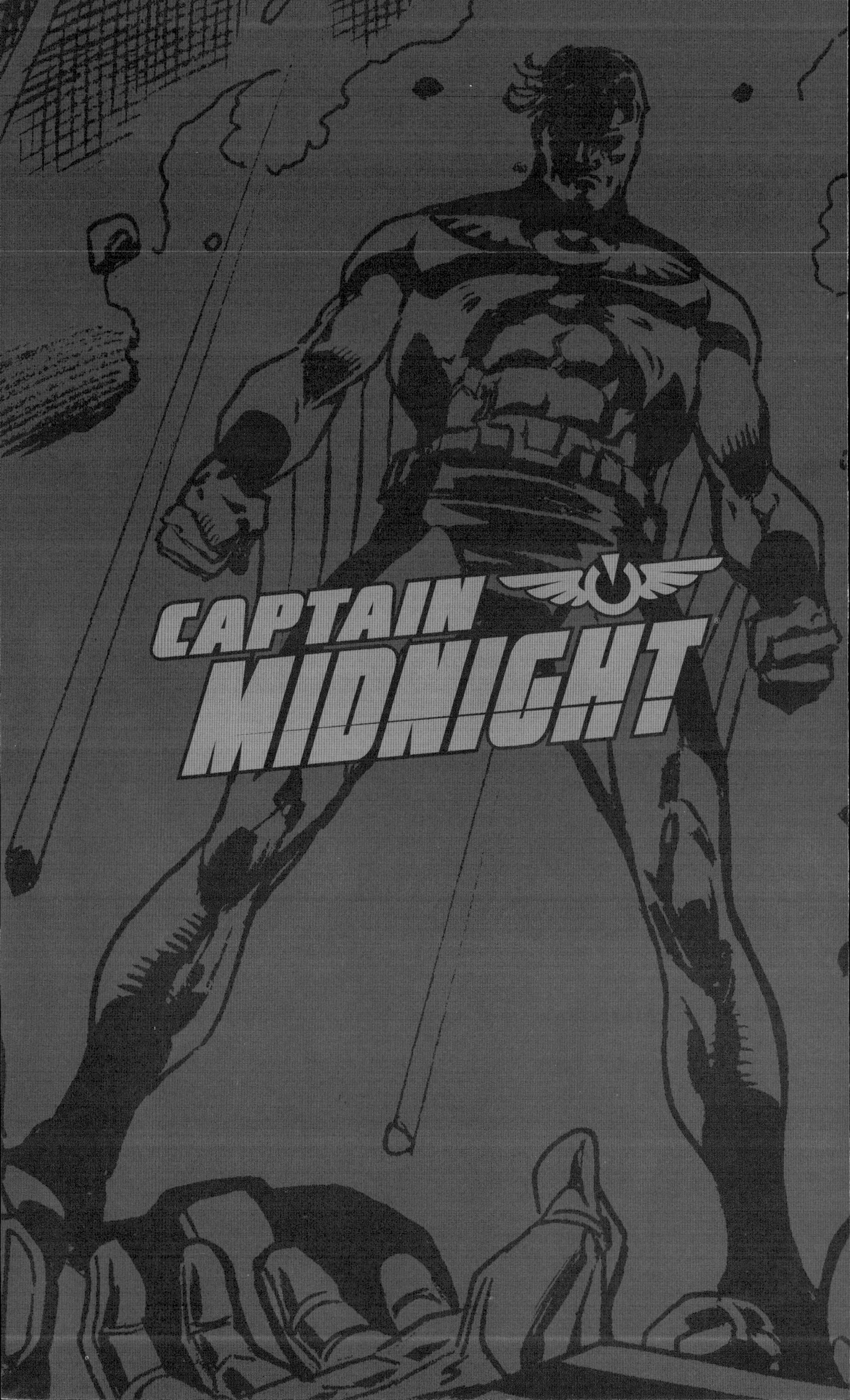
CAPTAIN
MIDNIGHT

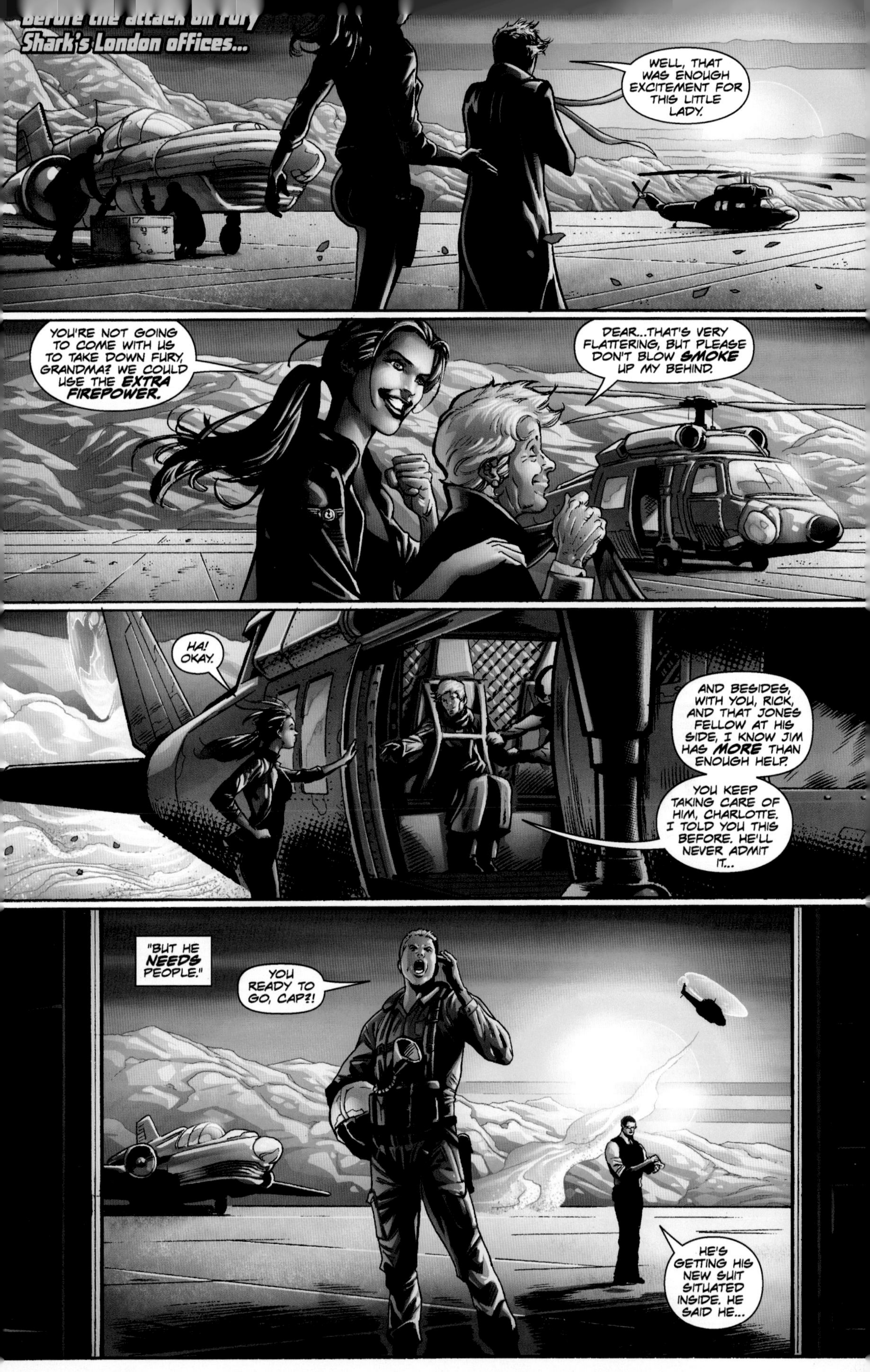
Before the attack on Fury
Shark's London offices...
WELL, THAT WAS ENOUGH EXCITEMENT FOR THIS LITTLE LADY.
YOU'RE NOT GOING TO COME DOWN WITH US TO TAKE DOWN FURY, GRANDMA? WE COULD USE THE EXTRA FIREPOWER.
DEAR...THAT'S VERY FLATTERING, BUT PLEASE DON'T BLOW SMOKE UP MY BEHIND.
HA! OKAY.
AND BESIDES, WITH YOU, RICK, AND THAT JONES FELLOW AT HIS SIDE, I KNOW JIM HAS MORE THAN ENOUGH HELP.
YOU KEEP TAKING CARE OF HIM, CHARLOTTE. I TOLD YOU THIS BEFORE. HE'LL NEVER ADMIT IT...
"BUT HE NEEDS PEOPLE."
YOU READY TO GO, CAP?!
HE'S GETTING HIS NEW SUIT SITUATED INSIDE. HE SAID HE...

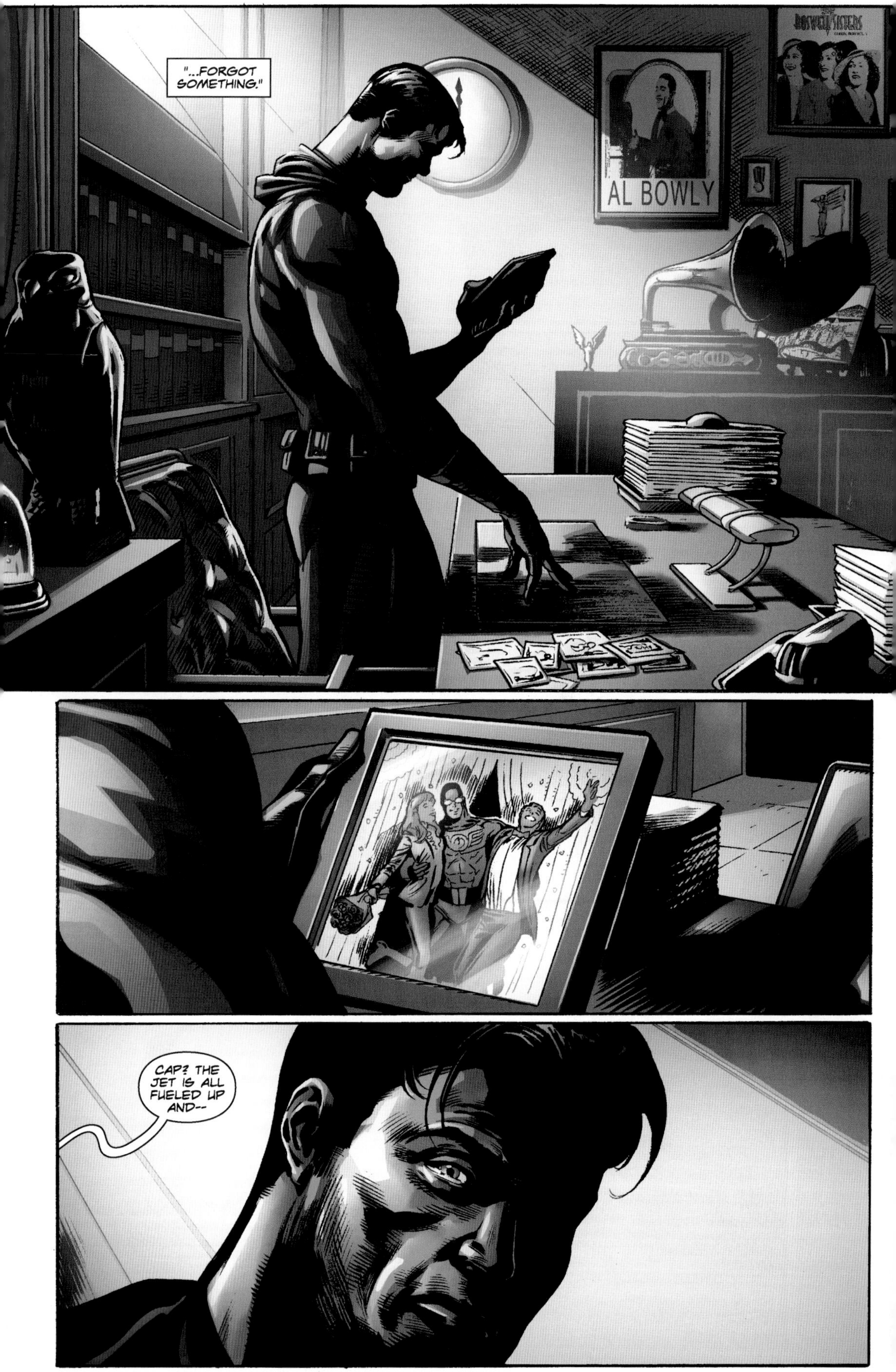
"...FORGOT SOMETHING."
AL BOWLY
CAP? THE JET IS ALL FUELED UP AND--

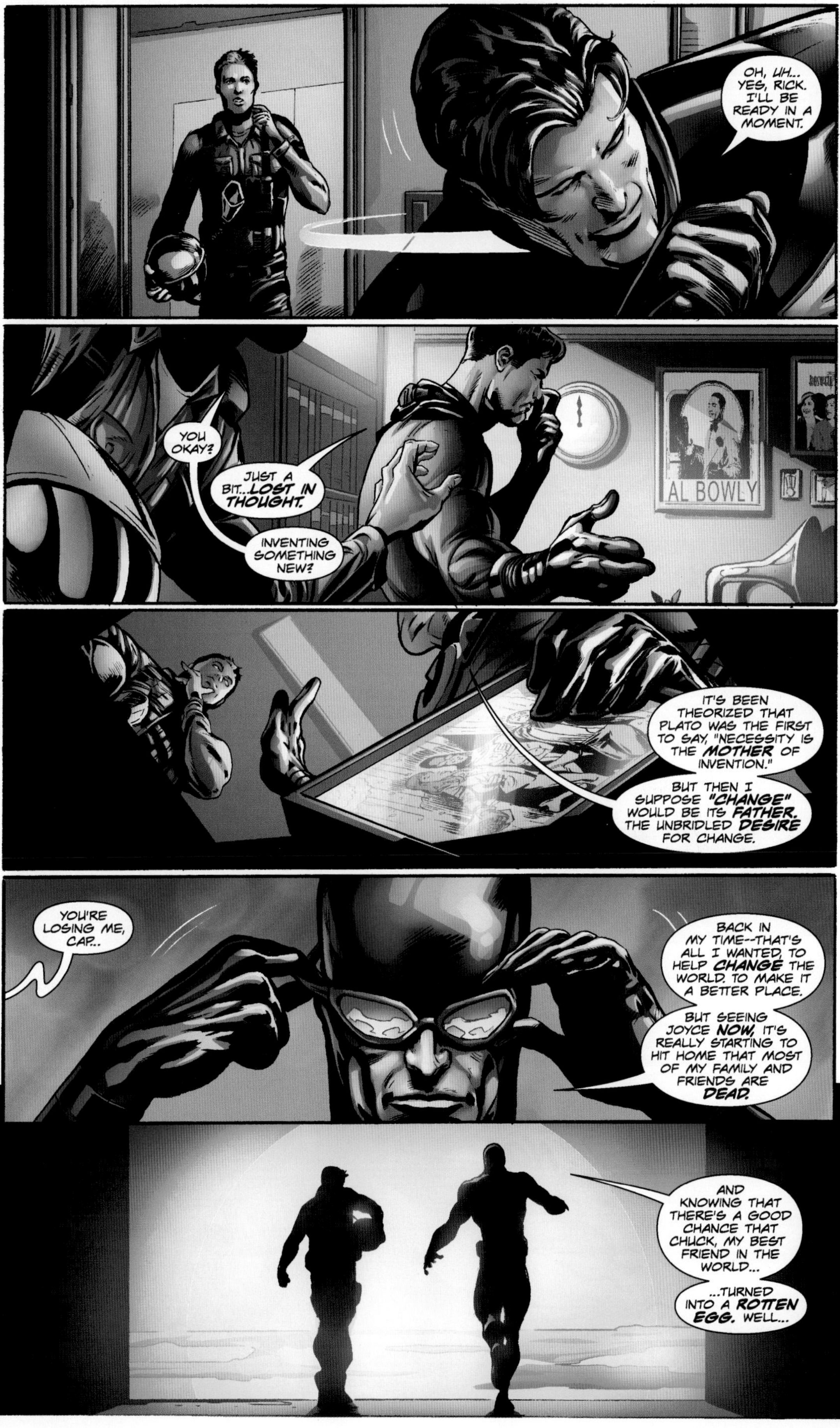

OH, UH... YES, RICK. I'LL BE READY IN A MOMENT.
YOU OKAY?
JUST A BIT...LOST IN THOUGHT.
INVENTING SOMETHING NEW?
AL BOWLY
IT'S BEEN THEORIZED THAT PLATO WAS THE FIRST TO SAY, "NECESSITY IS THE MOTHER OF INVENTION."
BUT THEN I SUPPOSE "CHANGE" WOULD BE ITS FATHER. THE UNBRIDLED DESIRE FOR CHANGE.
YOU'RE LOSING ME, CAP...
BACK IN MY TIME--THAT'S ALL I WANTED, TO HELP CHANGE THE WORLD. TO MAKE IT A BETTER PLACE.
BUT SEEING JOYCE NOW, IT'S REALLY STARTING TO HIT HOME THAT MOST OF MY FAMILY AND FRIENDS ARE DEAD.
AND KNOWING THAT THERE'S A GOOD CHANCE THAT CHUCK, MY BEST FRIEND IN THE WORLD...
...TURNED INTO A ROTTEN EGG. WELL...

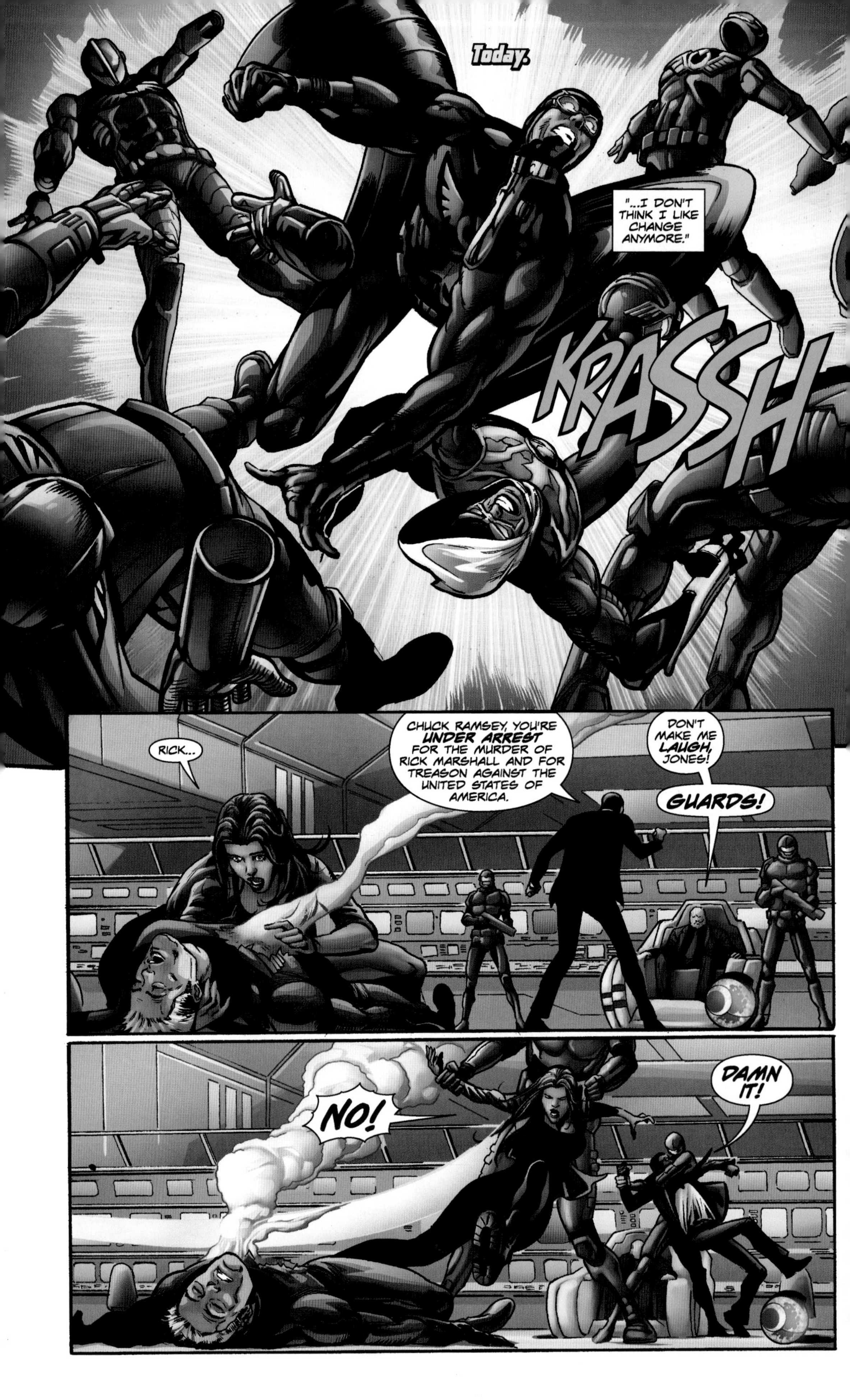
Today.
"...I DON'T THINK I LIKE CHANGE ANYMORE."
KRASSH
RICK...
CHUCK RAMSEY, YOU'RE UNDER ARREST FOR THE MURDER OF RICK MARSHALL AND FOR TREASON AGAINST THE UNITED STATES OF AMERICA.
DON'T MAKE ME LAUGH, JONES!
GUARDS!
NO!
DAMN IT!

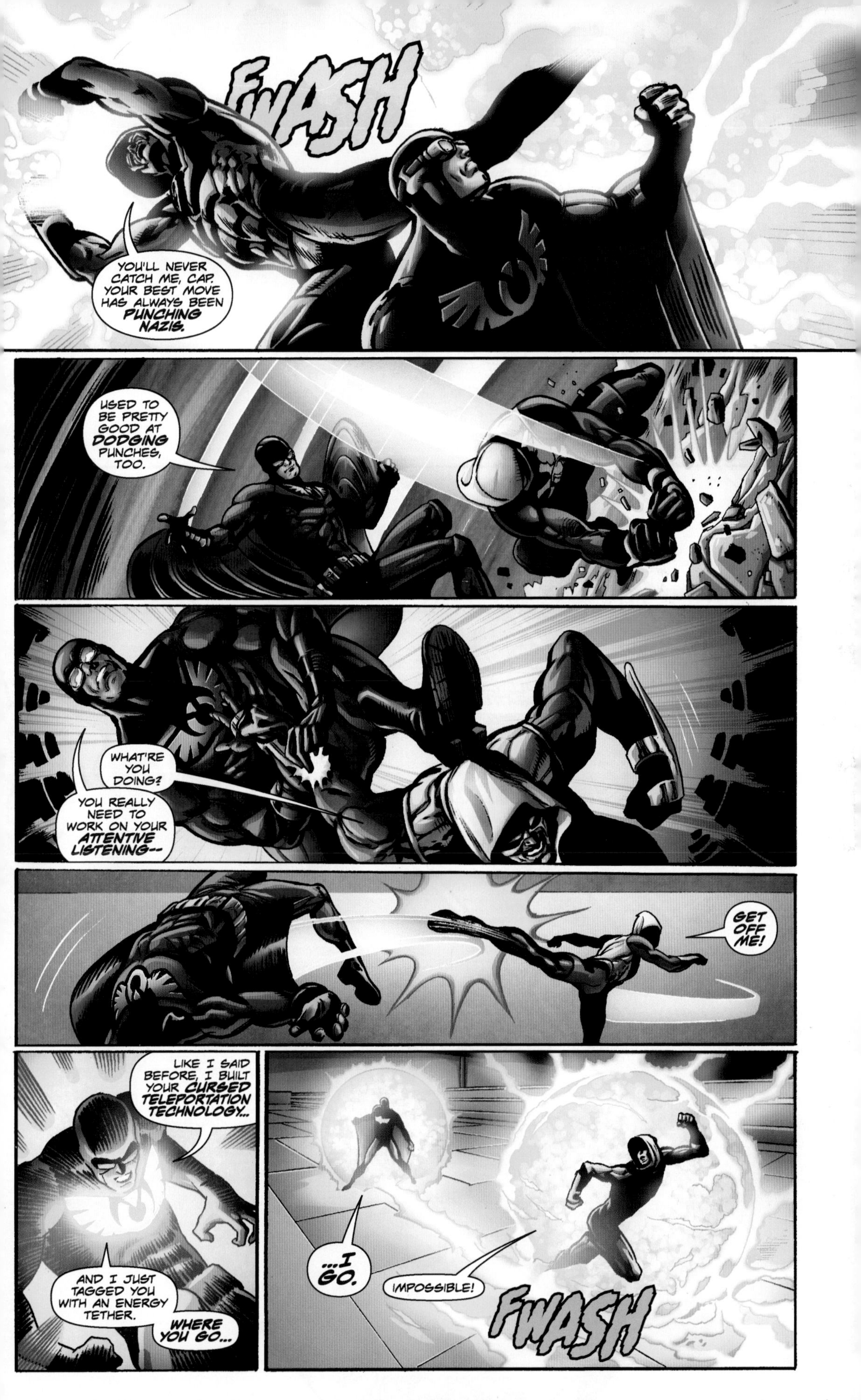
FWASH
YOU'LL NEVER CATCH ME, CAP. YOUR BEST MOVE HAS ALWAYS BEEN PUNCHING NAZIS.
USED TO BE PRETTY GOOD AT DODGING PUNCHES, TOO.
WHAT'RE YOU DOING?
YOU REALLY NEED TO WORK ON YOUR ATTENTIVE LISTENING--
GET OFF ME!
LIKE I SAID BEFORE, I BUILT YOUR CURSED TELEPORTATION TECHNOLOGY...
AND I JUST TAGGED YOU WITH AN ENERGY TETHER.
WHERE YOU GO...
...I GO.
IMPOSSIBLE!
FWASH

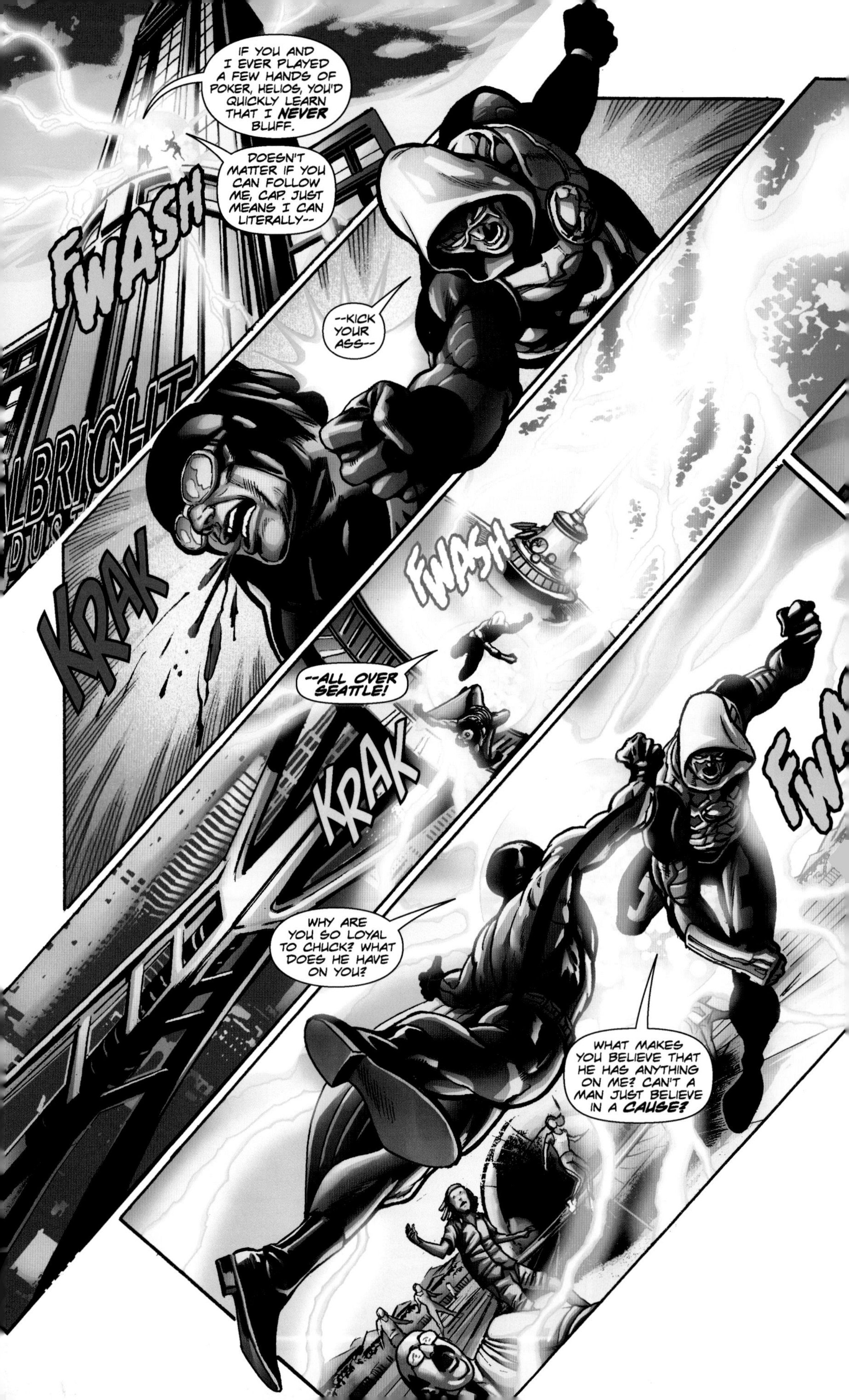
IF YOU AND I EVER PLAYED A FEW HANDS OF POKER, HELIOS, YOU'D QUICKLY LEARN THAT I **NEVER** BLUFF.
DOESN'T MATTER IF YOU CAN FOLLOW ME, CAP. JUST MEANS I CAN LITERALLY--
FWASH
--KICK YOUR ASS--
ALBRIGHT
KRAK
FWASH
--**ALL OVER SEATTLE!**
KRAK
WHY ARE YOU SO LOYAL TO CHUCK? WHAT DOES HE HAVE ON YOU?
WHAT MAKES YOU BELIEVE THAT HE HAS ANYTHING ON ME? CAN'T A MAN JUST BELIEVE IN A **CAUSE?**

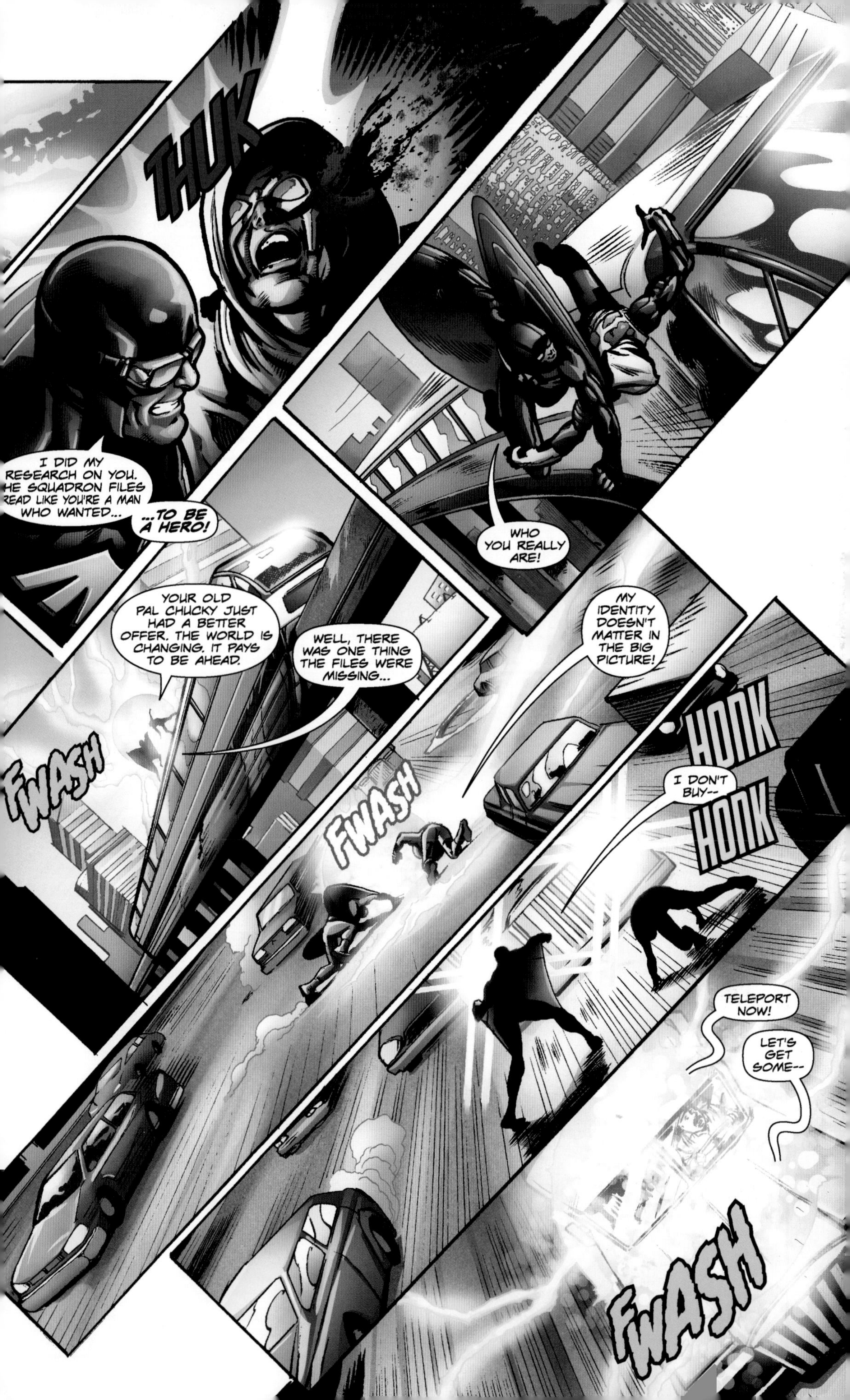
THUK
I DID MY RESEARCH ON YOU. HE SQUADRON FILES READ LIKE YOU'RE A MAN WHO WANTED...
...TO BE A HERO!
WHO YOU REALLY ARE!
YOUR OLD PAL CHUCKY JUST HAD A BETTER OFFER. THE WORLD IS CHANGING. IT PAYS TO BE AHEAD.
WELL, THERE WAS ONE THING THE FILES WERE MISSING...
FWASH
MY IDENTITY DOESN'T MATTER IN THE BIG PICTURE!
FWASH
HONK
I DON'T BUY--
HONK
TELEPORT NOW!
LET'S GET SOME--
FWASH

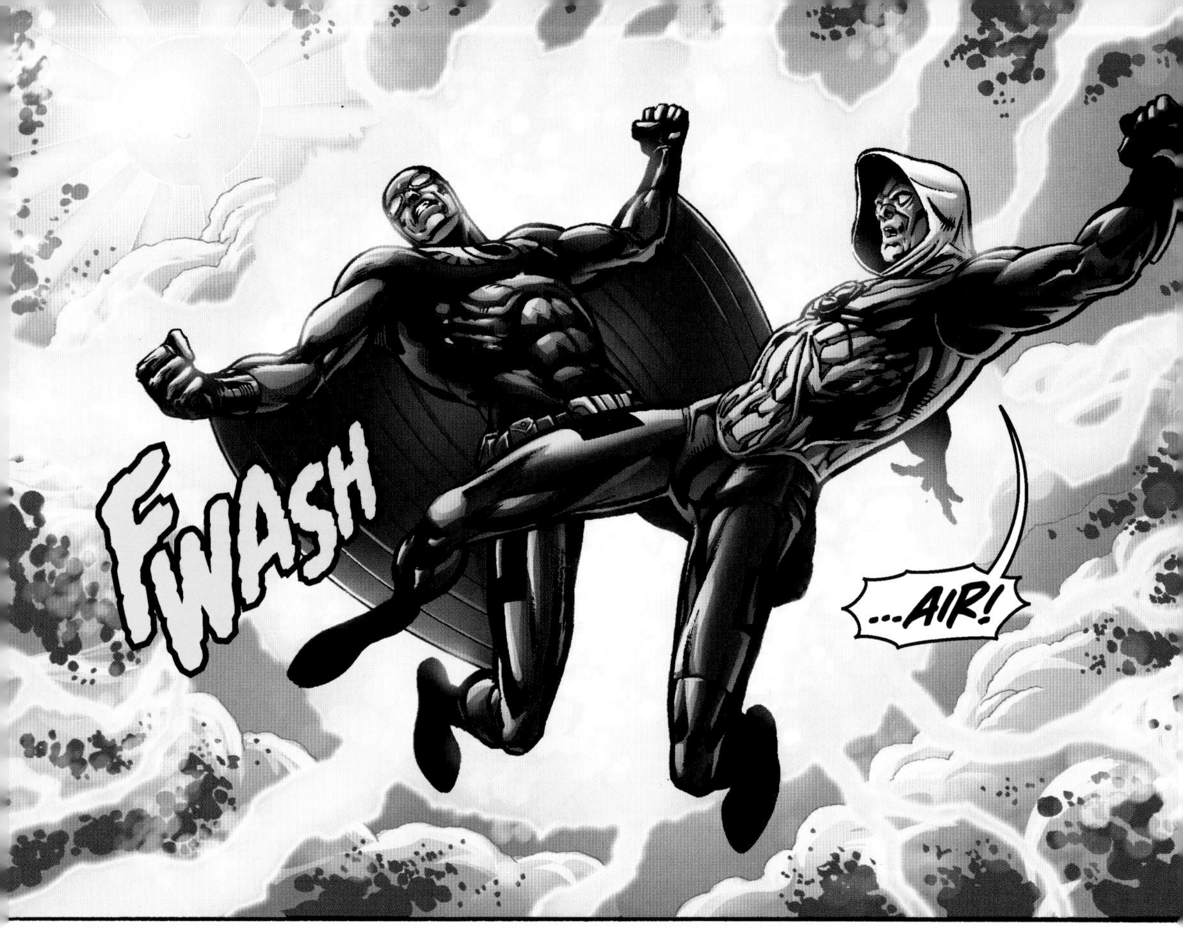
FWASH
...AIR!

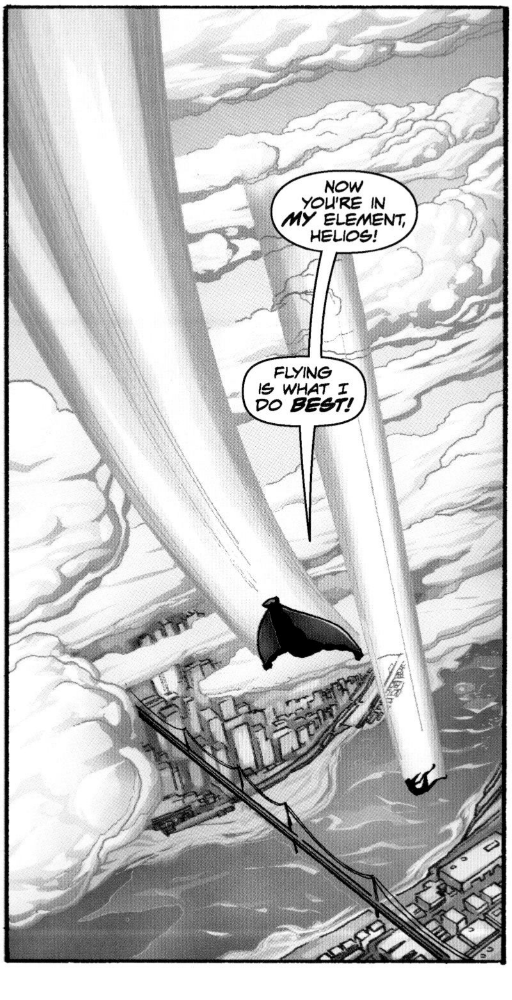
NOW YOU'RE IN MY ELEMENT, HELIOS!
FLYING IS WHAT I DO BEST!

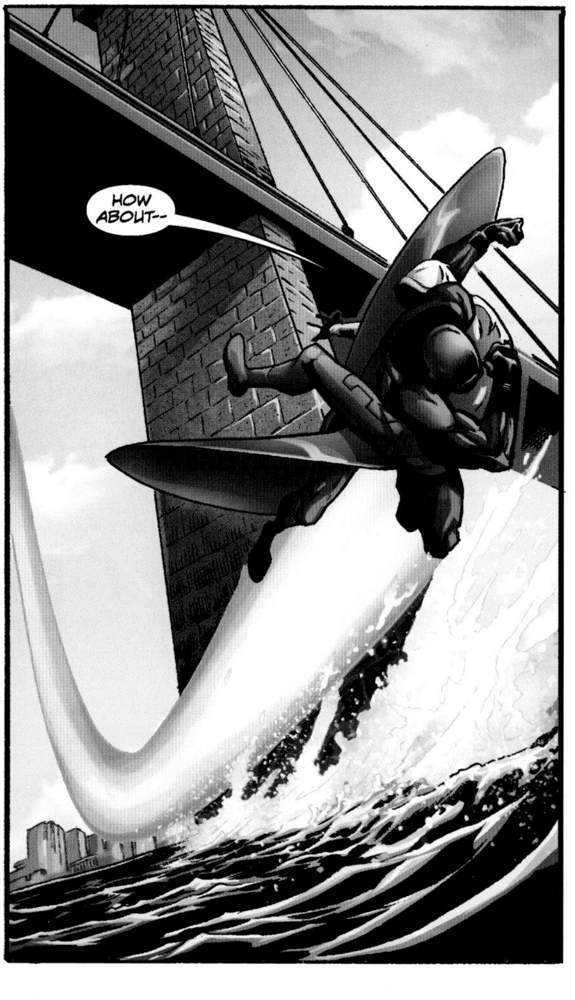
HOW ABOUT--

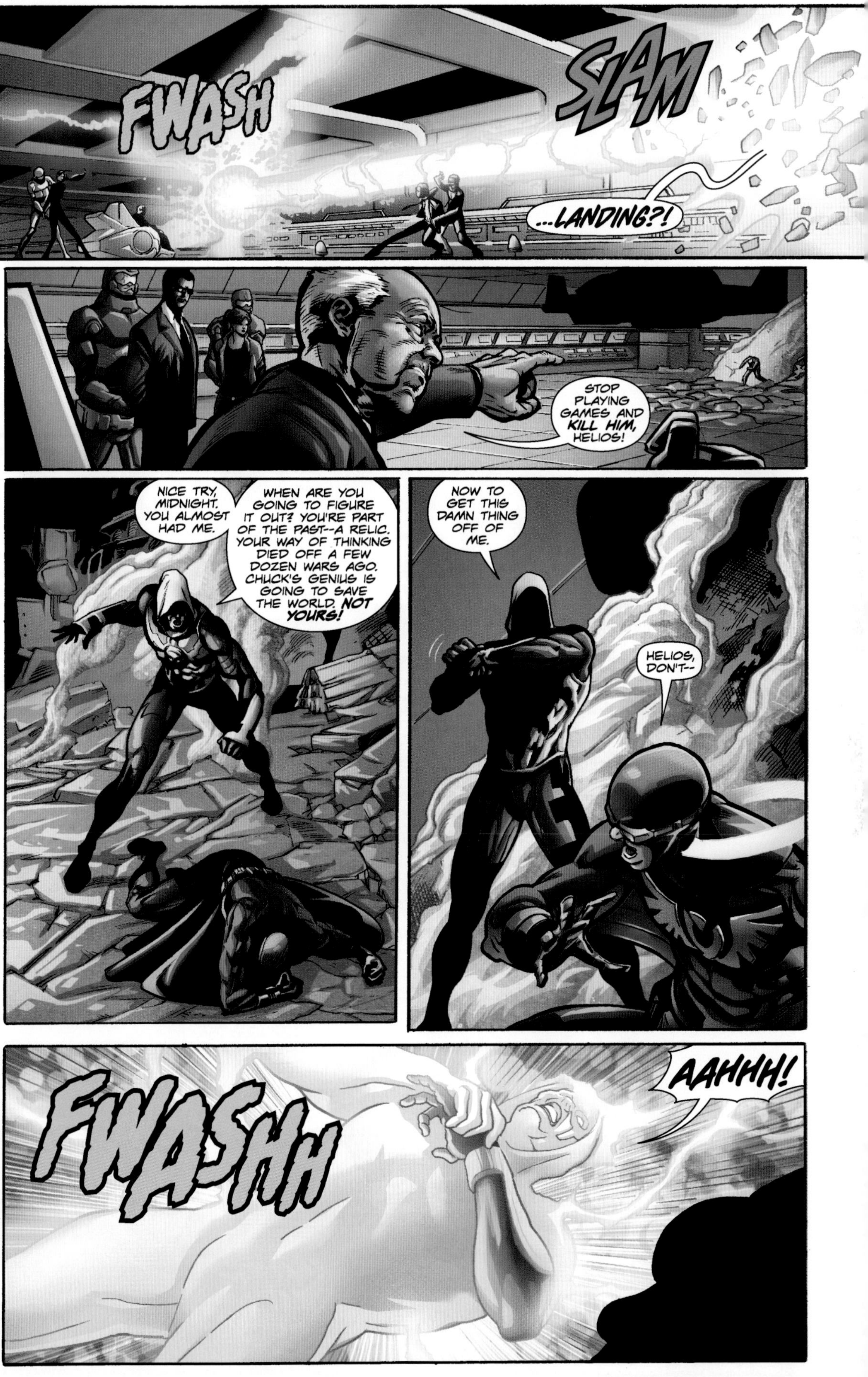
FWASH
SLAM
...LANDING?!
STOP PLAYING GAMES AND KILL HIM, HELIOS!
NICE TRY, MIDNIGHT. YOU ALMOST HAD ME.
WHEN ARE YOU GOING TO FIGURE IT OUT? YOU'RE PART OF THE PAST--A RELIC. YOUR WAY OF THINKING DIED OFF A FEW DOZEN WARS AGO. CHUCK'S GENIUS IS GOING TO SAVE THE WORLD. NOT YOURS!
NOW TO GET THIS DAMN THING OFF OF ME.
HELIOS, DON'T--
FWASHH
AAHHH!

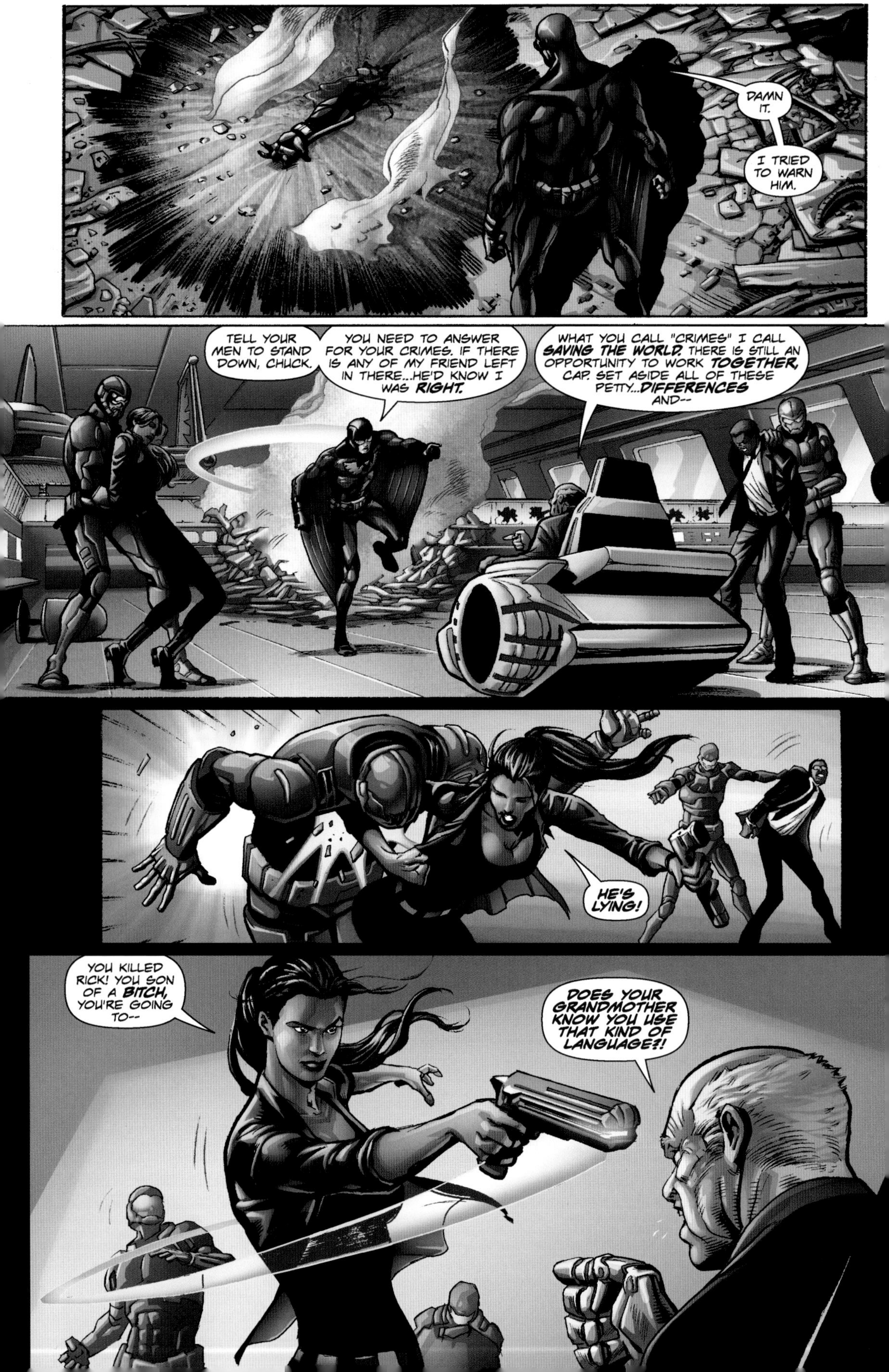
DAMN IT.
I TRIED TO WARN HIM.
TELL YOUR MEN TO STAND DOWN, CHUCK.
YOU NEED TO ANSWER FOR YOUR CRIMES. IF THERE IS ANY OF MY FRIEND LEFT IN THERE...HE'D KNOW I WAS RIGHT.
WHAT YOU CALL "CRIMES" I CALL SAVING THE WORLD. THERE IS STILL AN OPPORTUNITY TO WORK TOGETHER, CAP. SET ASIDE ALL OF THESE PETTY...DIFFERENCES AND--
HE'S LYING!
YOU KILLED RICK! YOU SON OF A BITCH, YOU'RE GOING TO--
DOES YOUR GRANDMOTHER KNOW YOU USE THAT KIND OF LANGUAGE?!

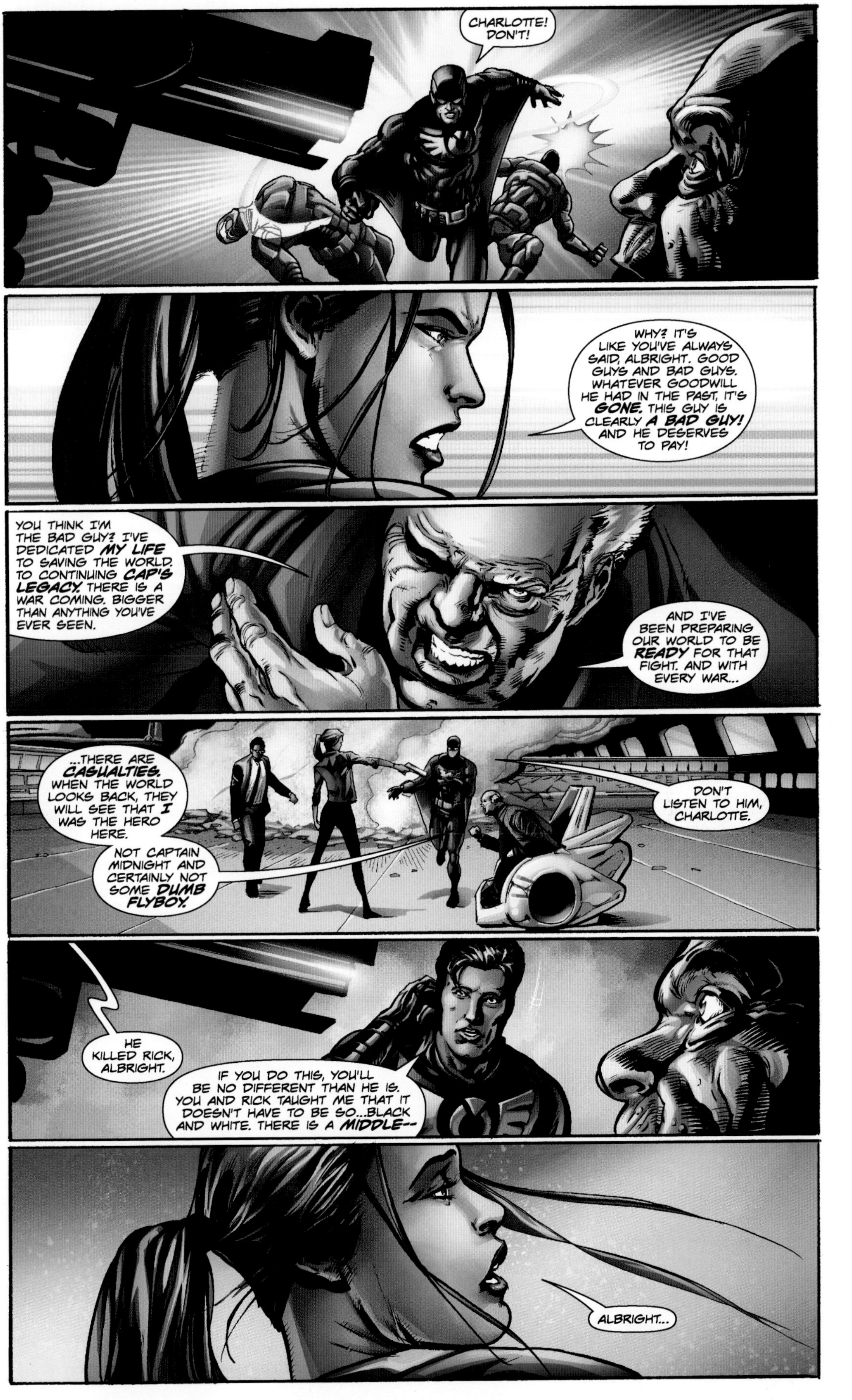
CHARLOTTE! DON'T!
WHY? IT'S LIKE YOU'VE ALWAYS SAID, ALBRIGHT. GOOD GUYS AND BAD GUYS. WHATEVER GOODWILL HE HAD IN THE PAST, IT'S GONE. THIS GUY IS CLEARLY A BAD GUY! AND HE DESERVES TO PAY!
YOU THINK I'M THE BAD GUY? I'VE DEDICATED MY LIFE TO SAVING THE WORLD. TO CONTINUING CAP'S LEGACY. THERE IS A WAR COMING. BIGGER THAN ANYTHING YOU'VE EVER SEEN.
AND I'VE BEEN PREPARING OUR WORLD TO BE READY FOR THAT FIGHT. AND WITH EVERY WAR...
...THERE ARE CASUALTIES. WHEN THE WORLD LOOKS BACK, THEY WILL SEE THAT I WAS THE HERO HERE.
NOT CAPTAIN MIDNIGHT AND CERTAINLY NOT SOME DUMB FLYBOY.
DON'T LISTEN TO HIM, CHARLOTTE.
HE KILLED RICK, ALBRIGHT.
IF YOU DO THIS, YOU'LL BE NO DIFFERENT THAN HE IS. YOU AND RICK TAUGHT ME THAT IT DOESN'T HAVE TO BE SO...BLACK AND WHITE. THERE IS A MIDDLE--
ALBRIGHT...

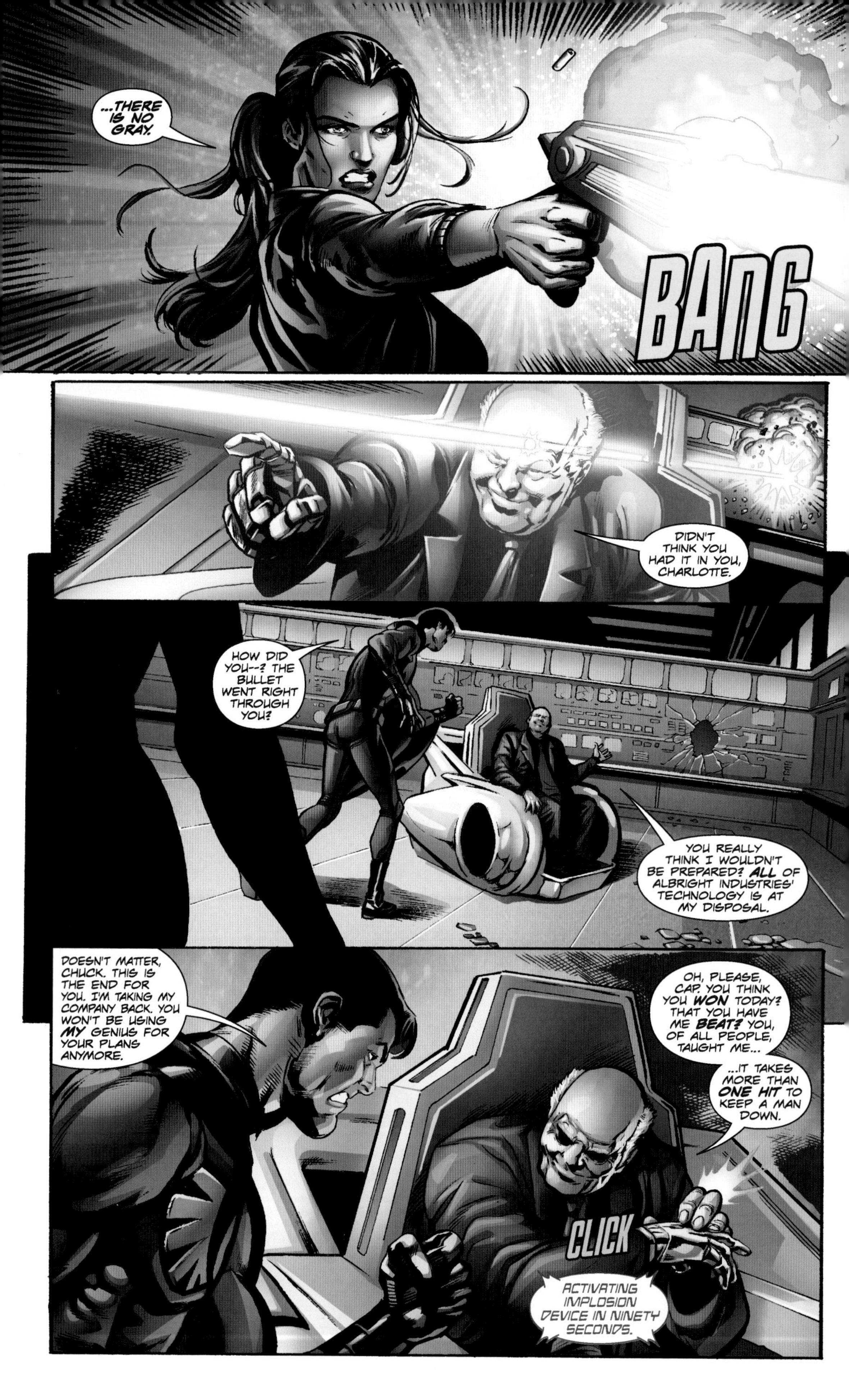
...THERE IS NO GRAY.
BANG
DIDN'T THINK YOU HAD IT IN YOU, CHARLOTTE.
HOW DID YOU--? THE BULLET WENT RIGHT THROUGH YOU?
YOU REALLY THINK I WOULDN'T BE PREPARED? ALL OF ALBRIGHT INDUSTRIES' TECHNOLOGY IS AT MY DISPOSAL.
DOESN'T MATTER, CHUCK. THIS IS THE END FOR YOU. I'M TAKING MY COMPANY BACK. YOU WON'T BE USING MY GENIUS FOR YOUR PLANS ANYMORE.
OH, PLEASE, CAP. YOU THINK YOU WON TODAY? THAT YOU HAVE ME BEAT? YOU, OF ALL PEOPLE, TAUGHT ME...
...IT TAKES MORE THAN ONE HIT TO KEEP A MAN DOWN.
CLICK
ACTIVATING IMPLOSION DEVICE IN NINETY SECONDS.

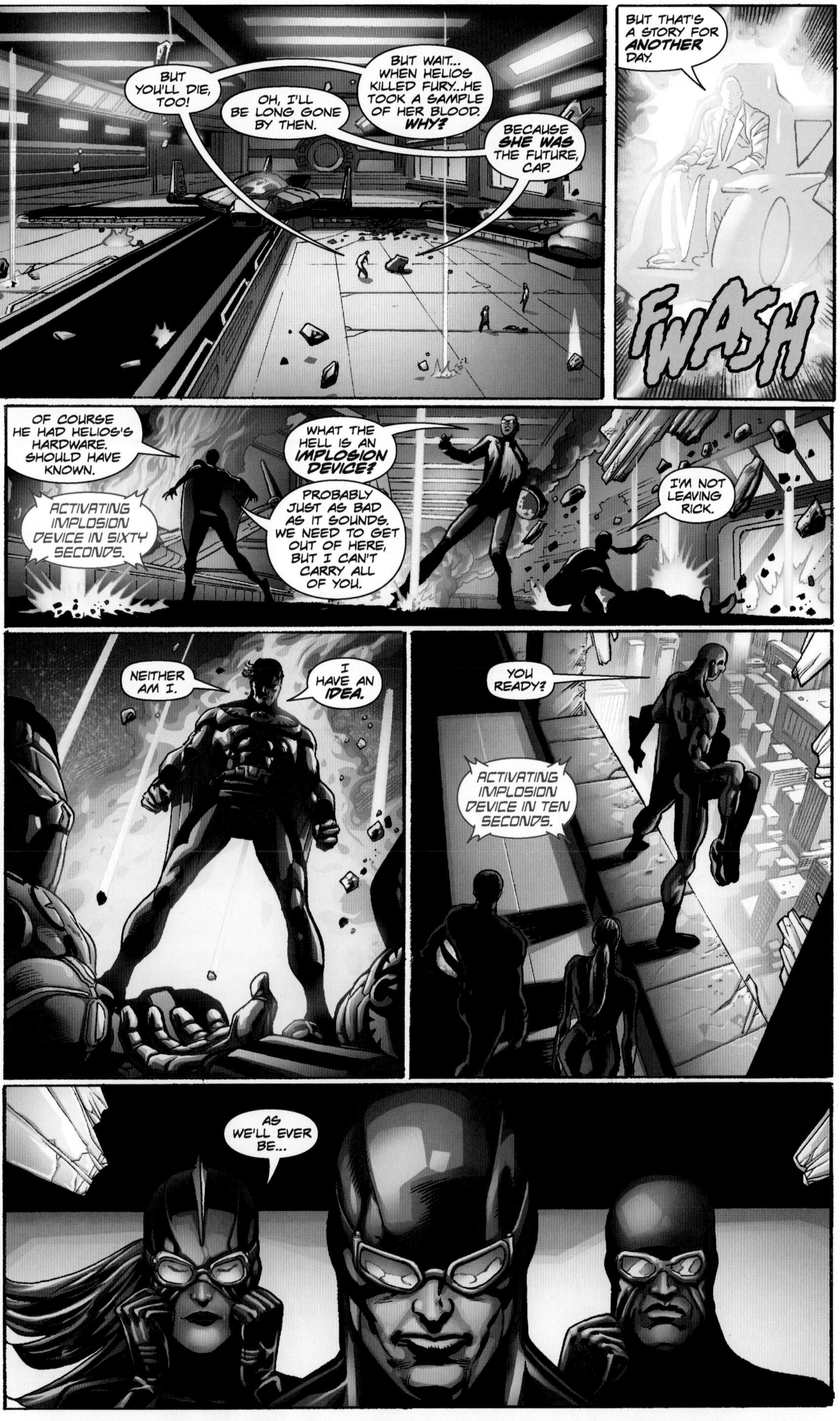
BUT YOU'LL DIE, TOO!
OH, I'LL BE LONG GONE BY THEN.
BUT WAIT... WHEN HELIOS KILLED FURY...HE TOOK A SAMPLE OF HER BLOOD. WHY?
BECAUSE SHE WAS THE FUTURE, CAP.
BUT THAT'S A STORY FOR ANOTHER DAY.
FWASH
OF COURSE HE HAD HELIOS'S HARDWARE. SHOULD HAVE KNOWN.
ACTIVATING IMPLOSION DEVICE IN SIXTY SECONDS.
WHAT THE HELL IS AN IMPLOSION DEVICE?
PROBABLY JUST AS BAD AS IT SOUNDS. WE NEED TO GET OUT OF HERE, BUT I CAN'T CARRY ALL OF YOU.
I'M NOT LEAVING RICK.
NEITHER AM I.
I HAVE AN IDEA.
YOU READY?
ACTIVATING IMPLOSION DEVICE IN TEN SECONDS.
AS WE'LL EVER BE...

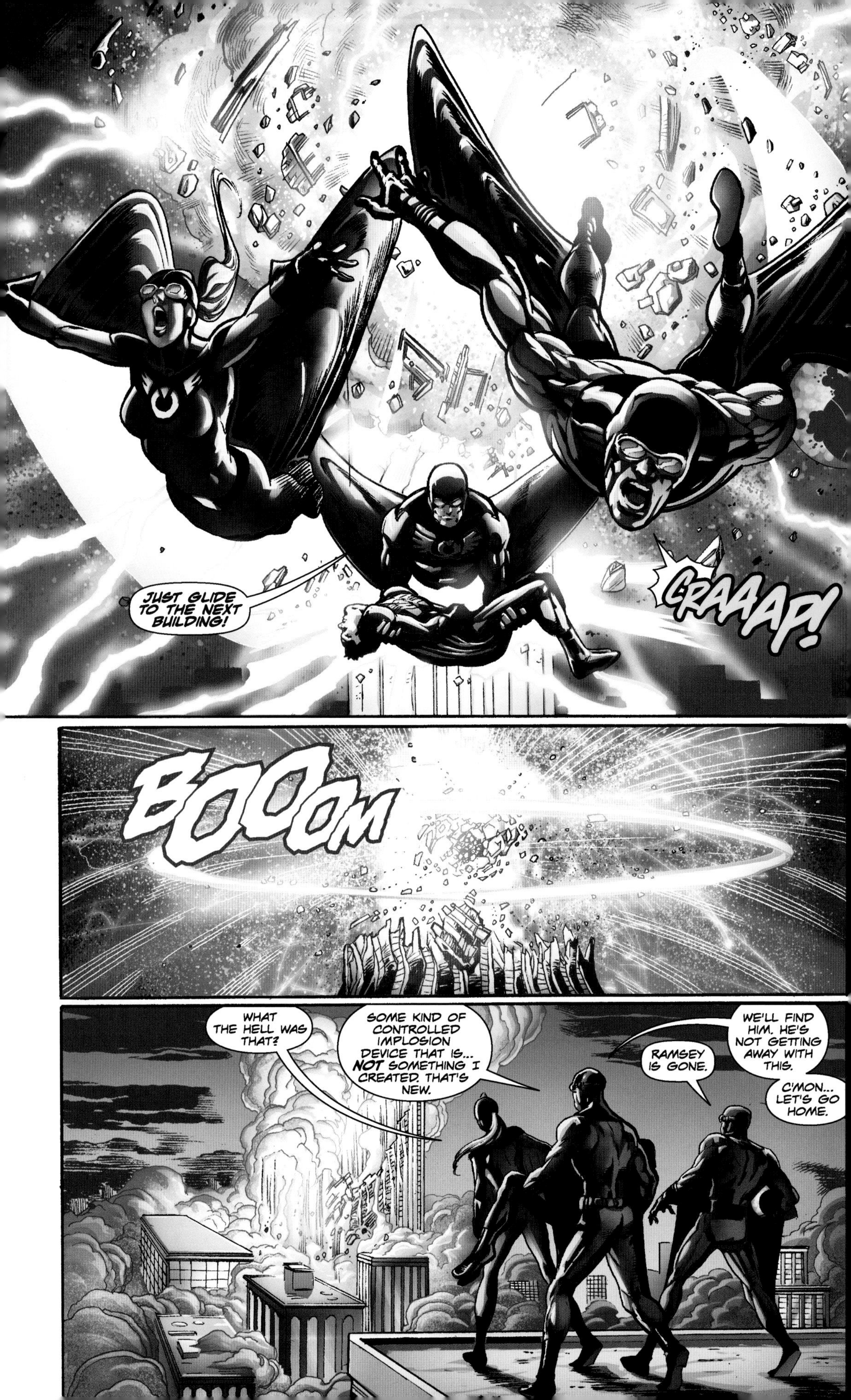
JUST GLIDE TO THE NEXT BUILDING!
CRAAAP!
BOOOM
WHAT THE HELL WAS THAT?
SOME KIND OF CONTROLLED IMPLOSION DEVICE THAT IS... **NOT** SOMETHING I CREATED. THAT'S NEW.
RAMSEY IS GONE.
WE'LL FIND HIM. HE'S NOT GETTING AWAY WITH THIS.
C'MON... LET'S GO HOME.

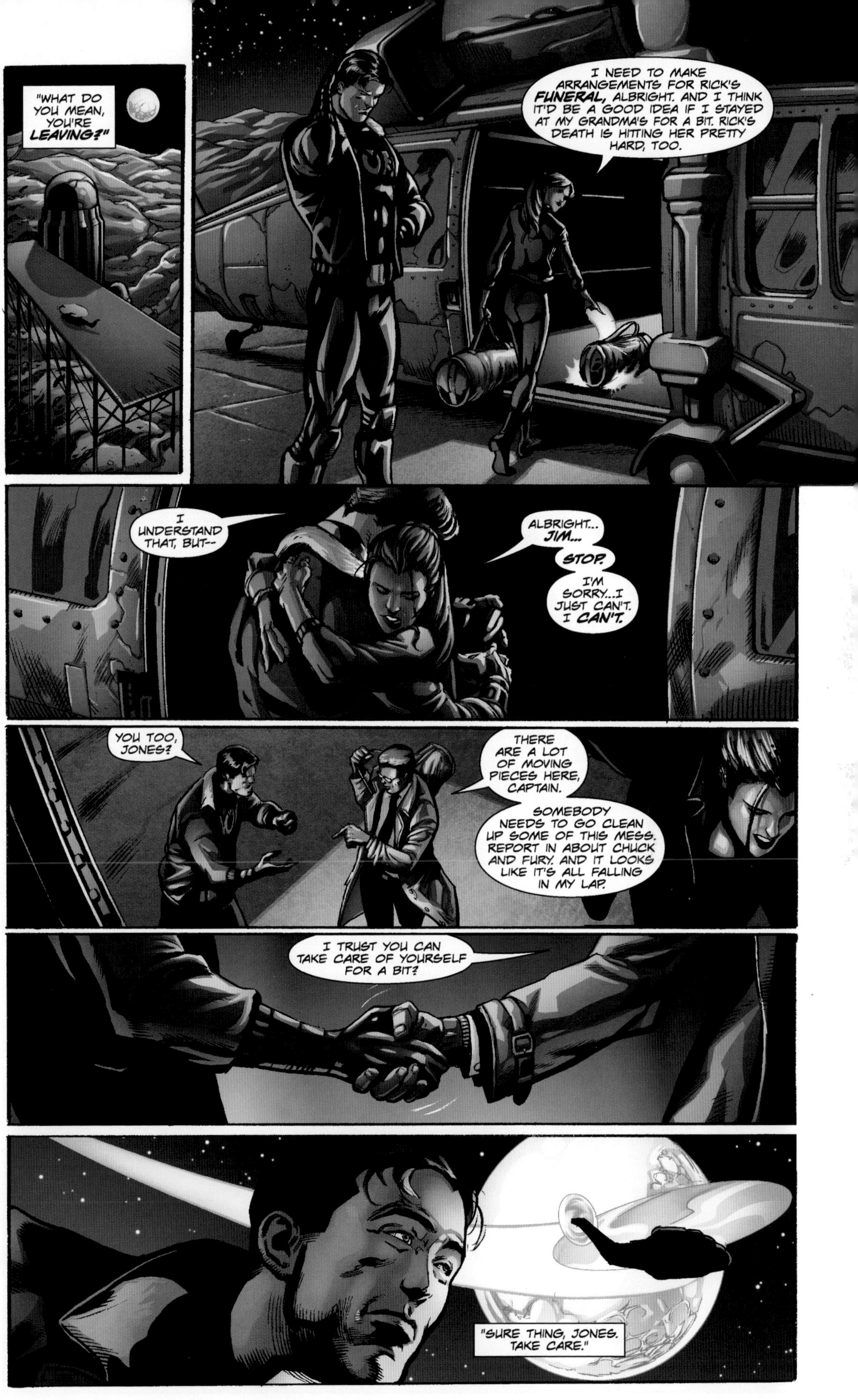
"WHAT DO YOU MEAN, YOU'RE LEAVING?"
I NEED TO MAKE ARRANGEMENTS FOR RICK'S FUNERAL, ALBRIGHT. AND I THINK IT'D BE A GOOD IDEA IF I STAYED AT MY GRANDMA'S FOR A BIT. RICK'S DEATH IS HITTING HER PRETTY HARD, TOO.
I UNDERSTAND THAT, BUT--
ALBRIGHT... JIM... STOP.
I'M SORRY...I JUST CAN'T. I CAN'T.
YOU TOO, JONES?
THERE ARE A LOT OF MOVING PIECES HERE, CAPTAIN.
SOMEBODY NEEDS TO GO CLEAN UP SOME OF THIS MESS. REPORT IN ABOUT CHUCK AND FURY. AND IT LOOKS LIKE IT'S ALL FALLING IN MY LAP.
I TRUST YOU CAN TAKE CARE OF YOURSELF FOR A BIT?
"SURE THING, JONES. TAKE CARE."

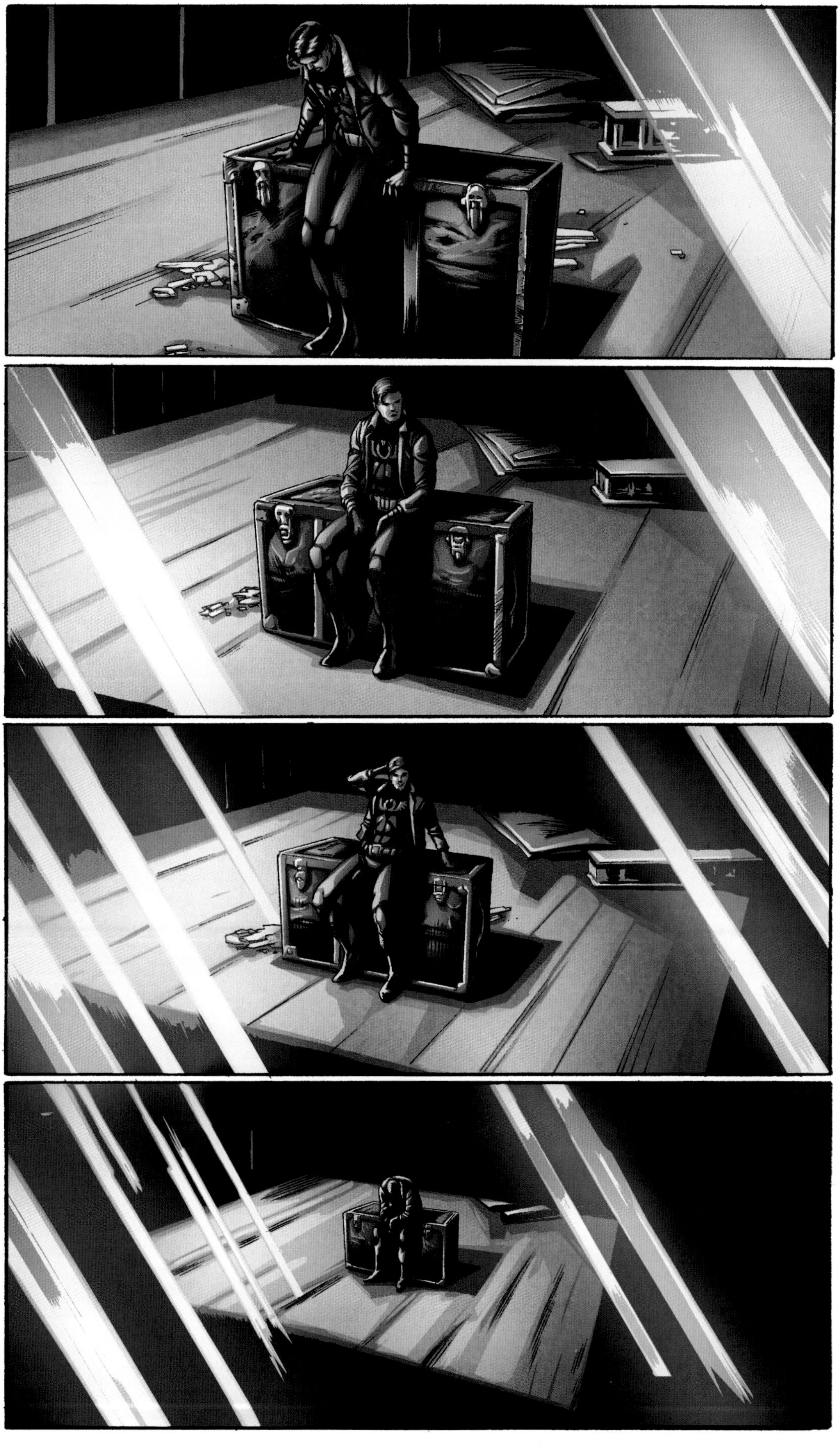

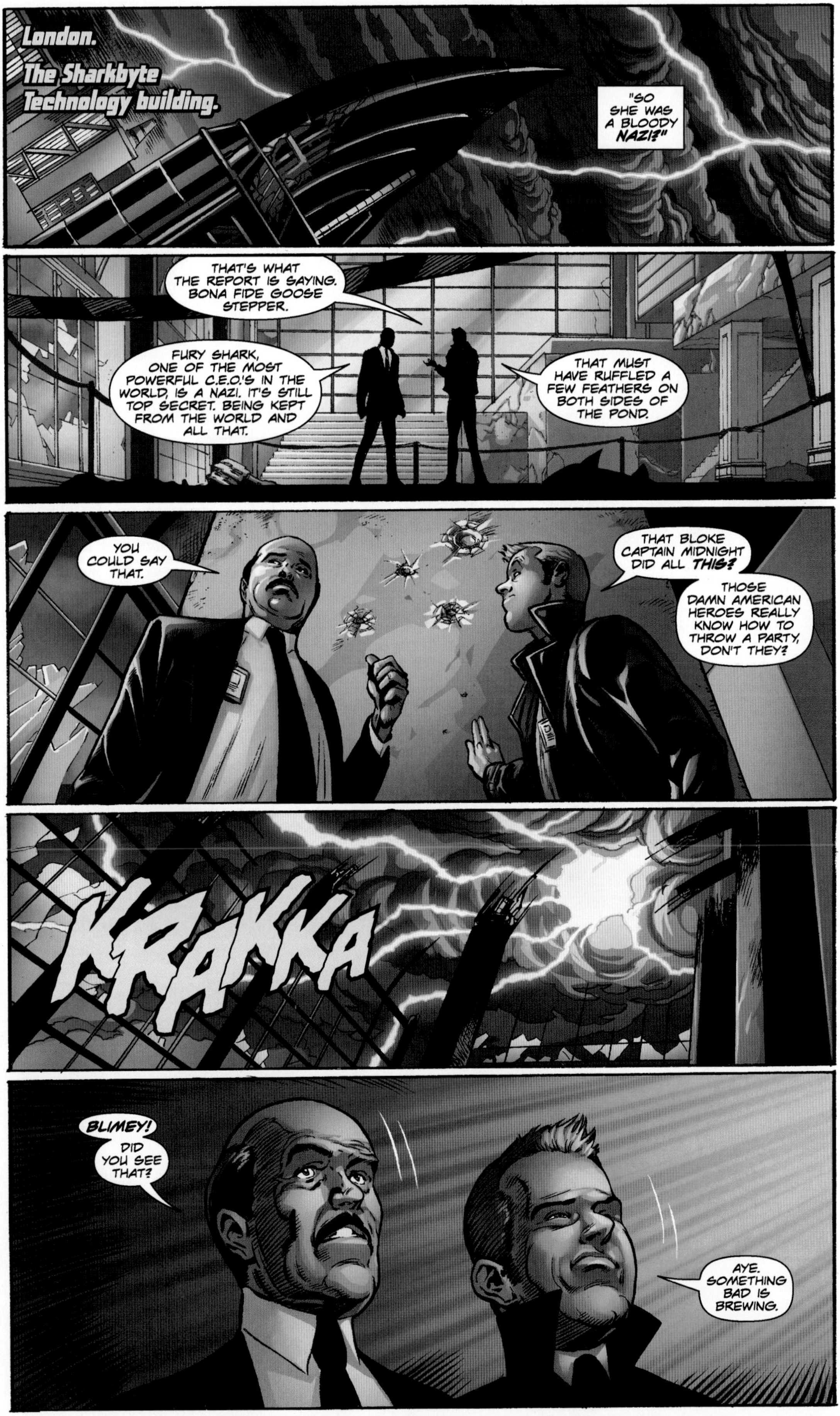
London.
The Sharkbyte Technology building.
"SO SHE WAS A BLOODY NAZI?"
THAT'S WHAT THE REPORT IS SAYING. BONA FIDE GOOSE STEPPER.
FURY SHARK, ONE OF THE MOST POWERFUL C.E.O.'S IN THE WORLD, IS A NAZI. IT'S STILL TOP SECRET. BEING KEPT FROM THE WORLD AND ALL THAT.
THAT MUST HAVE RUFFLED A FEW FEATHERS ON BOTH SIDES OF THE POND.
YOU COULD SAY THAT.
THAT BLOKE CAPTAIN MIDNIGHT DID ALL THIS?
THOSE DAMN AMERICAN HEROES REALLY KNOW HOW TO THROW A PARTY, DON'T THEY?
KRAKKA
BLIMEY! DID YOU SEE THAT?
AYE. SOMETHING BAD IS BREWING.

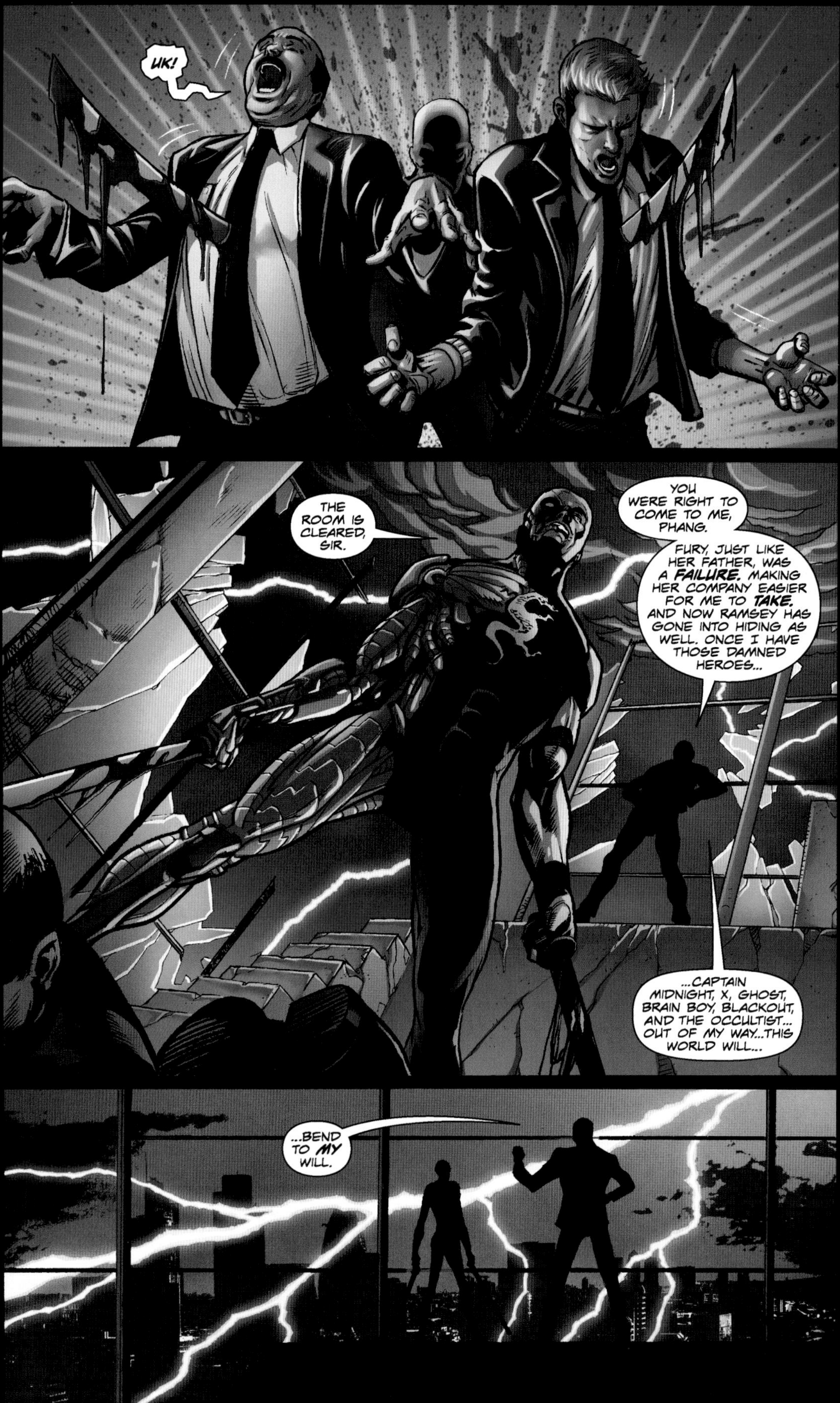
UK!
THE ROOM IS CLEARED, SIR.
YOU WERE RIGHT TO COME TO ME, PHANG.
FURY, JUST LIKE HER FATHER, WAS A FAILURE. MAKING HER COMPANY EASIER FOR ME TO TAKE. AND NOW RAMSEY HAS GONE INTO HIDING AS WELL. ONCE I HAVE THOSE DAMNED HEROES...
...CAPTAIN MIDNIGHT, X, GHOST, BRAIN BOY, BLACKOUT, AND THE OCCULTIST... OUT OF MY WAY...THIS WORLD WILL...
...BEND TO MY WILL.

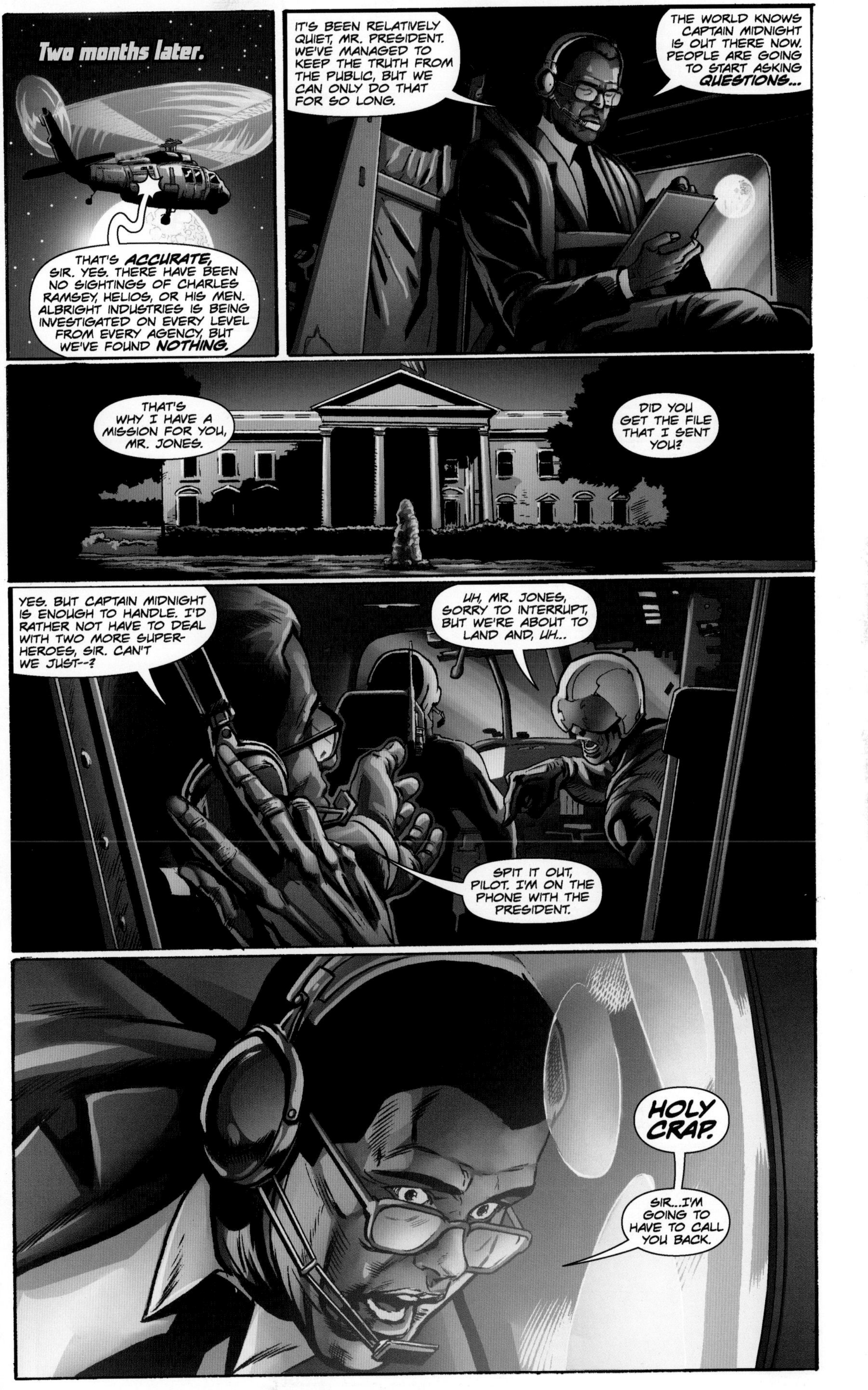
Two months later.
THAT'S ACCURATE, SIR. YES. THERE HAVE BEEN NO SIGHTINGS OF CHARLES RAMSEY, HELIOS, OR HIS MEN. ALBRIGHT INDUSTRIES IS BEING INVESTIGATED ON EVERY LEVEL FROM EVERY AGENCY, BUT WE'VE FOUND NOTHING.
IT'S BEEN RELATIVELY QUIET, MR. PRESIDENT. WE'VE MANAGED TO KEEP THE TRUTH FROM THE PUBLIC, BUT WE CAN ONLY DO THAT FOR SO LONG.
THE WORLD KNOWS CAPTAIN MIDNIGHT IS OUT THERE NOW. PEOPLE ARE GOING TO START ASKING QUESTIONS...
THAT'S WHY I HAVE A MISSION FOR YOU, MR. JONES.
DID YOU GET THE FILE THAT I SENT YOU?
YES. BUT CAPTAIN MIDNIGHT IS ENOUGH TO HANDLE. I'D RATHER NOT HAVE TO DEAL WITH TWO MORE SUPER-HEROES, SIR. CAN'T WE JUST--?
UH, MR. JONES, SORRY TO INTERRUPT, BUT WE'RE ABOUT TO LAND AND, UH...
SPIT IT OUT, PILOT. I'M ON THE PHONE WITH THE PRESIDENT.
HOLY CRAP.
SIR...I'M GOING TO HAVE TO CALL YOU BACK.

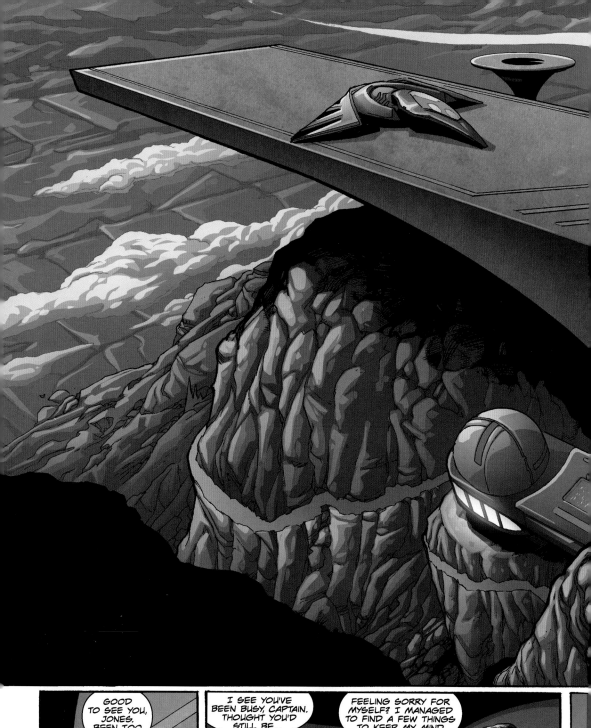

GOOD TO SEE YOU, JONES. BEEN TOO LONG.

I SEE YOU'VE BEEN BUSY, CAPTAIN. THOUGHT YOU'D STILL BE...

FEELING SORRY FOR MYSELF? I MANAGED TO FIND A FEW THINGS TO KEEP MY MIND *OCCUPIED.*

RICK WOULDN'T HAVE WANTED ME TO JUST SIT AROUND.

CAPTAIN MIDNIGHT®

SKETCHBOOK

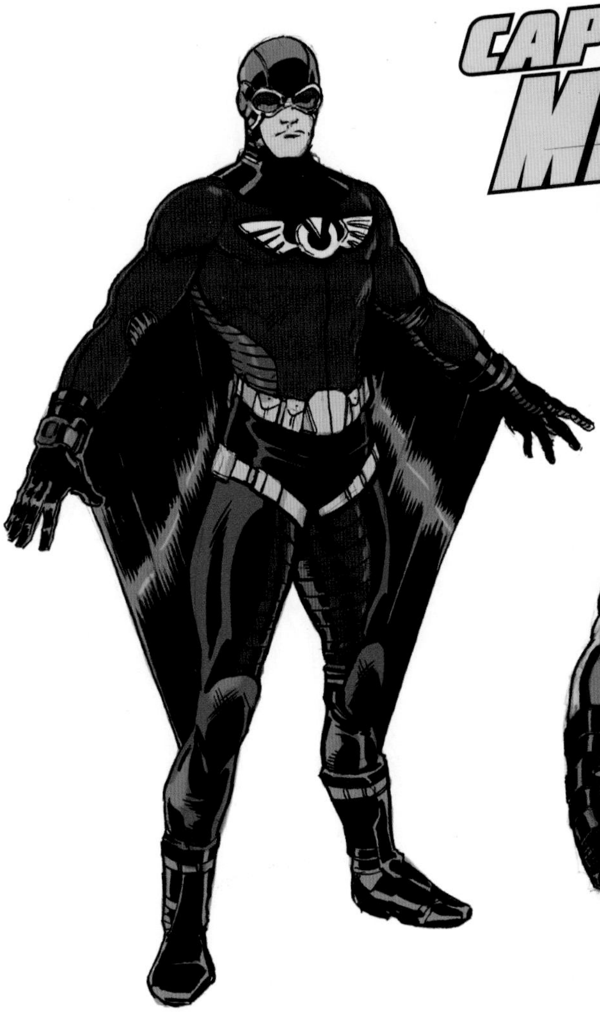

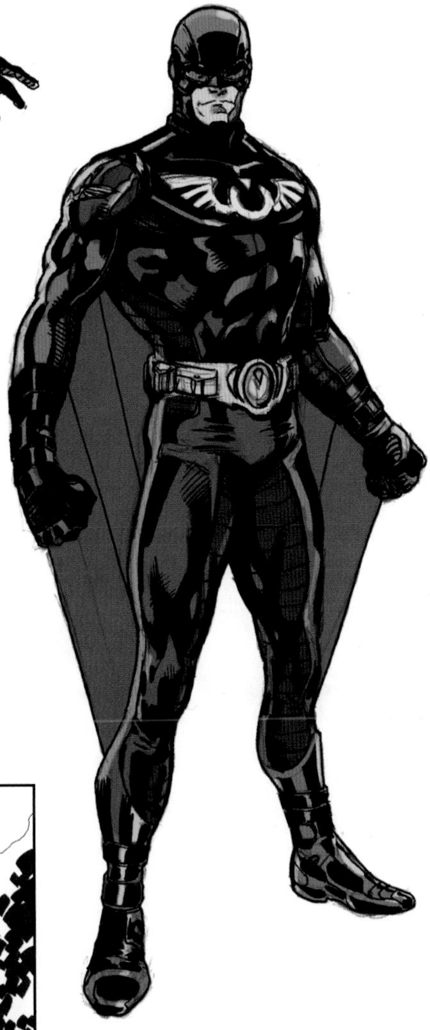

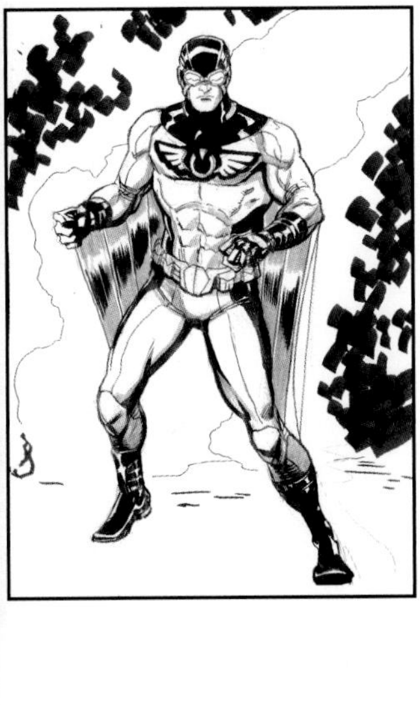

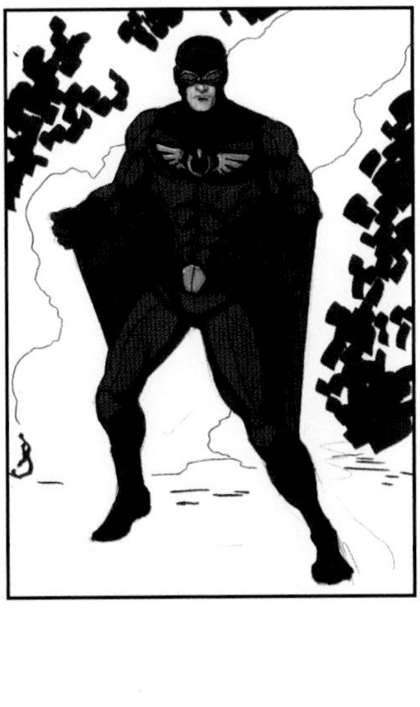

MIDNIGHT'S NEW SUIT

Initially dubbed a "stealth suit," as it would be used in a midnight attack on Sharkbyte Technology, Cap's new suit was designed by Fernando Dagnino for issue #9 (chapter 2 of this volume), with a focus on a more black-ops look. Though very cool, these suits got a little too far away from Cap's classic look, so we went with a design halfway between the classic and the stealth looks (seen in the lower left).

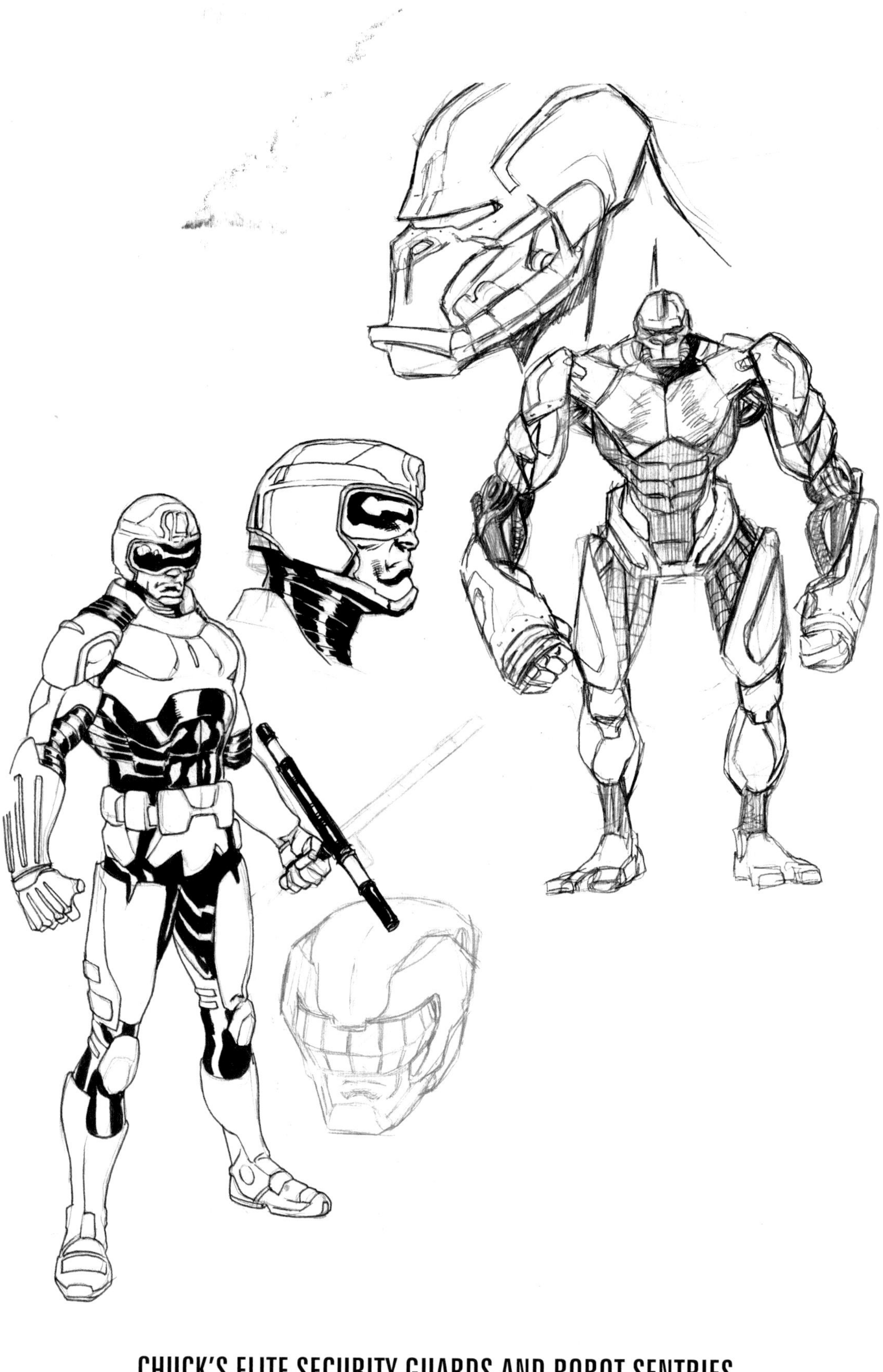

CHUCK'S ELITE SECURITY GUARDS AND ROBOT SENTRIES

Being the headquarters of one of the most advanced companies on the planet and home to its greatest resource (Chuck Ramsey), naturally Albright Industries in Seattle would have some pretty heavy security—thus the heavily armored guards and the heavy-hitter robots by Fernando Dagnino. The gorilla-like design of the robot was chosen because, obviously, gorilla robots are super cool!

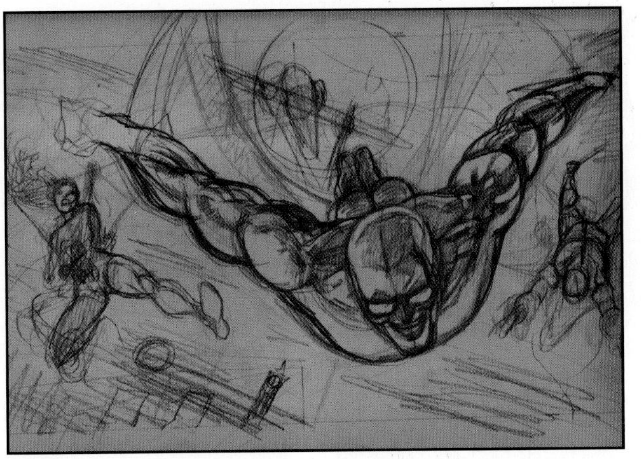

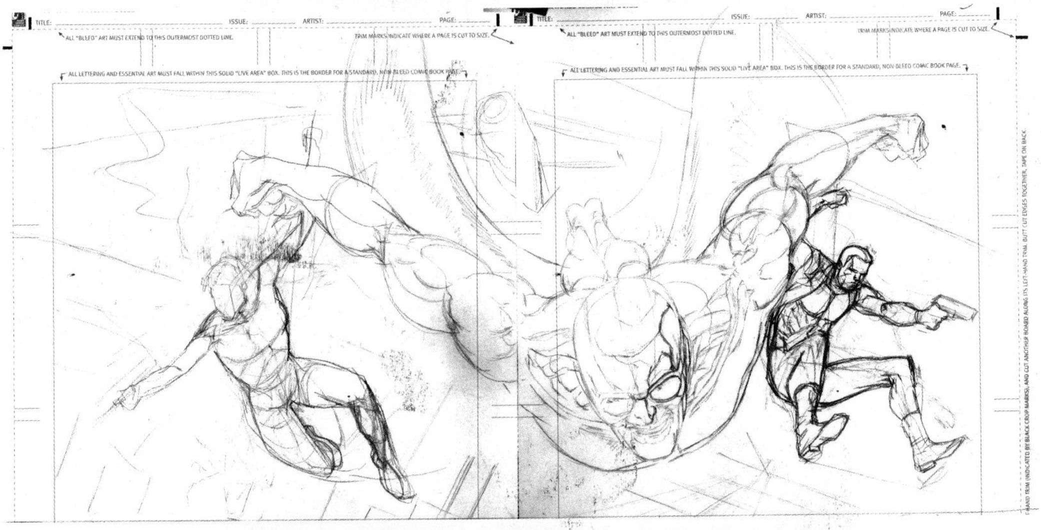

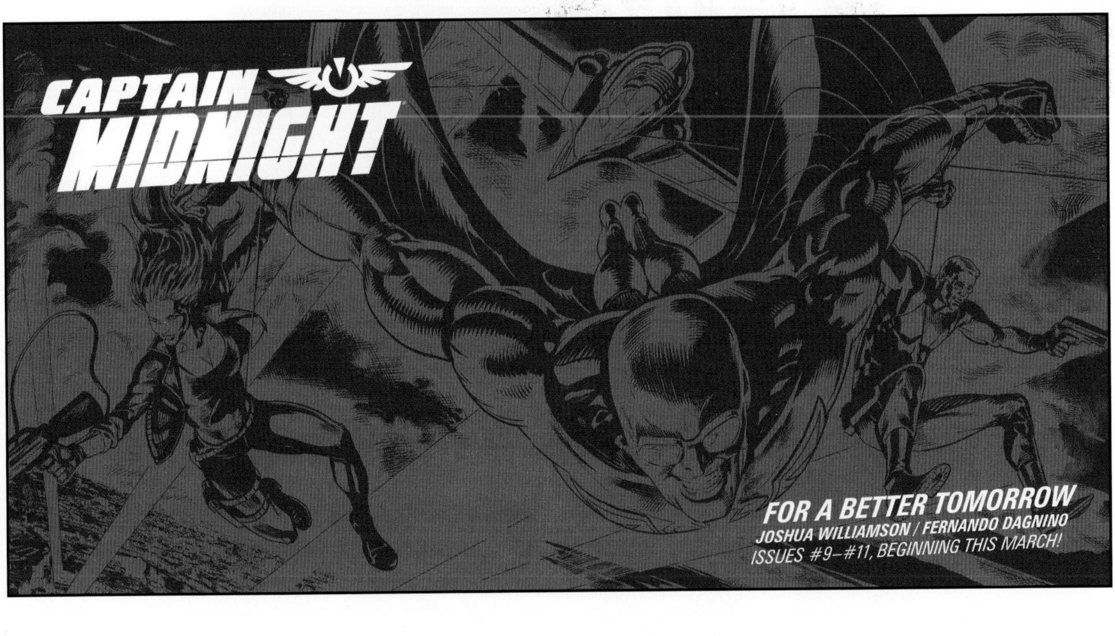
CAPTAIN
MIDNIGHT
FOR A BETTER TOMORROW
JOSHUA WILLIAMSON / FERNANDO DAGNINO
ISSUES #9–#11, BEGINNING THIS MARCH!

"FOR A BETTER TOMORROW" LOBBY CARD TEASER IMAGE

Issues #9–#11 (chapters 2–4 of this volume) compose the largest and most important arc of Cap's story so far. After seeing the incredible art for the issue #9 opening spread, from Fernando Dagnino, we knew that we needed to use this killer art for marketing purposes. Here you can see the rough version of the page, the pencils, and the eventual teaser image.

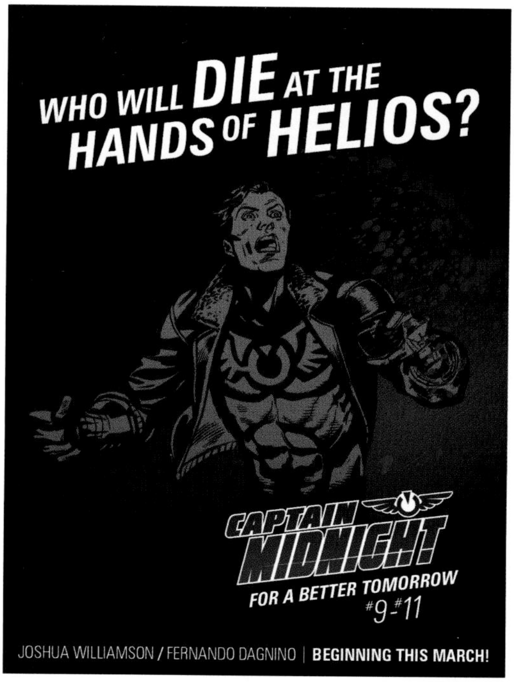
WHO WILL DIE AT THE HANDS OF HELIOS?
CAPTAIN MIDNIGHT
FOR A BETTER TOMORROW
#9-#11
JOSHUA WILLIAMSON / FERNANDO DAGNINO | BEGINNING THIS MARCH!

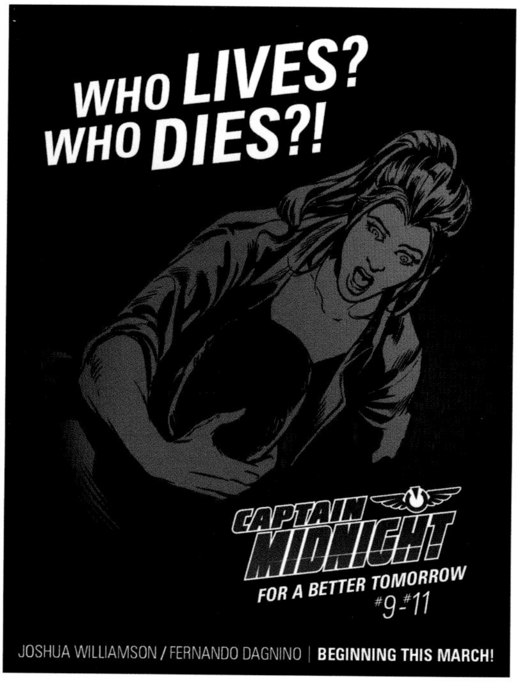
WHO LIVES? WHO DIES?!
CAPTAIN MIDNIGHT
FOR A BETTER TOMORROW
#9-#11
JOSHUA WILLIAMSON / FERNANDO DAGNINO | BEGINNING THIS MARCH!

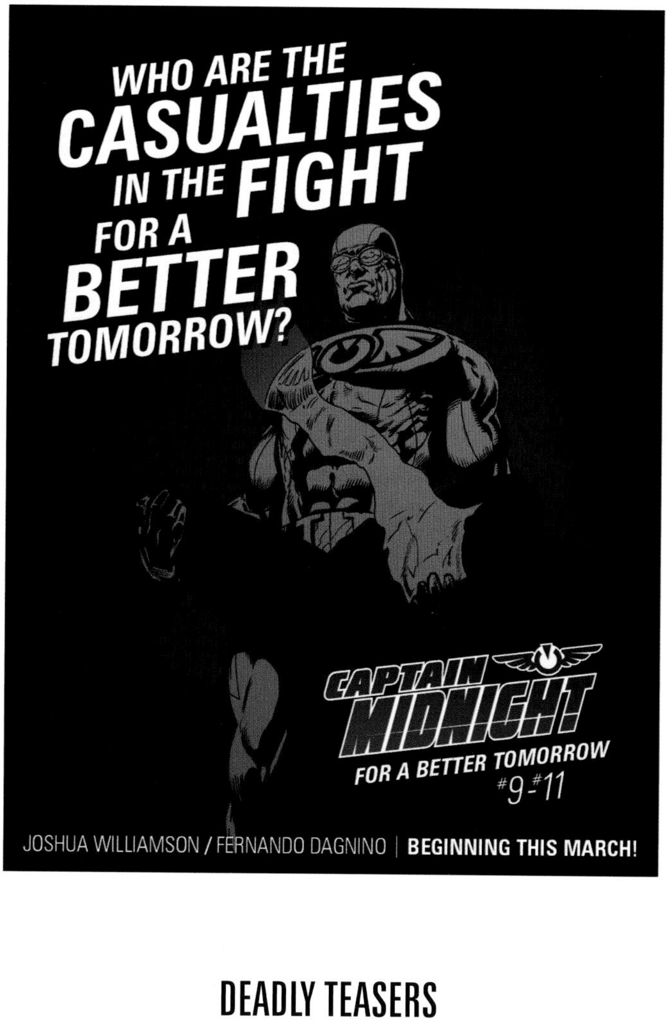
WHO ARE THE CASUALTIES IN THE FIGHT FOR A BETTER TOMORROW?
CAPTAIN MIDNIGHT
FOR A BETTER TOMORROW
#9-#11
JOSHUA WILLIAMSON / FERNANDO DAGNINO | BEGINNING THIS MARCH!

DEADLY TEASERS

With two major deaths occurring in this arc (the assassination of Fury Shark and the murder of Rick Marshall), teaser images were created to fuel fan speculation as to what game-changing and tragically permanent events lay ahead in "For a Better Tomorrow."

TRAGEDY DECONSTRUCTED

Here are Fernando Dagnino's pencils and inks for the heroic death of Rick Marshall, whose sacrifice will continue to affect Captain Midnight in the next volume of this series.

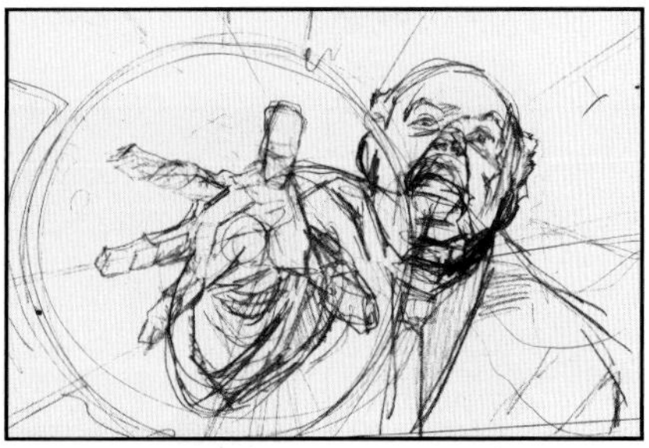

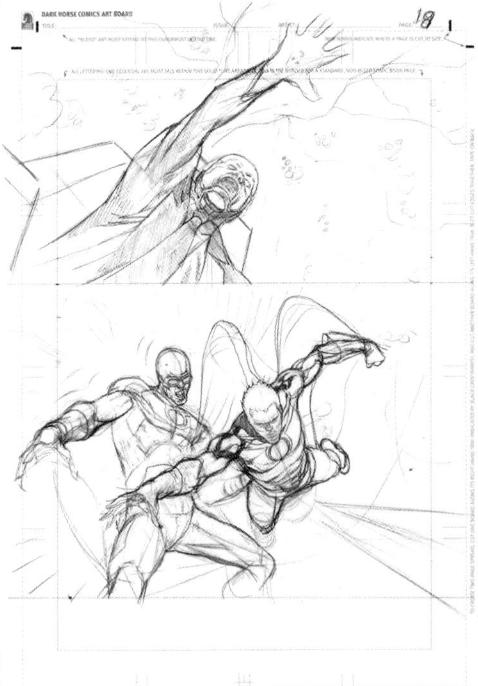

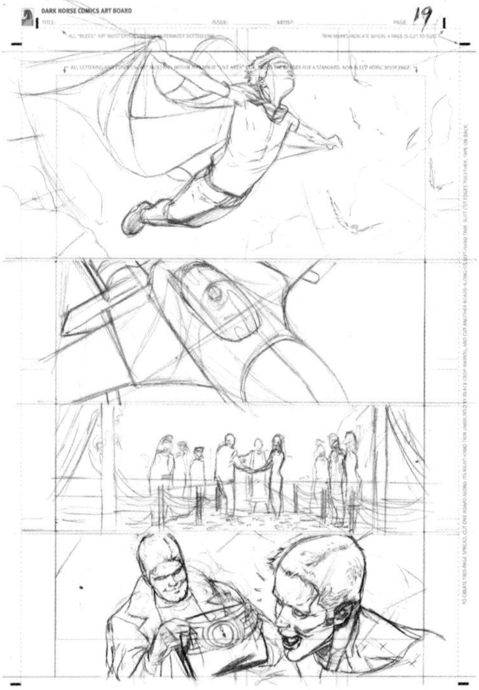

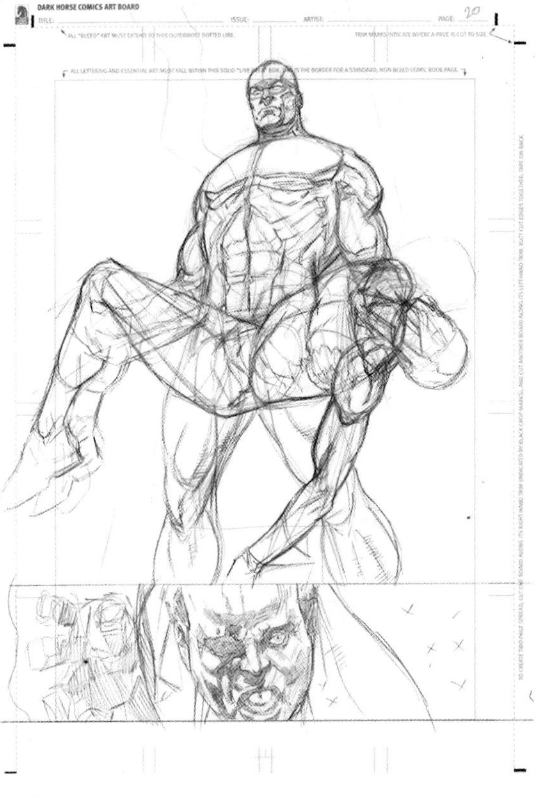

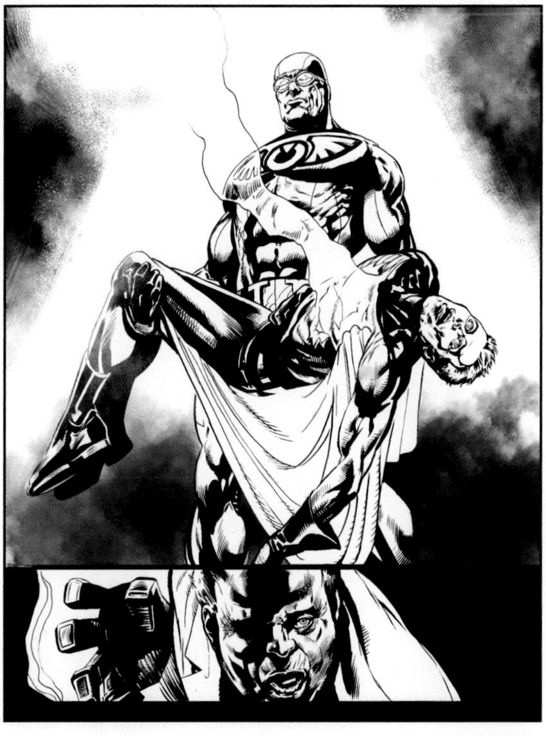

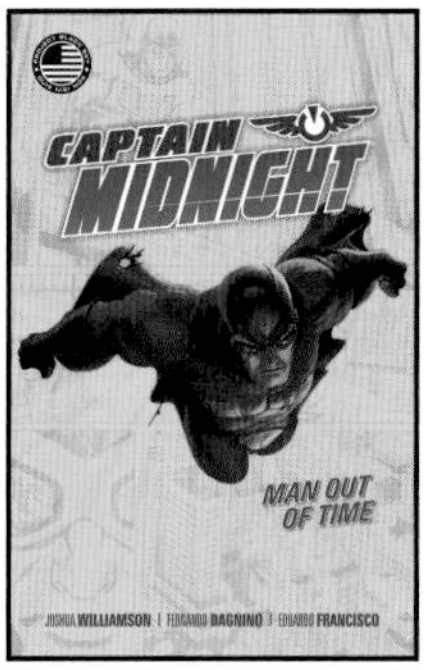
CAPTAIN MIDNIGHT
MAN OUT OF TIME
JOSHUA WILLIAMSON | FERNANDO DAGNINO | EDUARDO FRANCISCO
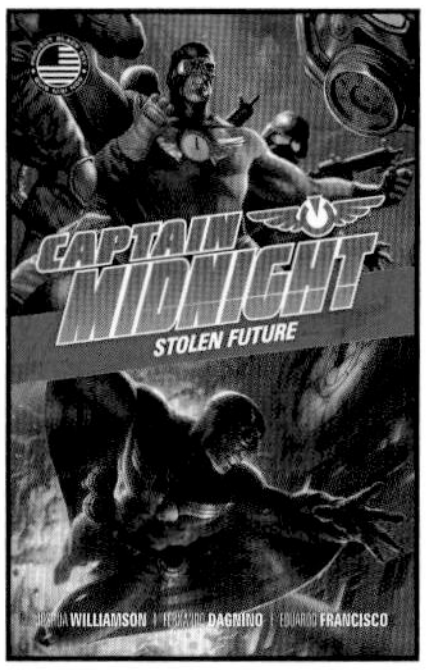
CAPTAIN MIDNIGHT
STOLEN FUTURE
JOSHUA WILLIAMSON | FERNANDO DAGNINO | EDUARDO FRANCISCO
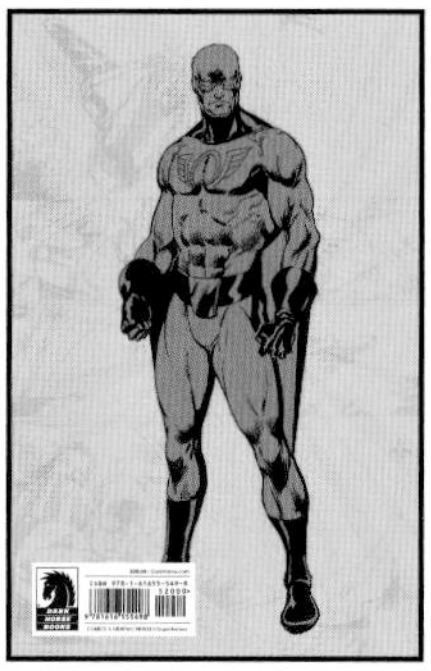
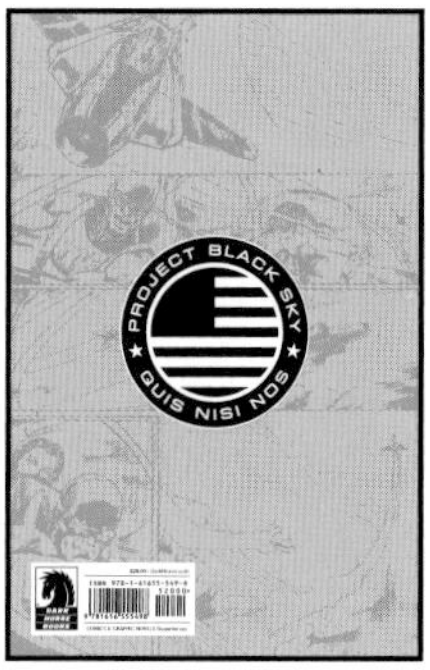
PROJECT BLACK SKY
QUIS NISI NOS
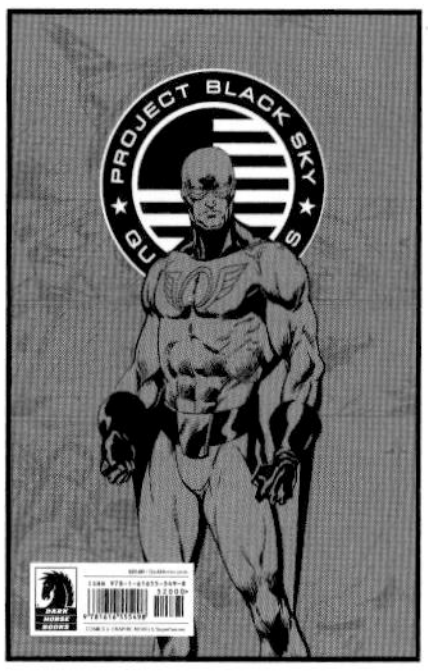
PROJECT BLACK SKY

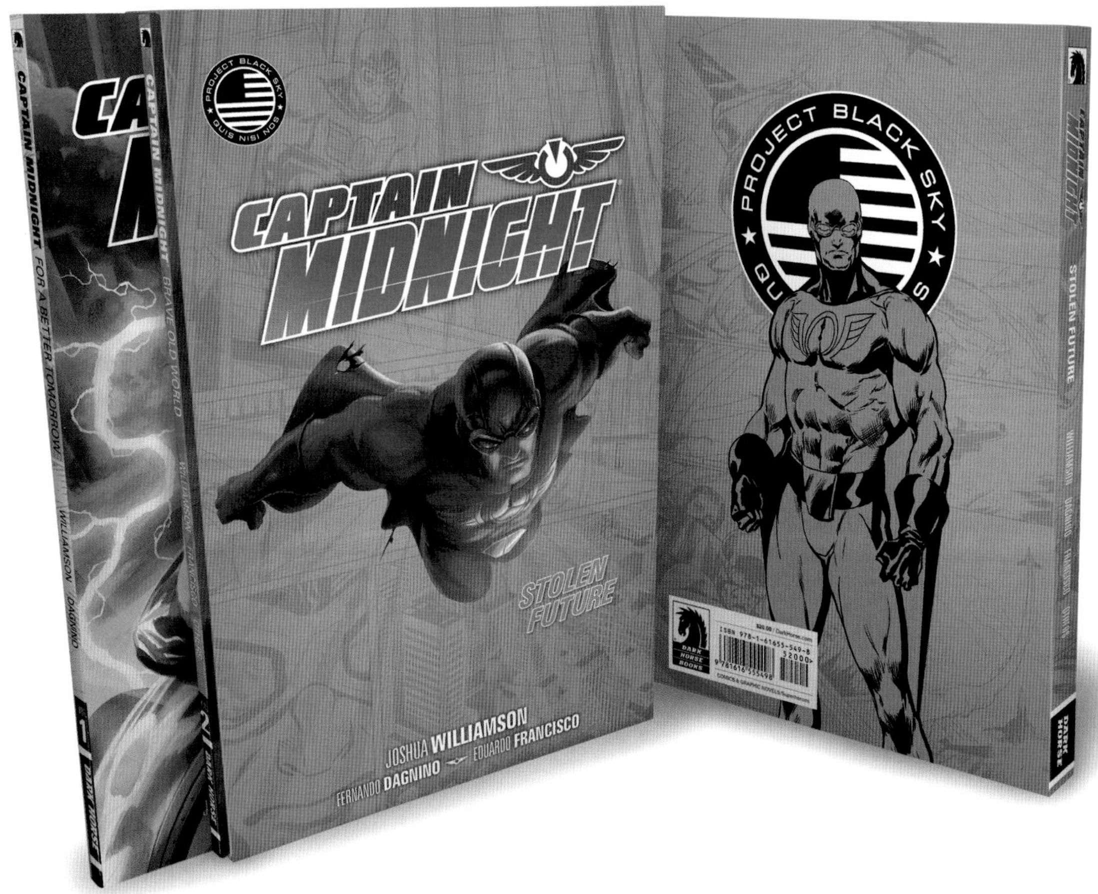
CAPTAIN MIDNIGHT FOR A BETTER TOMORROW
WILLIAMSON
DAGNINO
CAPTAIN MIDNIGHT BRAVE OLD WORLD
PROJECT BLACK SKY
QUIS NISI NOS
CAPTAIN MIDNIGHT
STOLEN FUTURE
JOSHUA WILLIAMSON
FERNANDO DAGNINO
EDUARDO FRANCISCO
STOLEN FUTURE
WILLIAMSON
DAGNINO
FRANCISCO

CAPTAIN MIDNIGHT: STOLEN FUTURE SLIPCASE DESIGNS

Early designs (above) and the final product of the slipcase entitled *Stolen Future*, initially available only at conventions, which features *Captain Midnight* Volumes 1 and 2.

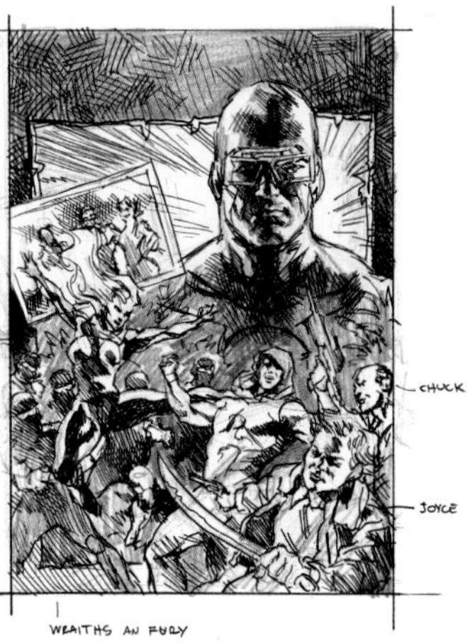
CHUCK
JOYCE
WRAITHS AN FURY

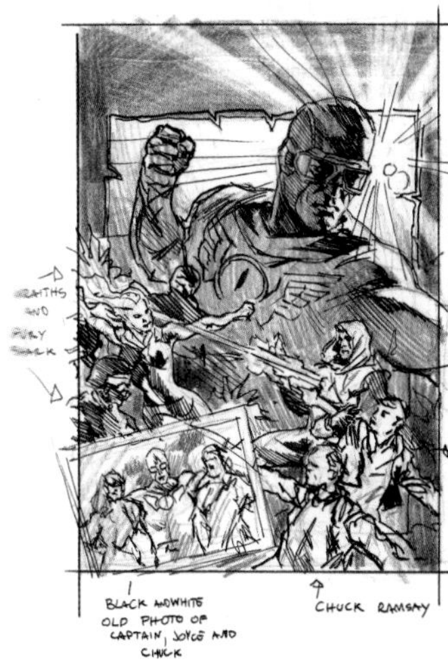
HELIOS
JOYCE RYAN
BLACK AND WHITE OLD PHOTO OF CAPTAIN, JOYCE AND CHUCK
CHUCK RAMSAY

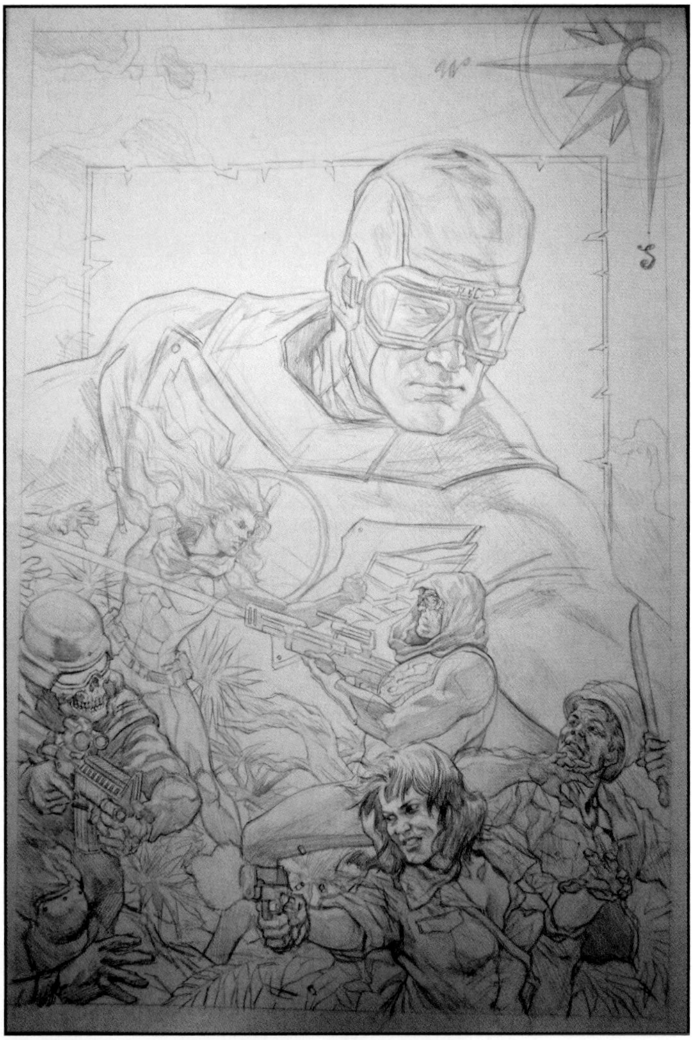

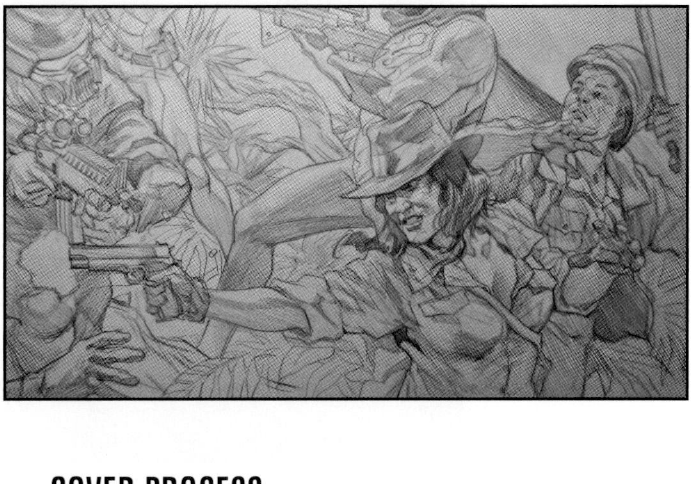

COVER PROCESS

#8 COVER

Initial sketches (upper right) and final pencils for the *Captain Midnight* #8 cover from Felipe Massafera, an homage to Drew Struzan's *Indiana Jones* art, as issue #8 (the first chapter of this collection) had a very "pulp story set in the jungle" feel. You can see that Joyce's hat was later removed—it was a bit too on the money for an Indy homage.

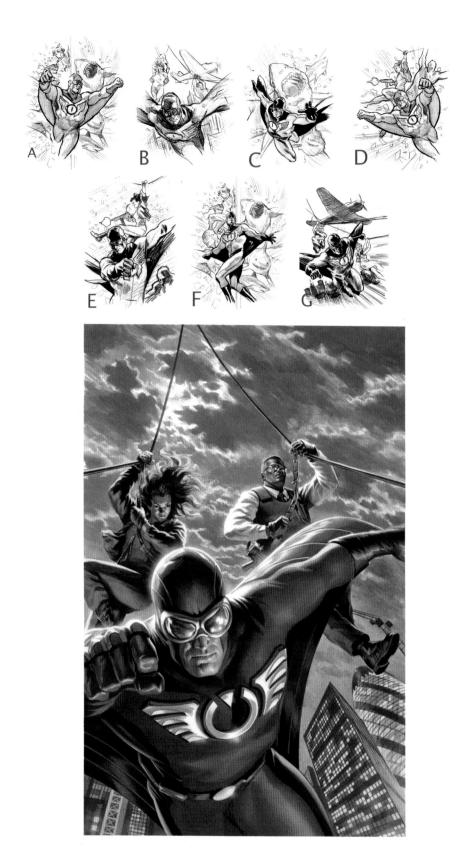

#9 COVER

Massafera's sketches and final art for *Captain Midnight* #9's cover.

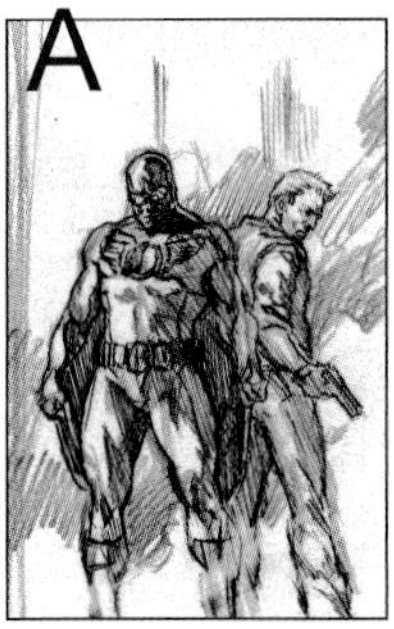
A
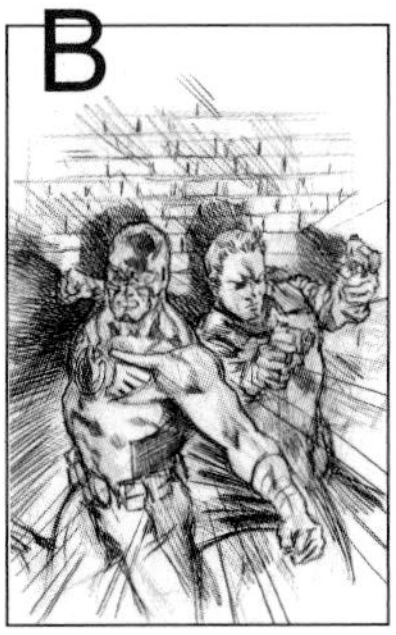
B
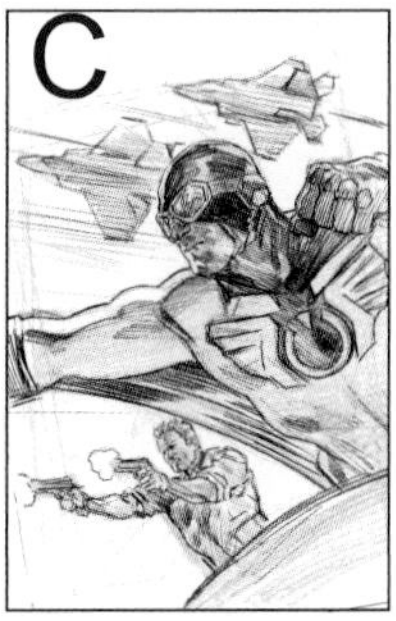
C
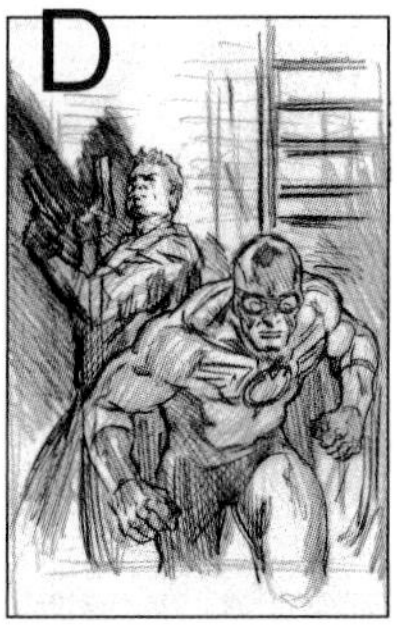
D
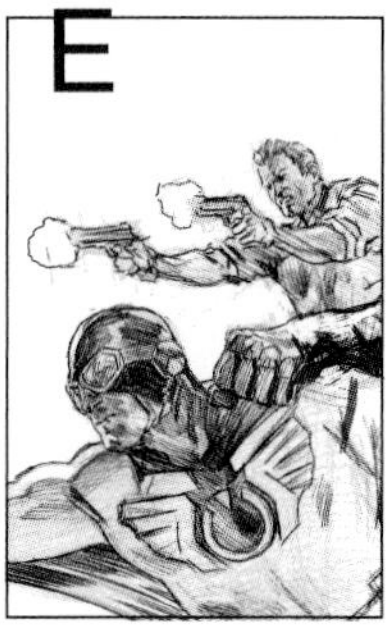
E
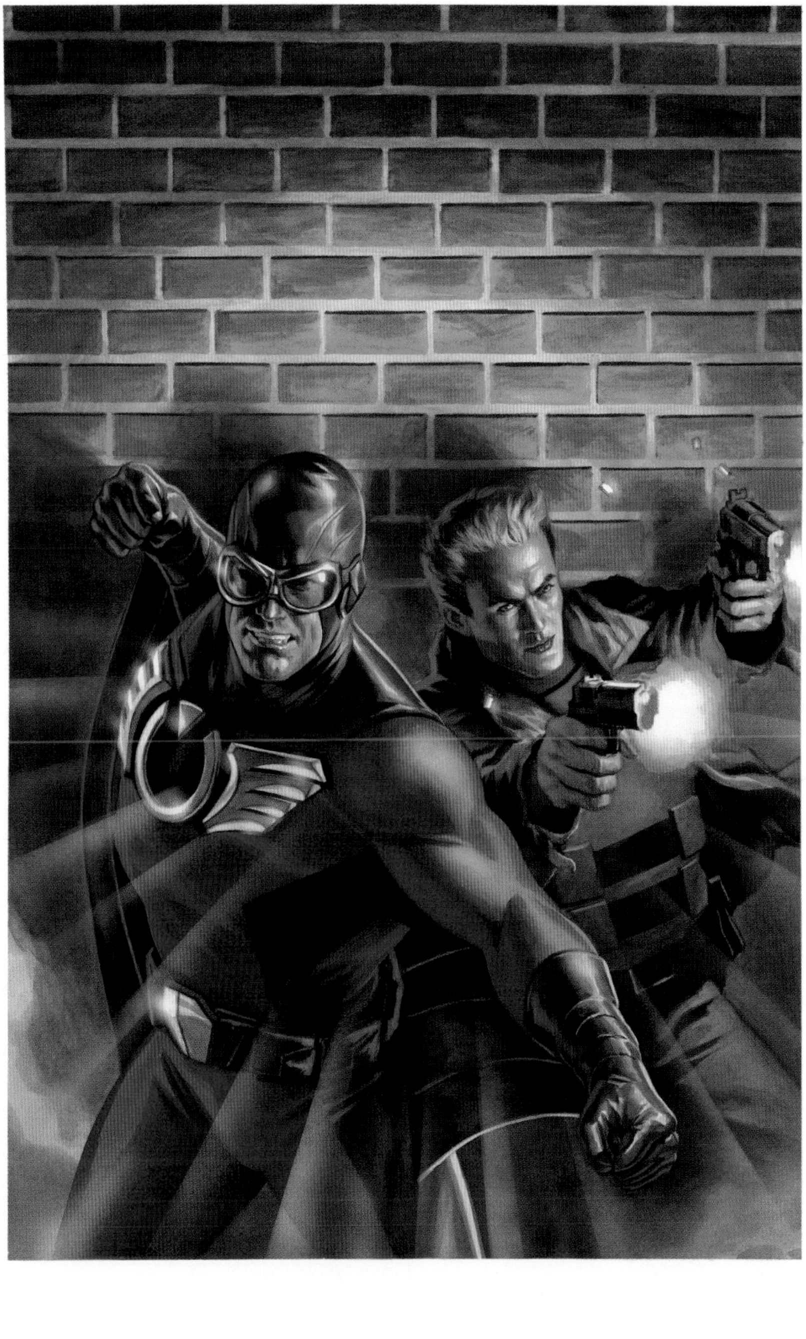

#10 COVER

As issue #10 would feature Rick Marshall's heroic sacrifice, it only seemed fitting to feature him on the cover, fighting alongside his hero, Captain Midnight. These are Massafera's sketches and final art for that cover.

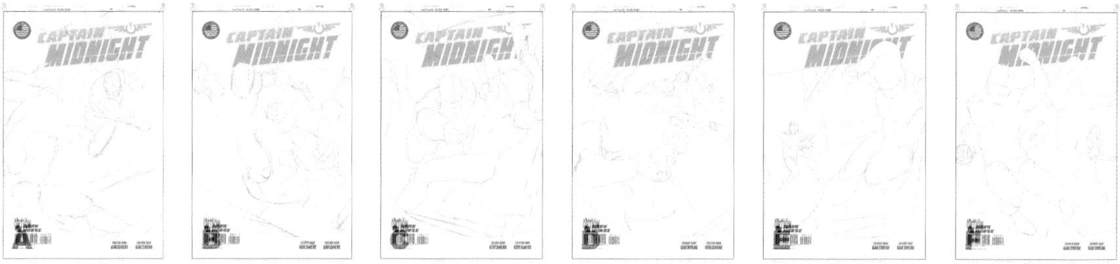
CAPTAIN MIDNIGHT

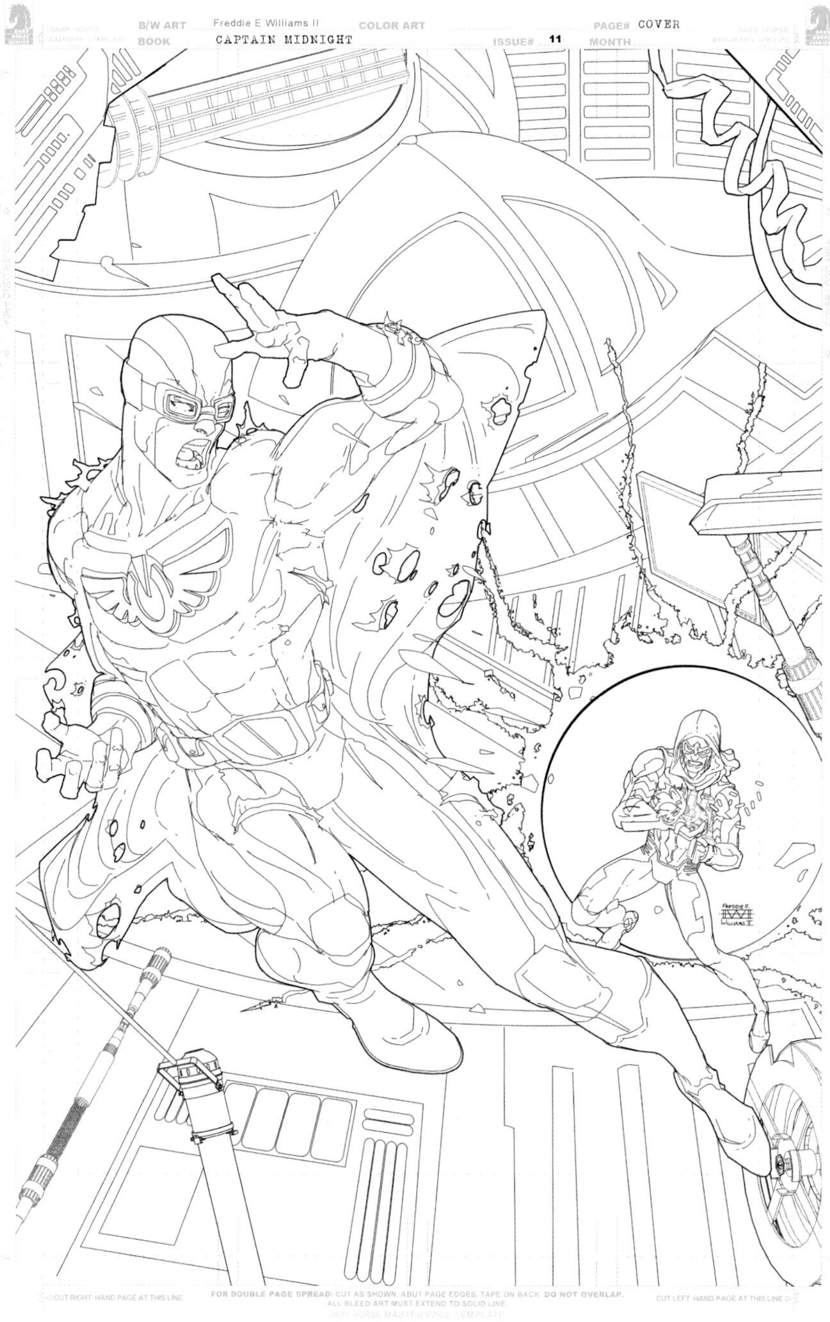
B/W ART Freddie E Williams II
COLOR ART
PAGE# COVER
BOOK CAPTAIN MIDNIGHT
ISSUE# 11
MONTH
FOR DOUBLE PAGE SPREAD: CUT AS SHOWN. ABUT PAGE EDGES. TAPE ON BACK. DO NOT OVERLAP.
ALL BLEED ART MUST EXTEND TO SOLID LINE.

#11 COVER

Issue #11 (chapter 4 of this volume) featured the long-awaited showdown between Captain Midnight and Helios, and provided the perfect opportunity for a great action cover. Freddie Williams II (who did the line art for the covers of *Captain Midnight* #6 and #7, as well as all four issues of *Skyman*) teamed with Jeremy Roberts (colorist on *Skyman* #3 and #4) for this epic cover! Here are Williams II's sketches and wireframes, before they were colored by Roberts.

PROJECT BLACK SKY

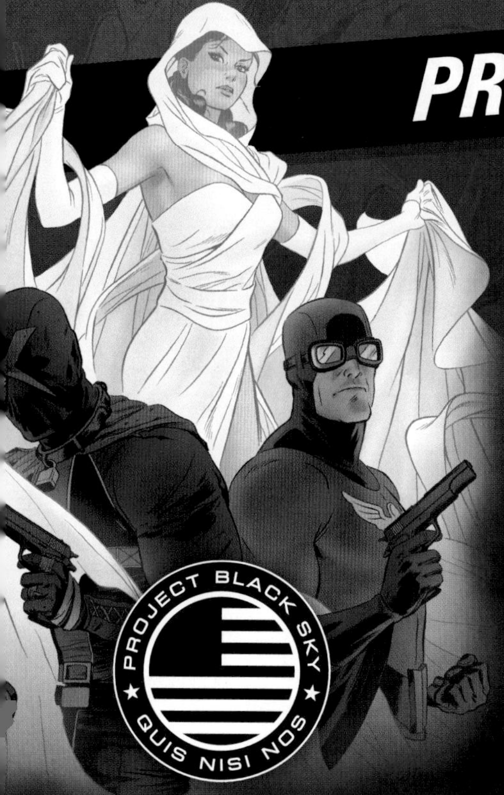
PROJECT BLACK SKY
QUIS NISI NOS

X

Duane Swierczynski and Eric Nguyen

A masked vigilante dispenses justice without mercy to the criminals of the decaying city of Arcadia. Nonstop, visceral action, with Dark Horse's most brutal and exciting character—X!

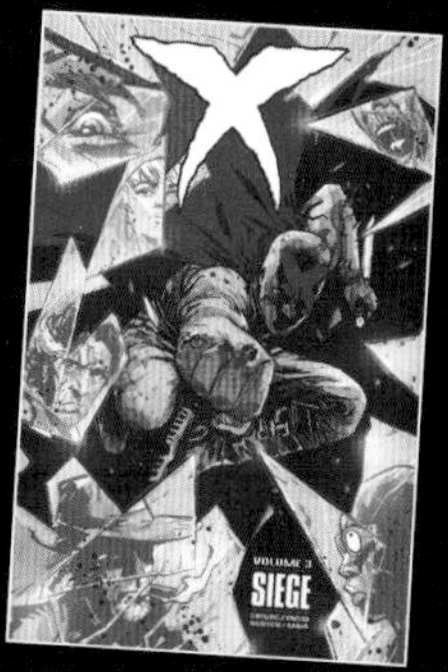
X
SIEGE

VOLUME 1: BIG BAD
978-1-61655-241-1 | $14.99

VOLUME 2: THE DOGS OF WAR
978-1-61655-327-2 | $14.99

VOLUME 3: SIEGE
978-1-61655-458-3 | $14.99

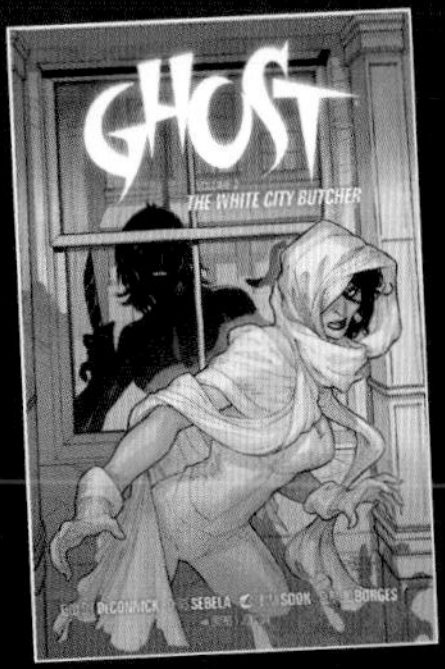
GHOST
THE WHITE CITY BUTCHER

GHOST

Kelly Sue DeConnick, Chris Sebela, Phil Noto, and Ryan Sook

Paranormal investigators accidentally summon a ghostly woman. The search for her identity uncovers a deadly alliance between political corruption and demonic science! In the middle stands a woman trapped between two worlds!

VOLUME 1: IN THE SMOKE AND DIN
978-1-61655-121-6 | $14.99

VOLUME 2: THE WHITE CITY BUTCHER
978-1-61655-420-0 | $14.99

THE OCCULTIST

Mike Richardson, Tim Seeley, and Victor Drujiniu

With a team of hit mages hired by a powerful sorcerer after him, it's trial by fire for the new Occultist, as he learns to handle his powerful magical tome, or suffer at the hands of deadly enemies. From the mind of Dark Horse founder Mike Richardson (*The Secret*, *Cut*, *The Mask*)!

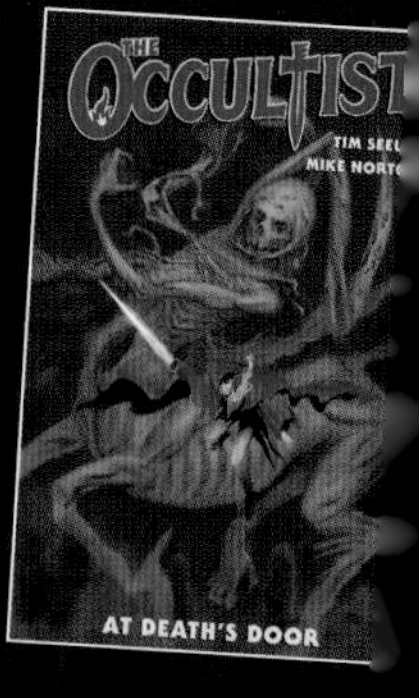
THE OCCULTIST
AT DEATH'S DOOR

VOLUME 1
978-1-59582-745-6 | $16.99

VOLUME 2: AT DEATH'S DOOR
978-1-61655-463-7 | $16.99

PROJECT BLACK SKY

CAPTAIN MIDNIGHT
BRAVE OLD WORLD

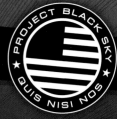

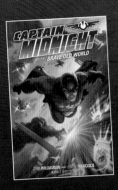

CAPTAIN MIDNIGHT

Joshua Williamson, Fernando Dagnino, Eduardo Francisco, Victor Ibáñez, Pere Pérez, and Roger Robinson

In the forties, he was an American hero, a daredevil fighter pilot, a technological genius . . . a superhero. Since he rifled out of the Bermuda Triangle and into the present day, Captain Midnight has been labeled a threat to homeland security. Can Captain Midnight survive in the modern world, with the US government on his heels and an old enemy out for revenge?

VOLUME 1: ON THE RUN
978-1-61655-229-9 | $14.99

VOLUME 2: BRAVE OLD WORLD
978-1-61655-230-5 | $14.99

BRAIN BOY

Fred Van Lente, Freddie Williams II, and R. B. Silva

Ambushed while protecting an important statesman, Matt Price Jr., a.k.a. Brain Boy, finds himself wrapped up in political intrigue that could derail a key United Nations conference and sets the psychic spy on a collision course with a man whose mental powers rival his own!

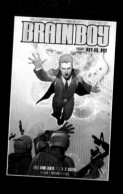

VOLUME 1: PSY VS. PSY
978-1-61655-317-3 | $14.99

BRAIN BOY
PSY VS. PSY

SKYMAN
THE RIGHT STUFF

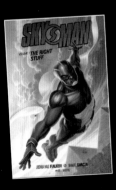

SKYMAN

Joshua Hale Fialkov and Manuel Garcia

The Skyman Program turns to US Air Force Sgt. Eric Reid: a wounded veteran on the ropes, looking for a new lease on life. *Ultimates* writer Joshua Hale Fialkov pens an all-new superhero series from the pages of *Captain Midnight*!

VOLUME 1: THE RIGHT STUFF
978-1-61655-439-2 | $14.99

BLACKOUT

Frank Barbiere, Colin Lorimer, and Micah Kaneshiro

Scott Travers possesses a special suit bearing technology that allows Travers to move in and out of our world through a shadowy parallel dimension–but he doesn't know how the device works or where it came from. With his benefactor missing, and powerful adversaries after his "Blackout" gear, Scott must master the suit's mysterious powers and find answers before the answers find him!

VOLUME 1: INTO THE DARK
978-1-61655-555-9 | $12.99

INTO THE DARK

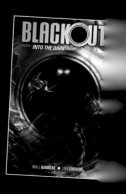